'A really fascinating and wonderful book, and beautifully written. Not many writers could have pulled this off with such grace and elegance. You won't regret buying this one, for sure' Nigel Warburton, *fivebooks.com*, Best Philosophy Books of 2021

'Ypi excels at describing the fall and aftermath of Albanian communism from the perspective of her childhood . . . rich and remarkable' *Literary Review*

'Essential reading. Lea Ypi's gorgeously written text – part memoir, part *bildungsroman* – tells a very personal story of socialism and post-socialism. Poignant and timely' Kristen Ghodsee, *Jacobin*

'A powerful and thought-provoking memoir . . . wonderfully human, it is a story of missed opportunities, disillusionment and hope that ultimately invites readers to ask themselves what it means to be free' Katja Hoyer, *History Today*

'This vivid rendering of life amid cultural collapse is nothing short of a masterpiece' *Publishers Weekly*

'Unique, insightful, and often hilarious . . . Albania on the cusp of change, chaos and civil war is the setting for the best memoir to emerge from the Balkans in decades' Craig Turp-Balazs *Emerging Europe*

'A probing personal history, poignant and moving. A young life unfolding amidst great historical change – ideology, war, loss, uncertainty. This is history brought memorably and powerfully to life' Tara Westover, author of *Educated*

'A lyrical memoir, of deep and affecting power, of the sweet smell of humanity mingled with flesh, blood and hope' Philippe Sands, author of *East West Street*

'*Free* is astonishing. Lea Ypi has a natural gift for storytelling. It brims with life, warmth, and texture, as well as her keen intelligence. A gripping, often hilarious, poignant, psychologically acute masterpiece and the best book I've read so far this year' Olivia Sudjic, author of *Asylum Road*

'Lea Ypi's teenage journey through the endtimes of Albanian communism tells a universal story: ours is an age of collapsed illusions for many generations. Written by one of Europe's foremost left-wing thinkers, this is an unmissable book for anyone engaged in the politics of resistance' Paul Mason, author of *Postcapitalism*

'This extraordinary coming-of-age story is like an Albanian *Educated*, but it is so much more than that. It beautifully brings together the personal and the political to create an unforgettable account of oppression, freedom and what it means to acquire knowledge about the world. Funny, moving but also deadly serious, this book will be read for years to come' David Runciman, author of *How Democracy Ends*

'A new classic that bursts out of the global silence of Albania to tell us human truths about the politics of the past hundred years . . . It unfolds with revelation after revelation – both familial and national – as if written by a master novelist. As if it were, say, a novella by Tolstoy. That this very serious book is so much fun to read is a compliment to its graceful, witty, honest writer. A literary triumph' Amy Wilentz, author of *Farewell, Fred Voodoo*

'Illuminating and subversive, *Free* asks us to consider what happens to our ideals when they come into contact with imperfect places and people and what can be salvaged from the wreckage of the past' Azar Nafisi, author of *Reading Lolita in Tehran*

'I haven't in many years read a memoir from this part of the world as warmly inviting as this one. Written by an intellectual with story-telling gifts, *Free* makes life on the ground in Albania vivid and immediate' Vivian Gornick, author of *Unfinished Business*

ABOUT THE AUTHOR

Lea Ypi is a professor of Political Theory at the London School of Economics. Her first trade book, *Free* was shortlisted for the Baillie Gifford Prize and the Costa Biography Award and won the Slightly Foxed Best First Biography Prize. It is being translated into nineteen languages.

PENGUIN BOOKS

FREE

'One of the non-fiction titles of the year, destined for literary accolades and popular success' Luke Harding, *Observer*

'A classic, moving coming-of-age story ... Ypi is a beautiful writer and a serious political thinker, and in just a couple hundred readable pages, she takes turns between being bitingly, if darkly, funny (she skewers Stalinism and the World Bank with equal deadpan) and truly profound' Max Strasser, *New York Times*

'The first book since *My Brilliant Friend* that I have pressed on family, friends and colleagues, insisting they read it. Ypi vividly and lyrically evokes her childhood in communist Albania ... a truly riveting memoir and a profound meditation on what it means to be free' Ruth Scurr, *Spectator*, Books of the Year

'Ypi's deliciously smart memoir of her Albanian girlhood at the end of the Cold War is a brilliant disquisition on the meanings of freedom – its lures, false hopes, disappointments and possibilities – in our time' Lyndsey Stonebridge, *New Statesman*, Books of the Year

'An absorbing memoir of Ypi's Albanian childhood and its ideological delusions. The freedom she discovers is far more complex than we might expect' Terri Apter, *TLS*, Books of the Year

'Branded Europe's last Stalinist outpost, precious little was known about life in communist Albania under Enver Hoxha. That strange world and its legacy is now stunningly brought to life in Lea Ypi's *Free*. From protective doublespeak round the kitchen table to the uncertain, and unfulfilled promises of post-communism, Ypi offers a moving and compelling memoir of growing up in turbulent times, as well as a frank questioning of what it really means to be "free"' Frederick Studemann, *FT*, Books of the Year

'A beautifully written account of life under a crumbling Stalinist system in Albania and the shock and chaos of what came next. In telling her story and examining the political systems in which she was raised, the author and LSE professor asks tough questions about the nature of freedom' Fiona Sturges, *Guardian*, Books of the Year

'A tart and tender childhood memoir. But also a work of social criticism, and a meditation on how to live with purpose ... A quick read, but like Marx's spectre haunting Europe, it stays with you' *New Yorker*, Best Books of 2021

'*Free* is a rare and nuanced glimpse into the history of Albania, offering the personal perspective of a childhood spent in the shadow of an oppressive regime, and the long and turbulent transition that came after' *Geographical*, Books of the Year

'A coming-of-age story in Albania that interweaves her growing up with the small Stalinist state's collapse. It is beautifully written, funny and moving, but also tells us something about all the preconceived truths we inherit without nationhood, religion, family and ideology' *Irish Independent*, Books of the Year

'Gripping. A book of political reality as lived from day to day by a young girl coming of age. It shows what can arrive all too easily in the void left by a suddenly discarded political system. Unforgettable' *Daily Mail*

'A wonderful memoir ... a uniquely engaging and illuminating account of a young life during a period of intense turmoil. So readable, yet Ypi does not sacrifice profound observations about politics and culture. Detailing the absurdities of the regime from a child's perspective, she pulls off the remarkable feat of emphasizing their cruelty with a light and often humorous touch' Misha Glenny, *TLS*

'Five stars ... deserves to be added to the history curriculum' *Daily Telegraph*

'A rightly acclaimed account of loss of innocence in Albania from a master of subtext ... Precise, acute, often funny and always accessible' *Irish Times*

'A remarkable story, stunningly told' Emma Duncan, *The Times*

'Lea Ypi's experiences inspire a moving and profound reflection on the nature of freedom that avoids either liberal triumphalism or Stalinist nostalgia. She is most concerned with the futures that were lost in between' George Eaton, *New Statesman*

'With its delicious sour-sweet comedy and pages of precise observation, Free opens a window on to one of the most bleakly isolationist regimes in human history' Ian Thomson, *Spectator*

Free

Coming of Age at the End of History

LEA YPI

PENGUIN BOOKS

PENGUIN BOOKS

UK | USA | Canada | Ireland | Australia
India | New Zealand | South Africa

Penguin Books is part of the Penguin Random House group of companies
whose addresses can be found at global.penguinrandomhouse.com

First published by Allen Lane 2021
Published in Penguin Books 2022
001

Typeset by Integra Software Services Pvt. Ltd, Pondicherry

Printed and bound in Great Britain by Clays Ltd, Elcograf S.p.A.

The authorized representative in the EEA is Penguin Random House Ireland,
Morrison Chambers, 32 Nassau Street, Dublin D02 YH68

A CIP catalogue record for this book is available from the British Library

ISBN: 978–0–141–99510–6

www.greenpenguin.co.uk

To the memory of my grandmother
Leman Ypi (Nini), 1918–2006

'Human beings do not make history of their own free will. But they make history nevertheless.'

— Rosa Luxemburg

Contents

PART I

1. Stalin   3
2. The Other Ypi   17
3. 471: A Brief Biography   32
4. Uncle Enver Has Left Us for Ever   43
5. Coca Cola Cans   55
6. Comrade Mamuazel   68
7. They Smell of Sun Cream   81
8. Brigatista   98
9. Ahmet Got His Degree   113
10. The End of History   123

PART II

11. Grey Socks   141
12. A Letter from Athens   157
13. Everyone Wants to Leave   174
14. Competitive Games   187
15. I Always Carried a Knife   199
16. It's All Part of Civil Society   212

17. The Crocodile   227

18. Structural Reforms   240

19. Don't Cry   251

20. Like the Rest of Europe   263

21. 1997   274

22. Philosophers Have Only Interpreted
     the World; the Point is to Change It   294

     Epilogue   305

     Acknowledgements   311

PART I

I.

Stalin

I never asked myself about the meaning of freedom until the day I hugged Stalin. From close up, he was much taller than I expected. Our teacher, Nora, had told us that imperialists and revisionists liked to emphasize how Stalin was a short man. He was, in fact, not as short as Louis XIV, whose height, she said, they – strangely – never brought up. In any case, she added gravely, focusing on appearances rather than what really mattered was a typical imperialist mistake. Stalin was a giant, and his deeds were far more relevant than his physique.

The thing that made Stalin really special, Nora went on to clarify, was that he smiled with his eyes. Can you believe it? Smiling with your eyes? That's because the friendly moustache that adorned his face covered his lips, so that if you focused only on the lips, you would never know if Stalin was really smiling or doing something else. But you just had to take one look at his eyes, piercing, intelligent and brown, and then you knew. Stalin was smiling. Some people were unable to look you in the eye. They clearly had something to hide. Stalin looked straight at you, and if he felt like it, or if you behaved well, his eyes would smile. He always wore an unassuming coat and plain brown shoes, and he liked to put his right hand under the left side of his coat, as if holding his heart. The left hand, he often kept in his pocket.

'In his pocket?' we asked. 'Isn't it rude to walk with your hand in your pocket? Grown-ups always tell us to take our hands out of our pockets.'

'Well, yes,' said Nora. 'But it is cold in the Soviet Union. And anyway,' she added, 'Napoleon also always had his hand in his pocket. Nobody ever said that was rude.'

'Not in his pocket,' I said timidly. 'In his waistcoat. In his time, that was a sign of good upbringing.'

Teacher Nora ignored me and was about to take another question.

'*And* he was short,' I interrupted.

'How do you know?'

'My grandmother told me.'

'What did she tell you?'

'She told me that Napoleon was short but when Marx's teacher Hangel, or Hegel, I can't remember, saw him, he said one could see the spirit of the world standing on a horse.'

'Hangel,' she corrected. 'Hangel was right. Napoleon changed Europe. He spread the political institutions of the Enlightenment. He was one of the greats. But not as great as Stalin. If Marx's teacher Hangel had seen Stalin standing, obviously not on a horse, but perhaps on a tank, he would have also claimed to have seen the spirit of the world. Stalin was a vital source of inspiration for many more people, for millions of our brothers and sisters in Africa and Asia, not only in Europe.'

'Did Stalin love children?' we asked.

'Of course, he did.'

'Even more than Lenin?'

'About the same, but his enemies always tried to hide that. They made Stalin sound worse than Lenin because Stalin was stronger and far, far more dangerous for them. Lenin changed Russia but Stalin changed the world. This is why the fact that Stalin loved children just as much as Lenin was never properly reported.'

'Did Stalin love children as much as Uncle Enver?'

Teacher Nora hesitated.

'Did he love them more?'

'You know the answer,' she said with a warm smile.

It is possible that Stalin loved children. It is likely that children loved Stalin. What is certain, dead certain, is that I never loved him more than on that wet December afternoon when I scampered from the port to the little garden near the Palace of Culture, sweaty, shaky, and with my heart pounding so hard I thought I would spit it on the ground. I had run as fast as I could for more than a mile when I finally spotted the tiny garden. When Stalin appeared on the horizon, I knew I would be safe. He stood there, solemn as usual, with his unassuming coat, plain bronze shoes and his right hand under his coat. as if supporting his heart. I stopped, looked around to ensure nobody was following me, and went closer. With my right cheek pressed against Stalin's thigh and my arms struggling to circle the back of his knees, I was not visible. I tried to catch my breath, closed my eyes and began to count. One. Two. Three. When I got to thirty-seven, I could no longer hear the dogs barking. The thundering sound of shoes stamping on concrete had become a distant echo. Only the slogans of protesters occasionally reverberated: '*Freedom, democracy, freedom, democracy.*'

When I became certain of my safety, I let go of Stalin. I sat on the ground and took a more careful look. The last drops of rain on his shoes were drying out and the paint on his coat had begun to fade. Stalin was just as teacher Nora had described him: a bronze giant with hands and feet much larger than I'd expected. Tilting my neck backwards, I lifted my head to confirm that his moustache really did cover the upper lip and that he smiled with his eyes. But there was no smile. There were no eyes, lips, nor even a moustache. The hooligans had stolen Stalin's head.

I covered my mouth to suffocate a scream. Stalin, the bronze giant with the friendly moustache who had been standing in the garden of the Palace of Culture since long before I was born, decapitated? Stalin, of whom Hangel would have said that he had seen the spirit of the world on a tank? Why? What did they want? Why did they shout, '*Freedom, democracy, freedom, democracy*'? What did it mean?

I had never given much thought to freedom. There was no need to. We had plenty of freedom. I felt so free that I often perceived my freedom as a burden and, occasionally, like on that day, as a threat.

I had not meant to end up in a protest. I hardly knew what a protest was. Only a few hours before, I had been standing in the rain by the school gate, wondering which way to walk back home, whether to turn left, turn right or walk straight on. I was free to decide. Each path raised different questions, and I had to weigh causes and consequences, reflect on their implications and make a decision I knew I might come to regret.

Certainly, I was regretting it that day. I chose freely which way to walk home, and I made the wrong decision.

I had just finished my cleaning shift in school, after the end of the lessons. We took turns cleaning our classroom in groups of four, but the boys often made excuses and only the girls were left. I shared the shift with my friend Elona. On a normal day, Elona and I would leave the school after cleaning, stop by the old woman who sat on the pavement at the corner of the road selling sunflower seeds, and we would ask her: 'Can we try them? Are they salted or unsalted? Roasted or unroasted?' The woman would open one of the three sacks she carried, the roasted and salted one, the roasted and unsalted, the unroasted and unsalted, and we would try a couple of seeds from each. When we had spare coins, there was plenty of choice.

After, we would turn left to go to Elona's house, munching sunflower seeds and struggling a little to let ourselves in with the rusty keys attached to her mother's necklace which she wore beneath her school uniform. There, we would have to choose which game to play. In December it was easy. At that time of the year preparations for the national song contest started, and we would make up our own songs and pretend we were going to appear on national television. I wrote the lyrics while Elona sang them, and sometimes I offered a drum accompaniment by using a large wooden spoon to beat the pans in the kitchen. Recently, though, Elona had lost interest in the song contest. She was more likely to want to play Brides and Babies. Instead of beating pans in the kitchen, she wanted us to stay in her parents' room, try out her mother's hair clips, change into her old wedding dress or wear her make-up, and pretend to nurse dolls until it was time for lunch. At that point I would have to decide whether to carry on playing, as Elona wanted, or convince her to fry eggs, or if there were no eggs, whether to eat bread and oil, or perhaps only bread. But these were trivial choices.

The real dilemma emerged after an argument Elona and I had about cleaning the classroom that day. She insisted we ought to both sweep and mop, otherwise we would never get the flag for the best cleaners of the month, which her mother had always been very keen on. I replied that we always swept on odd days of the week, and swept and mopped on even ones, and since it was an odd day, we could go home early and still receive the cleaning flag. She replied that this was not what the teacher expected and reminded me of the time when my parents had been summoned to the school because I had been negligent with my cleaning. I said she was wrong; the real reason had been the Monday-morning control team, who had discovered that my nails were too long. She maintained that it didn't matter, that in any case the right way to clean the classroom was to both sweep and mop, and even if we did receive the flag at the end of the month it would feel as if we had cheated. Moreover, she added, as if no further argument could be had, that is how she cleaned at home because that is how her mother used to do it. I told Elona she could not use her mother like that every time just to get her own way. I left in anger, and while standing in the rain by the school gate I wondered if Elona had a right to expect everyone to be nice to her, even when she was wrong. I wondered if I should have pretended that I loved sweeping and mopping just as I pretended that I loved playing Brides and Babies.

I had never told her, but I hated that game. I hated being in her mother's room and trying on the wedding dress. I found it unnerving to wear a dead person's clothes, or to touch the make-up they had been putting on only a few months before, as if we were them. But it was all recent, and Elona had been looking forward to having a baby sister who was going to play with my little brother. Instead, her mother died, the baby sister was sent to the orphanage, and only the wedding dress was left. I did not want to hurt her by refusing to wear it, or to tell her that I was repelled by the hair clips. Of course, I was free to tell her what I thought about Brides and Babies, just as I had been free to leave her to mop the classroom on her own; nobody stopped me. But I decided it was better to let Elona hear the truth, even if it might hurt her, than to lie indefinitely just to keep her happy.

If I did not turn left to go to Elona's house, I could turn right. That would have been the shortest route home, following two narrow alleyways that joined the main road in front of a biscuit workshop. Here a different dilemma emerged. A sizeable group of children assembled each day after the end of school, at the critical time when the distribution lorry was expected. If I chose that route, I would have to join what we called the 'action for biscuits'. I would form a line with the other children against the outside walls of the workshop, nervously awaiting the arrival of the lorry, monitoring the doors, carefully listening for sounds of potentially disruptive traffic, such as people on bikes or the occasional horse and carriage. At one point, the workshop door would open and two transport workers would appear carrying biscuit cases, like twin Atlases carrying the Earth. There would be a small commotion, and we would all lurch forward to the chant of 'Oh greedy, oh greedy, biscuits, biscuits, oh greedy man!' The orderly line would then spontaneously divide into a vanguard of children in black uniforms waving their arms to try to grab hold of the transport workers' knees, and a rearguard that swarmed towards the workshop gate to obstruct the exit. The workers would twist the lower half of their bodies to release themselves from the hold, while stiffening the upper half so as to tighten their grip on the biscuit cases. A packet would slip, a fight would break out, and then a manager would emerge from inside the workshop, holding as many biscuits as necessary to satisfy everyone and triggering the dispersal of the assembly.

I was free to turn right or continue to walk straight, and if I turned right, that is what I could expect to happen. It was all perfectly innocent, and it was unreasonable, possibly unfair, to ask an eleven-year-old who was merely walking back home, without having set out to search for treats, to press ahead, ignoring the delicious smell of biscuits drifting from the workshop's open windows. It would be equally unreasonable to expect her to ignore the awkward, inquisitive looks of the other children by walking past, seemingly indifferent to the arrival of the lorry. Yet that was exactly what my parents had come to ask of me the night before that wretched December day in 1990, which is partly why the decision about which way to walk back home was directly relevant to the question of freedom.

It had been my fault, to some extent. I should never have gone home carrying biscuits like a trophy. But it was also the fault of the new workshop manager. Recently hired, she was unaccustomed to the ways of her new workplace and had mistaken the children's appearance on that day for a one-off event. Instead of offering one biscuit to each child like all the other managers before her, she had handed over whole packets. Alarmed by this change, and by its implications for the 'action for biscuits' in the following days, instead of eating on the spot we had all stored the packets in our school bags and hastily run away.

I confess I did not imagine my parents would kick up such a fuss when I showed them the biscuits and explained where I had found them. I certainly did not expect the first question to be: 'Did anybody see you?' Of course, somebody had seen me, not least the person who had handed over the packets. No, I did not remember her face *exactly*. Yes, she was middle-aged. Not tall, not short, maybe average. Wavy hair, dark. Big, hearty smile. At that point, my father's face turned pale. He stood up from his armchair, holding his head in his hands. My mother left the living room and made a sign for him to follow her into the kitchen. My grandmother started stroking my hair in silence, and my little brother, to whom I had given a spare biscuit, stopped chewing, sat in a corner and started crying from the tension.

I was made to promise that I would never linger in the workshop yard again, or join the line against the wall, and I had to declare that I understood the importance of letting workers carry on with their duties, and that if everyone behaved like me, soon biscuits would disappear from the shops altogether. RE-CI-PRO-CI-TY, my father emphasized. Socialism is built on reciprocity.

I knew when I made the promise that it would be hard to keep. Or perhaps not – who knows? But I had at least to make the effort in good faith. I did not have anyone to blame for walking straight on rather than turning right, or for not going back to collect Elona after the cleaning shift to play Brides and Babies, or for choosing to ignore the biscuits that day. They had all been my decisions. I had done my best and still ended up in the wrong place at the wrong time, and now the result of all that freedom was the sheer terror that the dogs might return to devour me or that I would be crushed in a stampede.

Not that I could have predicted that I would stumble on a protest, or that Stalin would provide shelter. If I had not recently seen scenes of unrest elsewhere on television, I would not even have known that the strange spectacle of people screaming slogans and the police with their dogs was called a 'protest'. A few months before, in July 1990, dozens of Albanians had climbed the walls of foreign embassies, forcing themselves inside. I was perplexed as to why anyone might want to lock themselves up in a foreign embassy. We talked about it in school, and Elona said there was once a family, an entire family of six people, two brothers and four sisters, who had smuggled themselves into the Italian embassy in Tirana dressed as foreign tourists. They lived there for five years – five whole years – in just two rooms. Then another tourist, a real one this time, called Javier Pérez de Cuéllar, visited our country and talked to the embassy climbers, and then to the Party to communicate their desire to live in Italy.

I was intrigued by Elona's story and asked my father what it meant. 'They are *uligans*,' he replied, 'as they said on TV.' He clarified that *hooligan* was a foreign word for which we had no Albanian translation. We didn't need it. Hooligans were mostly angry young men, who went to football matches, drank too much and got into trouble, who fought with supporters of the other team and burned flags for no reason. They lived mostly in the West, though there were some in the East too, but since we were neither in the East nor the West, in Albania they hadn't existed until recently.

I thought about hooligans as I tried to make sense of what I had just encountered. Clearly, if one was a hooligan, it would not be beyond the pale to climb up embassy walls, to shout at the police, to disrupt public order or to decapitate statues. Clearly, hooligans did the same in the West; perhaps they had smuggled themselves into our country just to provoke trouble. But the people who had climbed the embassy walls a few months before were definitely not foreigners. What did these different hooligans have in common?

I remembered vaguely something called the Berlin Wall protest the year before. We had talked about it in school, and teacher Nora explained it was related to the fight between imperialism and revisionism, and how they were each holding a mirror to the other, but both mirrors were broken. None of it concerned us. Our enemies regularly tried to topple our government, but they failed just as regularly. In the late forties, we split up with Yugoslavia when the latter broke with Stalin. In the sixties, when Khrushchev dishonoured Stalin's legacy and accused us of 'leftist nationalist deviationism', we interrupted diplomatic relations with the Soviet Union. In the late seventies, we abandoned our alliance with China when the latter decided to become rich and betray the Cultural Revolution. It didn't matter. We were surrounded by powerful foes, but knew ourselves to be on the right side of history. Every time our enemies threatened us, the Party, supported by the people, emerged stronger. Throughout the centuries, we had fought mighty empires and shown the rest of the world how even a small nation on the edge of the Balkans could find the strength to resist. Now we were leading the struggle to achieve the most difficult transition: that from socialist to communist freedom – from a revolutionary state governed by just laws to a classless society, where the state itself would wither away.

Of course, freedom had a cost, teacher Nora said. We had always defended freedom alone. Now *they* were all paying a price. *They* were in disarray. We were standing strong. We would continue to lead by example. We had neither money nor weapons, but we continued to resist the siren call of the revisionist East and the imperialist West, and our existence gave hope to all the other small nations whose dignity continued to be trampled on. The honour of belonging to a just society would be matched only by the gratitude felt for being sheltered from the horrors unfolding elsewhere in the world, places where children starved to death, froze in the cold or were forced to work.

'Have you seen this hand?' teacher Nora had said, lifting up her right hand at the end of the speech with a fierce look on her face. 'This hand will always be strong. This hand will always fight. Do you know why? It has shaken Comrade Enver's hand. I didn't wash it for days, after the Congress. But even after I washed it, the strength was still there. It will never leave me, never until I die.'

I thought about teacher Nora's hand, and the words she had spoken to us only a few months ago. I was still sitting on the ground in front of Stalin's bronze statue, collecting my thoughts, trying to summon the courage to lift myself up and retrace the steps back home. I wanted to remember her every word, to evoke her pride and strength when she told us how she was going to defend freedom because she had shaken Uncle Enver's hand. I wanted to be like her. I must defend my freedom too, I thought. It must be possible to overcome my fear. I had never shaken Uncle Enver's hand. I had never met him. But maybe Stalin's legs would be enough to give me strength.

I stood up. I tried to think like my teacher. We had socialism. Socialism gave us freedom. The protesters were mistaken. Nobody was looking for freedom. Everyone was already free, just like me, simply exercising that freedom, or defending it, or making decisions that they had to own, about which way to go home, whether to turn right or left or to walk straight. Perhaps also, just like me, they had stumbled near the port by mistake, ending up in the wrong place at the wrong time. Perhaps when they saw the police and the dogs, they were simply very afraid, and the same could be said for the police and the dogs, that they were very afraid in turn, especially when they saw people running. Perhaps both sides were simply chasing each other without knowing who was following whom, and that is why people had started to shout, '*Freedom, democracy*,' out of fear, and uncertainty, to explain that this was what they did not want to lose, rather than what they wanted.

And perhaps Stalin's head was entirely unrelated.

Perhaps it had been damaged in the night by the storm and the rain and someone had already collected it so that it could be repaired and would soon bring it back like new to take its old place, with the sharp, smiley eyes, and the thick, friendly moustache covering the upper lip, just as I had been told it looked, just as it had always been.

I hugged Stalin one last time, turned around, stared at the horizon to gauge the distance to my house, took a deep breath and started to run.

2.

The Other Ypi

'*Mais te voilà enfin! On t'attend depuis deux heures! Nous nous sommes inquiétés! Ta mère est déjà de retour! Papa est allé te chercher à l'école! Ton frère pleure!*',* thundered a tall, slim figure all dressed in black. Nini had been waiting at the top of the hill for more than an hour, asking passers-by if they had seen me, nervously wiping her hands on her apron, squinting harder and harder to try and spot my red leather rucksack.

I could tell my grandmother was angry. She had a bizarre way of scolding, making you feel responsible, reminding you of the consequences that your actions had for others, listing all the ways in which the pursuit of other people's goals was disrupted by the selfish prioritizing of yours. As her monologue in French continued unabated, my father, too, appeared at the bottom of the slope. He raced up the hill panting, holding his asthma pump like a miniature Molotov cocktail. He kept looking behind his back as if he suspected that he was being followed. I hid behind my grandmother.

* 'You're here at last! We've been waiting for two hours! We were worried. Your mother is already back! Papa went to look for you at the school! Your brother is crying!'

'She left the school after cleaning,' my father said, hurrying towards Nini. 'I tried to retrace her steps. I couldn't see her anywhere.' Visibly agitated, he paused to inhale from his pump. 'I think there's been a protest,' he whispered, indicating with a gesture that he would continue his explanation inside.

'She's here,' my grandmother replied.

My father breathed a sigh of relief and then, noticing me, turned severe.

'Go to your room,' he ordered.

'It was not a protest. They were *uligans*,' I muttered as I walked through the courtyard, wondering why my father had used that other word: protest.

Inside, I found my mother occupied with a large house-cleaning operation. She was in the process of bringing down from the attic things that had not been seen for years: a sack of wool, a rusty ladder and my grandfather's old books from his university years. I could tell she was agitated. She had a tendency to channel her frustration by finding new domestic chores: the greater the frustration, the more ambitious the scale of her projects. When she was angry with other people, she would say nothing but would bang pots and pans, curse the cutlery that slipped to the floor, fling trays into cupboards. When she was angry with herself, she would rearrange the furniture, drag tables across the room, pile up chairs and roll up the heavy carpet in our living room so she could scrub the floor.

'I saw *uligans*,' I said to her, eager to share my adventure.

'The floor is wet,' she replied in a menacing voice, tapping my ankle twice with the damp end of the mop to indicate that I ought to have left my shoes outside.

'Or maybe they weren't hooligans,' I continued, untying my shoelaces. 'Maybe they were protesters.'

She stopped and gave me a blank stare.

'The only hooligan here is you,' she said, raising the mop from the floor and waving it twice in the direction of my room. 'We don't have any protesters in this country.'

My mother had always been indifferent to political matters. In the past, only my father and my grandmother (his mother) had followed it closely. They spoke often about the Nicaraguan revolution and the Falklands War; they were enthusiastic about the start of negotiations to end apartheid in South Africa. My father said that if he had been American and called up in the Vietnam War, he would have refused the draft. We were lucky that our country supported the Viet Cong, he often emphasized. He had a tendency to make fun of the most tragic things, and his jokes about anti-imperialist politics were legendary among my friends. Whenever I invited them for a sleepover and we laid out mattresses on the bedroom floor, he would poke his head through the door at the end of the evening, and say: 'Sleep well, Palestinian camp!'

With recent developments in the East, or what we called 'the revisionist bloc', something felt different. I could not say what it was. I vaguely remembered hearing about *Solidarność* once on Italian television. It seemed to concern workers' protests and, as we lived in a workers' state, I thought it would be interesting to write about it in the 'political information' newsletter we had to prepare for school. 'I don't think it's that interesting,' my father said when I asked him about it. 'I have something else for your newsletter. The cooperative in the village where

I work surpassed the target for wheat production set in the current five-year plan. They didn't make enough corn, but they made up for it with wheat. They were in the news last night.'

Whenever protests came up, my family became reluctant to answer questions. They looked either tired or irked and they switched off the television or lowered the volume to the point that the news became unintelligible. Nobody seemed to share my curiosity. It was obvious that I couldn't rely on them to explain anything. It was wiser to wait until the class on moral education in school and to ask my teacher Nora. She always gave clear, unambiguous answers. She explained politics with the kind of enthusiasm my parents showed only when commercials featuring soaps and creams appeared on Yugoslav television. Whenever my father caught an advert on TV Skopje, especially if it was an advert for personal hygiene, he would immediately shout: '*Reklama! Reklama!*' My mother and grandmother would drop whatever they were doing in the kitchen and sprint to the living room to catch the last sight of a beautiful woman with a delightful smile on her face who showed you how to wash your hands. If they were held up for a while and arrived when the adverts were over, my father would declare apologetically: 'It's not my fault, I called you, you came late!' and this usually marked the beginning of an argument about how *they* were late because *he* never helped with anything around the house. The argument would soon turn into an exchange of insults, and the insults might deteriorate into a fight, often with Yugoslav basketball players continuing to score points in the background, until the next lot of adverts came up and peace was restored. My family always squabbled about everything. Everything except politics.

In the bedroom, I found my brother, Lani, sobbing. When he saw me, he wiped away his tears and asked if I had brought any biscuits.

'Not today,' I replied. 'I didn't walk that way.' He looked as if he was about to cry again.

'I have to stay here,' I said. 'To reflect. Do you want to hear a story? It's about a man on a horse who looked like the spirit of the world, but then his head was chopped off.'

'I don't want to hear it,' he replied, new tears flowing on to his cheeks. 'I'm scared. I'm scared of people with no heads. I want biscuits.'

'Do you want to play Teachers?' I offered, feeling vaguely guilty.

Lani nodded. He and I loved to play Teachers. He would sit at my desk, pretending to be a teacher and scribble notes while I prepared my homework. He was especially keen on history lessons. Once I had memorized the events, I would repeat the text out loud with dramatized dialogues between the main historical characters, often impersonated with the help of my dolls.

That day, both the characters and the events were familiar. We were studying the occupation of Albania by Italian fascists during the Second World War, focusing on the complicity of the country's tenth prime minister. That man, an Albanian quisling, as teacher Nora called him, was responsible for the transfer of sovereignty to Italy after the flight of King Zog. Zog's rule, and all that followed from it, marked the end of Albanian aspirations to become a truly free society. After centuries of servitude under the Ottoman empire, and decades of

struggle against the Great Powers who sought to partition the country, patriots from all regions came together
in 1912, defying ethnic and religious differences, to fight
for independence. Then Zog, teacher Nora explained,
eliminated his adversaries, concentrated power and
declared himself King of the Albanians, until the country was occupied by fascists, with the help of Albanian
collaborationists. On 7 April 1939, the official date of the
Italian invasion of Albania, many soldiers and ordinary
citizens bravely fought Italian warships, facing artillery
shells with few weapons of their own, until their last
breath on the defence lines. However, other Albanians –
the beys, the landowners and commercial elites, those
who had previously served that exploitative and blood-
thirsty king – now rushed to greet the occupying forces,
eager to take positions in the new colonial administration.
Some, including the country's former prime minister,
even thanked the Italian authorities for liberating the
country from King Zog's heavy yoke. A few months
later, this previous prime minister was killed by an aerial
bomb. His life as a traitor who had collaborated with the
king and his death as a fascist scoundrel were the subject
of my history assignment that day.

There was huge excitement when we talked about
fascism in school. There were animated discussions and
the children almost burst with pride. We were asked if we
could bring in examples of relatives who had fought in
the war or supported the resistance movement. Elona's
grandfather, for example, had, at just fifteen, joined the
ranks of the partisans in the mountains to fight against
the Italian invaders. After liberating Albania in 1944 he
had moved to Yugoslavia to help the resistance there. He

often came to speak to us about his time as a partisan and how Albania and Yugoslavia were the only countries to have won the war without the help of Allied forces. Other children mentioned grandparents or great-uncles and great-aunts who had supported the anti-fascists with food and shelter. Some brought to class clothes or personal objects that once belonged to young relatives who had sacrificed their lives for the movement: a shirt, a hand-embroidered handkerchief, a letter sent to the family only hours before execution.

'Do we have relatives who participated in the anti-fascist war?' I asked my family. They thought hard, rummaged through family pictures, consulted with relatives, then came up with Baba Mustafa: a great-uncle of the second cousin of my uncle's wife. Baba Mustafa had held the keys to a local mosque, where he sheltered a group of partisans one afternoon after their attack on a Nazi garrison when the Italians had left the country and been replaced by Germans. I enthusiastically recounted the episode in class. 'How is he related to you, again?' asked Elona. 'What was he doing at the mosque? Why did he have the keys?' quipped another friend, Marsida. 'What happened to the partisans after?' a third, Besa, wanted to know. I tried to answer the questions as best I could, but the truth was that I hadn't been given enough detail to satisfy my friends' curiosity. The discussion became confusing, then uncomfortable. After a few exchanges, both my relationship to Baba Mustafa and his contribution to the anti-fascist resistance started to look marginal, then exaggerated. By the end, it was difficult for me to suppress the impression that even Nora had quietly concluded he was a product of my imagination.

Every fifth of May, the day on which we commemorated heroes of the war, delegations of Party officials visited our neighbourhood to offer their renewed condolences to the families of martyrs, and to remind them of how the blood of their loved ones had not been spilt in vain. I sat by our kitchen window and observed with bitter envy my friends, dressed in their best clothes, carrying large bouquets of fresh red roses, waving flags and singing resistance songs while leading the way to their houses. Their parents lined up to shake hands with Party representatives, official photos were taken, and the albums that arrived a few days later were brought to the school to be put on display. I had nothing to offer.

It was not enough that my family had no socialist martyrs to commemorate. The Albanian quisling, the country's tenth prime minister, the national traitor, the class enemy, the deserving target of hatred and contempt in school discussions, happened to share a surname with me and a name with my father: Xhaferr Ypi. Each year, when he came up in the textbooks, I had to patiently explain that even though the surname was the same, we were not related. I had to explain that my father was named after his grandfather, who simply happened to carry the same name and surname as our old prime minister. Each year, I hated that conversation.

I held my breath while reading through the history assignment, then thought for a moment and stood up in anger, clutching the book in one hand. 'Come with me,' I ordered Lani. 'It's about the other Ypi again.' He followed me submissively, still sucking the pen with which he had been drawing. I slammed the door behind me and marched towards the kitchen.

'I am not going to school tomorrow!' I announced.

At first, nobody noticed. My mother, father and grand-mother were lined up on the same side of a small oak table, facing away from the entrance, sitting precariously on three folding chairs placed tightly next to each other. Their elbows rested on the table, the palms of their hands covered their temples, and their heads leaned so far from their centre of gravity that they looked like they were about to detach. All three seemed engrossed in a mys-terious collective ritual involving an enigmatic object that their figures shielded from view.

I waited to hear the reaction to my verdict. Nothing but a hushing sound came back. I stood on my toes and bent my head forward. At the centre of the table, I rec-ognized the family radio.

'I am not going to school tomorrow!'

I raised my voice, taking more steps into the kitchen, with the history book open on the prime minister's photo. Lani stamped one foot on the floor and looked at me complicitly. My father twisted brusquely with the guilty expression of someone caught in a subver-sive act. My mother turned the radio off. I caught the last two words before the sound disappeared: 'political pluralism'.

'Who told you to leave your bedroom?' My father's question sounded like a threat.

'It's about him again,' I said, ignoring his reproach, my voice still high but starting to tremble. 'It's Ypi the quisling. I am not going to school tomorrow. I am not going to waste my time explaining that we have nothing to do with *that man*. I've already told everyone before, I've said it over and over. But they will ask again, they will, as if they'd never heard, as if they don't know. They will ask again, they always do, and I've run out of explanations.'

I had recited that monologue before, each time fascism came up in history or literature lessons or in the moral education class. My family always refused to let me skip school. I knew they would refuse this time too. I could never explain to them what it was like to feel the pressure from my friends. I could never explain to my friends what it was like to live in a family where the past seemed irrelevant and all that mattered was debating the present and planning for the future. I could not explain to myself the lingering feeling I had then, and which I am able to articulate only now, that the life I lived, inside the walls of the house and outside, was in fact not one life but two, lives that sometimes complemented and supported each other but mostly clashed against a reality I could not fully grasp.

My parents stared at each other. Nini looked at them, then turned towards me and said in a tone of voice intended to be both firm and reassuring:

'Of course you will go. You have done nothing wrong.'

'*We* have done nothing wrong,' my mother corrected. She stretched her hand to the radio to indicate that she wanted to listen further, and that my presence in the room would soon no longer be welcome.

'It's not about me,' I insisted. 'It's not about us. It's about the quisling man. If we had someone whose heroism we could celebrate, I could mention him in class and people wouldn't be so obsessed with asking about my relationship to that other Ypi. But we have no one, no one in our family, not even in the extended family, no relative who ever tried to defend our freedom. No one has ever cared about freedom in this house.'

'That's not right,' my father said. 'We have someone. We have you. You care about freedom. You're a freedom fighter.'

The dialogue was playing out as it had countless times before: my grandmother arguing that it would be irrational to miss school just because of a surname, my father deflecting attention with a joke, and my mother eager to return to whatever I had inconveniently interrupted.

But this time, something unexpected followed. My mother suddenly let go of the radio, stood up and turned towards me. 'Tell them Ypi did nothing wrong,' she said.

Nini frowned, then stared at my father, perplexed. He reached for his asthma pump and tried to avoid her eyes, turning towards my mother with an expression of concern. My mother stared back fiercely, her eyes flashing with anger. She had the air of someone who has calculated her actions to be disruptive. Ignoring my father's silent reproach, she continued where she had broken off.

'He did nothing wrong. Was he a fascist? I don't know. Maybe. Did he defend freedom? It depends. To be free, you have to be alive. Maybe he was trying to save lives. What chance did Albania have to stand up to Italy? It was dependent on it in every way. What was the point of bloodshed? The *fascists* had already taken over the country. The fascists controlled the markets. It was Zog who gave them shares in all the major state companies. Italian goods arrived long before Italian weapons. Our very roads were built by fascists. Mussolini's architects designed our government buildings long before his officials occupied them. What they call the fascist *invasion . . .*'

She paused, twisting her mouth in a sarcastic smile as she pronounced the word *invasion.*

'This is not the time,' Nini interrupted. She turned to me. 'What matters is that *you* have done nothing wrong. *You* have nothing to fear.'

'Who are *they*?' I asked, confused and curious about my mother's words. I could not understand everything she had said but was intrigued by the length of her intervention. It was quite unlike her to engage in extensive explanations. It was the first time I had heard my mother offer opinions about politics and history. I had never known her to have any.

'They say Zog was a tyrant and a fascist,' my mother continued, ignoring both my question and Nini's warning. 'If you comply with one tyrant, what is the point of fighting another? What is the point of dying to defend the independence of a country that is already occupied in all but name? The real enemies of the people – Don't pull my sleeve,' she said, interrupting herself, and turned aggressively to my father, who was now very close to her and had started to breathe heavily. 'They say he was a traitor, well . . .'

'Who are *they*?' I asked again, increasingly puzzled.

'They, they are . . . she means the revisionists,' my father rushed to explain on her behalf. Then he hesitated and, not knowing how to continue, he changed the topic: 'I asked you to reflect in your bedroom. Why did you come out?'

'I reflected. I don't want to go to school.'

My mother gave a snort of derision. She left the table

and started banging pots and pans and smashing cutlery into the sink.

The morning after, Nini did not wake me for school as usual. She did not say why. I knew something was different, that something had happened the day before, something that changed the way I looked at my family and thought about my parents. It is difficult to say if what happened was related to my encounter with Stalin, the radio programme, or that prime minister whose exploits, death and presence in my life I tried in vain to ignore. I wondered why my father whispered when he discussed the protest with my grandmother. Why did he not call them hooligans? I also wondered why my mother had tried to justify the actions of a fascist politician. How could she have sympathy for an oppressor of the people?

In the following days, the protests multiplied. Now state television knew them by that name too. Initiated by university students in the capital, they spread to the rest of the country. There were rumours that workers were preparing to walk out of the factories and join the young people on the streets. What had started as a wave of unrest about economic conditions, with students lamenting the shortage of food, poor heating in dormitories and frequent power cuts in lecture halls, soon turned into something else, a demand for change whose exact nature was unclear even to those calling for it. Prominent academics, including former Party members, gave unprecedented interviews to *Voice of America*, explaining that it would be a mistake to reduce the grievances of the students to economic matters. What the movement campaigned for, they explained, was the end of the one-party system and the recognition of political pluralism. They wanted *real* democracy and *real* freedom.

I had grown up believing that my family shared my enthusiasm for the Party, the desire to serve the country, the contempt for our enemies and the concern that we had no war heroes to remember. This time it felt different. My questions about politics, the country, the protests and how to explain what was going on found only curt, evasive answers. I wanted to know why everyone demanded freedom if we were already one of the freest countries on Earth, as teacher Nora always said. When I mentioned her name at home, my parents rolled their eyes. I started to suspect they were not in the best position to answer me and that I could no longer trust them. Not only did my questions about the country go unanswered; I now also wondered about what kind of family I had been born into. I doubted them and, by doubting, found that my grip on who I was began to slip.

I am now aware of something that I did not understand clearly at the time; the patterns that shaped my childhood, those invisible laws that had given structure to my life, my perception of the people whose judgements helped me make sense of the world – all these things changed for ever in December 1990. It would be an exaggeration to suggest that the day I hugged Stalin was the day I became an adult, the day I realized I was in charge of making sense of my own life. But it would not be far-fetched to say it was the day I lost my childhood innocence. For the first time I wondered whether freedom and democracy might not be the reality in which we lived but a mysterious future condition about which I knew very little.

My grandmother always said that we don't know how to think about the future; we must turn to the past. I started to wonder about the story of my life, of how I was born, of how things were before I was there. I tried to check back on details I might have got confused, too young to remember them correctly. It was a story I had heard countless times before; the story of a fixed reality in which I had gradually found my part, however complicated. This time it was different. This time, there were no fixed points, everything had to be remade from scratch. The story of my life was not the story of the events that had occurred in any particular period but the story of searching for the right questions, the questions I had never thought to ask.

3.

471: A Brief Biography

I come from a family of what my teacher Nora used to call 'intellectuals'. 'There are too many children of intellectuals in this class,' she would say in school, with a vaguely disapproving look on her face. 'An intellectual,' my father reassured me, 'is simply someone with a university education. Don't worry, though. Ultimately, everyone is a worker. We all live in a working-class state.'

Although both my parents were officially 'intellectuals' because they went to university, neither studied what they wanted to study. My father's story was the more confusing of the two. He was gifted in the sciences and while still in secondary school had won Olympiads in maths, physics, chemistry and biology. He wanted to continue studying maths but was told by the Party that he had to join the real working class because of his 'biography'. My family often mentioned that word, but I never understood it. It had such wide applications that you could not make out its significance in any particular context. If you asked my parents how they met and why they married, they would answer: 'Biography.' If my mother was preparing a file for work, she would be reminded: 'Don't forget to add a few lines about your biography.' If I made a new friend in school, my parents would ask each other: 'Do we know anything about their biography?'

Biographies were carefully separated into good and bad, better or worse, clean or stained, relevant or irrelevant, transparent or confusing, suspicious or trustworthy, those that needed to be remembered and those that needed to be forgotten. Biography was the universal answer to all kinds of questions, the foundation without which all knowledge was reduced to opinion. There are words after whose meaning it is absurd to enquire, either because they are so basic they explain themselves and everything that is related to them, or because you might be embarrassed to reveal that after so many years of hearing it, you still don't understand. *Biography* was like that. Once the word was said, you just had to accept it.

My father was an only child. His official name was Xhaferr, like the Albanian quisling, but everyone called him Zafo, which spared him having to apologize each time he introduced himself. Zafo had been raised by his mother. In 1946, when he was three years old, my grandfather, Asllan, who I never met, left him to go to university somewhere; this was part of his biography. When Asllan returned after fifteen years, the family held a party to celebrate it and Nini wore lipstick. My father had never seen his mother with lipstick and declared he did not recognize her, that she looked like a clown and that she would no longer live with them. Then he had a huge fight with his father; Nini wiped off her lipstick and never wore make-up again. The two men continued to have arguments over the years. My father refused to recognize Asllan's authority, while my grandfather said that my father's willpower was 'like butter', and that he was merely living like 'a satisfied pig'. Nini liked to report her

33

husband's full sentence: 'It is better to be a dissatisfied human being than a satisfied pig.' But my father never looked particularly satisfied. Instead, he had frequent anxiety attacks, which usually came when his asthma worsened and which he did his best to conceal.

Zafo had contracted asthma as a child, around the time when he and Nini were asked by the Party to move out of their house and into a mouldy barn. This, too, was part of their biography. My grandfather was not there when it happened, but he apparently later pointed out that a lot of people had asthma and that my father should not complain too much. He also said that my father should thank the government every day that we were under socialism. If we lived in the West, my father would have become a tramp, singing *bobdylan* songs under a bridge to make money. I found that part mysterious too, not only because nobody ever explained what *bobdylan* was but because my father was completely tone-deaf and had never played any instrument. Instead, he was obsessed with two things, both of which he tried to teach me: how to dance 'like little Ali' and what he called the 'magic of Vieta's formulas' to solve algebra problems. The first was a set of boxing moves, but the training tended to stop just when I thought I had mastered them because my father ran out of breath. The latter could go on for days, sometimes even weeks, and his excitement about Vieta's formulas grew in proportion to my frustration.

The confusing part in my father's biography was not that he had been told he could not go to university but that he had ended up going in spite of this. A few days before the beginning of the academic year, he appeared in front of a panel of doctors, and my grandmother told the panel that unless my father was allowed to study at university he would kill himself. Then the panel asked him a few questions and sent him home with a letter that instructed the relevant officials to authorize him to continue with higher education. He could not study maths because then he might become a teacher, and he was not allowed to become a teacher because of his biography. He was sent to do forestry, but it was clearly good enough for him, since he never tried to kill himself. Instead, he commuted to Tirana from Kavajë, the little town where his family lived, alongside many other families whose biographies were similar to theirs.

If maths was one of my father's greatest passions, there was nothing in the world my mother loathed more. This, too, was unfortunate, because not only did she have to study maths at university, she also had to teach it to secondary-school children. The fact that my mother could be trusted with a teacher's role, whereas my father would not be, suggested that her biography was better than his, though only marginally, because, if it had been much better, they would not have married each other. My mother loved Schiller and Goethe, went to concerts of Mozart and Beethoven and had learned to play the guitar with the Soviets who visited the House of the Pioneers before we broke our alliance with them just after their Party's 20th Congress. She was allowed to study literature, but her parents encouraged her to switch degrees because they struggled financially and, with a science degree, she could get a scholarship.

My mother was the third of seven children: five

girls and two boys. Her mother, Nona Fozi, worked in a factory that made chemicals, and her father, who we called Baçi, cleaned gutters. In the few photos we have of my mother as a child she appears extremely slim, fragile and with dark circles under her eyes, as if she were anaemic. She never spoke about her childhood, but it must have been miserable because when my father once suggested watching a historical documentary about the Great Bengal Famine, she replied: 'Zafo, I know what hunger is, I don't need to watch it on television.' She was mostly hostile to television. The only programme for which she made an exception was *Dynasty* on the Yugoslav channel, not necessarily because she followed the plot but because she liked to inspect the interior decoration. 'It's very pretty,' she would say, with a longing expression. 'Very, very pretty.'

My mother's family lived and shared their earnings with two grandmothers and a first cousin of her father's called Hysen, who had been with them since he had been orphaned at the age of thirteen. My mother was extremely fond of Hysen. When she was brought home from the maternity hospital one day during the war, Hysen refused to call her by her name, Vjollca, declaring she was as beautiful as a doll. That gave her the nickname Doli, by which everyone called her. Hysen had been to boarding school in Vienna and had taught her how to dance the waltz and how to recite Goethe's *Erlkönig* in German. Sometimes my mother would go around the house declaiming: '*Wer reitet so spät durch Nacht und Wind? Es ist der Vater mit seinem Kind,*'* alternating between a

---

* 'Who is riding so late on a windy night? It is the father and his child.'

very loud voice for the question and a hushed tone for the answer. I'd always assumed the poem told the story of a child who could not fall asleep, until she recited the whole thing to me one winter night while there was a storm outside our window and we roasted chestnuts on the fire. She then translated it, and I can still feel the chills down my spine when I remember the last two lines: 'He reaches his home with trouble and dread, with the boy in his arms; but the boy is dead.'

My mother and Hysen also shared a passion for making cars, boats, trains and planes out of scrap paper; all to be sent on imaginary travels. Hysen suffered from some kind of mental illness and had frequent strokes, and after each stroke he fell into a deep sleep, almost like a coma. When he woke up, he spoke only German, then a mixture of German and Albanian, and when he was well enough to leave the bed, he and my mother would draw maps of our town, Durrës, circling particular areas of land around it, marking buildings and roads, then making paper boats which he claimed carried the family's gold. The boats were all named after Teuta, the ancient Illyrian queen who had sent pirates to fight the Romans, though each had a different number: *Teuta I, Teuta II, Teuta III.* My mother said Hysen prepared for what he called 'the time of peacey'. In the time of peacey, he promised, my mother and her siblings would move to a castle, wander around on the land they owned, mount racehorses and dress like princes and princesses. Whenever Hysen told her the story of what they could expect once 'peacey' arrived, my mother forgot that she had gone a whole day without eating.

Hysen had also taught my mother how to play chess,

and her family encouraged her to join the city's club, because she could get tracksuits for free and travel to tournaments. At twenty-two, she became the national chess champion, and defended the title for a few years. I remember the rhythmic sound of her heels as she paced a large hall in the Palace of Sport, where she trained teams of youngsters, gliding from one row of tables to the next, accompanied only by the *tick tock* of the large wooden chess clocks placed between the players. She observed each game for a few minutes without saying a word, and if a child was about to make a mistake, she would raise her index finger and tap once or twice on the threatening knight or bishop, then proceed to inspect the next table. 'It's a sport for the brain,' she would say, when she encouraged me to play, and took it as a personal offence when I waited for her to be distracted with other children and ran away to watch ping-pong in a different room. 'The beauty of chess,' she insisted, 'is that it has nothing to do with biography. It's all up to you.'

When my mother was ill, she had a tendency to describe changes in her body with the same monotonous and dispassionate precision with which she explained the basic rules for moving chess pieces on the board. She always described only what happened, never how she felt about it. She hardly complained; I never saw her cry. She emanated supreme confidence and absolute authority; the kind enjoyed by those who somehow manage to convince others that it would be against their self-interest to question their subordination to her. She was always in control. Always, except once – the time I was born. On the morning of the day she was due to be admitted to hospital, she locked herself in the bathroom, trying to style her hair like someone she had recently seen on television, a woman who had recently become the United Kingdom's first female prime minister. Since my mother hardly ever brushed her hair, let alone styled it, this was a clear sign of, if not panic, unprecedented anxiety.

On 8 September 1979, *Zëri i Popullit*, the Party's official organ, reported an attack by the racist Rhodesian government of Abel Muzorewa on Mozambique, criticized new nuclear explosions at USA testing sites, highlighted a recent case of corruption among Houston police officers as a prime example of the degeneration of capitalism, and denounced child exploitation in Madrid's textile factories. A long editorial condemned *Voice of America* and *Novosti* as weapons of ideological aggression by the world's two largest superpowers. The foreign news page included a message of solidarity with the ongoing strikes around the world: naval workers at the port of Rotterdam, mechanics at British Leyland, teachers in Peru, Costa Rica and Colombia. I was born at 10 a.m.

It had taken my parents a few years to conceive; more or less since the Helsinki Accords were signed in August 1975, as my father liked to point out. When I was born, the chances of survival were put at thirty per cent. My parents dared not give me a name but celebrated the hospital number I was assigned: 471. Only dead babies did not receive numbers and, since I was not dead yet, there was life to celebrate.

'We had been grieving for decades,' my grandmother later said. 'When you were born there was hope. Hope is something you have to fight for. But there comes a point when it turns into illusion; it's very dangerous. It all comes down to how one interprets the facts.' 471 was enough to give my family hope, but only just.

My mother and I were divided from the minute I was born: she stayed in the maternity ward until she recovered from her operation, and I was sent to a different hospital, where I lived attached to various machines, showing no signs of improvement until my grandmother decided to ask for permission to take me back home. When I left the incubator, aged five months and just under three kilograms, the size of a newborn, the odds of my survival had increased to fifty per cent. 'About the same as the American diplomats in Tehran,' my father later joked, 'but if Nini had not insisted, you might have been held hostage for longer.' The fact that my grandmother's request had been accepted was a good sign for our biography.

In the early months of my life, the single bedroom my family rented from a former cooperative worker was transformed into an intensive care unit. My father brought wood from the garden to keep the fire going, my mother stayed up late sewing clothes for me, and my grandmother sterilized everything that caught her eye: cutlery, scissors, pots and pans, but also unrelated things like hammers and pliers. Visitors were prohibited unless they came wearing masks but, since masks were scarce, they soon disappeared altogether.

'In any other family, she wouldn't have made it,' Dr Elvira, who regularly came to check on my health, declared on my first birthday. 'Congratulations! You can stop calling her 471. Look at those chubby cheeks. Better call her "stuffed pepper".'

I must have been given strange immunity boosters

when I was little because, with the exception of those first few months, I hardly ever became ill again. As a child, I was sick so rarely that I came to idealize disease, to think of convalescence as some kind of prize distributed to only a chosen few, wondering what challenges one had to overcome to become worthy of a high temperature, a chesty cough, or even just a plain sore throat. Whenever an infection did the rounds in my class, I asked the children who had been off school if I could give them extra hugs in the hope of catching their illnesses. On the rare occasions when I succeeded in contracting something, I stayed at home, sipping bay-leaf tea, and asked my grandmother to tell me the story of how 471 survived to become the stuffed pepper. 'What's my biography like?' I wondered. 'You were a premature child,' was always her first sentence. 'You came before we were ready. Apart from that, your biography so far is as good as it gets.'

It was only when Elona lost her mother in circumstances very similar to the ones my mother and I had survived that I realized things could have gone differently for us too. I started to think of my life as a miraculous adventure story. But Nini never admitted to it being a miracle; she always rejected the possibility that things could have gone otherwise. She recounted the first few months of my existence with such an exact attribution of cause and effect that it sounded more like the analysis of a scientific theory, a reconstruction of the laws of nature than a description of events that could have taken a different course. Success was always due to the right people making the right choices, fighting for hope when it seemed justified, and interpreting the facts in such a way as to distinguish hope from illusion.

In the end, my grandmother said, we are always in charge of our fate. 'Biography' was crucial to knowing the limits of your world but, once you knew those limits, you were free to choose and you became responsible for your decisions. There would be gains and there would be losses. You had to avoid being flattered by victories and learn how to accept defeat. Like the moves in chess my mother used to describe, the game was yours to play if you mastered the rules.

4.

Uncle Enver Has Left Us for Ever

'Something awful happened,' our nursery teacher, Flora, said, urging all the five- and six-year-olds to sit on coloured wooden chairs laid out in a semicircle. It was 11 April 1985. 'Uncle Enver has . . . has . . . left us . . . for ever.' She uttered those words as if on her last breath herself, as if this were the last sentence she would muster. After that, she dropped on to one of the small chairs herself, holding a hand on her heart as if it hurt, shaking her head, taking deep breaths: inhale, exhale, inhale, exhale. A long silence followed.

Then Flora stood up with great resolve and rubbed her eyes. During those few minutes of quiet, she had turned into a different person. 'Children,' she said solemnly. 'Listen carefully. It's very important that you understand. Uncle Enver has passed away. But his work lives on. The Party lives on. We will all continue his work and follow his example.'

We spoke extensively about death that day. My friend Marsida, whose father repaired shoes but whose grandfather had been the head of the local mosque before religion was abolished, said that in the olden days people believed that we don't really die when we die. Of course, we replied, of course we don't die. All our work, like Uncle Enver's, continues to live.

But Marsida protested that this was not what she had meant. She had not meant to say that our work lives on while we are dead. Instead, she meant that when people die, there is a part of them that continues to live, and that goes off to a different place, depending on how you had behaved during your life. She could not remember what that part was called. Her grandfather had explained it to her.

We were incredulous. A different place? 'How can anyone go anywhere when they are dead?' I said. 'When you're dead you can't move. They put you straight into a coffin.'

'Have you ever seen a dead person for real?' Marsida asked.

I told her I had not. But I had seen coffins. And I had seen where they go, very deep underground, with the help of ropes. I saw them when we visited my grandfather's grave at the cemetery on Sunday. I had even seen children's graves. I once scratched the marble of one with a piece of glass I found on the ground, and my grandmother scolded me. There was a black-and-white photo on the gravestone, showing a smiling little girl who was wearing a large ribbon that looked a bit like mine. She had died by falling from a tree. Nini told me that this is why we have cemeteries, so that we know where dead people are and we can visit their graves and talk to them about how we are continuing their work.

Marsida replied that she had seen coffins too, many times. She had seen not just the ones made for grownups, which were black; once she had also seen a small coffin, which was red and less heavy to lift than the others because only one man was needed to carry it.

Then another friend, Besa, who was slightly older, joined the conversation. She had seen a dead person for real. She had seen her uncle. She had peeked through the keyhole into the room where he was waiting to be washed and dressed in his best clothes before being put into his coffin. There it was, open, ready, right next to him. He lay still across the sofa. He was as white as chalk, and had blood on his head because he had just fallen off an electricity pole at work. 'My aunt complained that nobody had closed his eyes when it happened,' she said. 'There's no way any part of him could have gone anywhere.'

'Yeah.' I nodded. 'My grandmother told me that when people die and we bury them, insects feed off their bodies, then they melt into the earth, and become compost, which is needed for other things to grow, like flowers or plants or whatever. They can't go anywhere,' I insisted.

'Plus, dead people stink,' Besa added. 'When my uncle died, I heard my aunt say that the funeral had to be organized quickly because if we didn't bury him right away, he would start stinking.'

'Yuck,' I said. 'We once had salami in the fridge that started stinking after a power cut. It was so stinky my dad was running around the house with a clothes peg clipped to his nose and his mouth wide open, gasping for air, crying, "Help! Help!"'

Everyone giggled. Teacher Flora heard us and sent us to stand in the corner, to reflect, she said, on how we could possibly laugh on such a sad day for our nation. When I returned home and told my grandmother that Uncle Enver was dead, and that I had been sent to stand in a corner because of rotten salami in our fridge, I could not hold back the tears flowing down my cheeks. I don't know if it was embarrassment at being scolded on the wrong day, the sadness for the loss of Uncle Enver, a combination of both, or perhaps something else, entirely unrelated.

That first conversation about death and what happens afterwards was repeated in school several years later. Teacher Nora told us that in the olden days people gathered in large buildings called churches and mosques to sing songs and recite poems dedicated to someone or something they called God, which we had to distinguish carefully from the gods of Greek mythology like Zeus, Hera or Poseidon. Nobody knew what that single God looked like, but different people had different interpretations. Some, such as Catholics and Orthodox Christians, believed that God had a child who was also half human. Others, the Muslims, thought that God was everywhere, from the smallest particles of matter to the entire universe. Others still, the Jews, thought that God would create a king who would save them at the end of the days. The prophets they recognized were also different. In the past, religious groups had bitterly fought each other, killing and maiming innocent people in disputes about whose prophet was right. But not in our country. In our country, the Catholics, Orthodox Christians, Muslims and Jews had always respected one another, because they cared about the nation more than they cared about their disagreements on what God looked like. Then the Party had come, more people started to read and write, and the more they learned about how the world worked, the more they discovered that religion was an illusion, something that the rich and powerful used to supply the poor with false hopes, promising them justice and happiness in another life.

We asked if there is another life after we die.

'There is not,' said teacher Nora with characteristic conviction. She explained it was all a way to make people stop fighting for their rights in the only life they had, so that the rich could benefit.

Capitalists, who did not necessarily believe in God themselves, wanted to keep him because it made it easier to exploit workers and blame a magical being rather than themselves for the misery they caused. But once people learned to read and write, and the Party was there to guide them, they stopped relying on God. And they also stopped believing in all kinds of other superstitions, like the evil eye, or carrying garlic to avoid bad luck, which were so many ways of pretending that people were not free to do what was right but were controlled by supernatural forces. Fortunately, with the help of the Party, we could finally understand that God was just an invention to make us afraid and reliant on those who pretended to have the power to translate the word of God, or to explain his rules.

'But it was hard to get rid of God completely,' teacher Nora said. 'Some people, some reactionaries, kept believing in him. When the Party was strong enough to fight them, voluntary action was taken to transform all the places of worship into spaces for youth training and development. Churches became sports centres; mosques became conference halls. This is why not only is there no God,' teacher Nora said in conclusion, 'but we also no longer have churches and mosques. We destroyed them all.' She raised her voice slightly. 'We must never return to those backward customs. There is no God anywhere. No God, no afterlife, no immortality of the soul. When we die, we die. The only thing that lives eternally is the work we have done, the projects we have created, the ideals we leave to others to pursue on our behalf.'

I sometimes thought about teacher Nora's words on my way back from school, as I walked past the building that housed the Party's headquarters and looked up towards one of the windows. I looked up instinctively, because that is what I had always seen my mother do, each time we walked past the building. I repeated her gesture. For some reason, I associated the Party headquarters with God, and with thoughts about the afterlife. It all started the time we were returning home from our usual Sunday outing, and I was cycling behind my parents when I overheard my mother whisper to my father: 'No, not the window with the flowerpot, the other one. He shouted, "Allahu-akbar!".'

'Allahu-akbar,' she repeated.

'Who is he?' I asked while still pedalling. 'What does "allahu-aka" mean?'

My father turned abruptly. 'Nothing,' he replied. 'It doesn't mean anything.'

'You just said "allahu-aka",' I insisted, riding ahead and stopping my bike in front of him.

'It is a very bad habit to listen to grown-up conversations,' my father said, visibly irritated. '"Allahu-akbar" is what people who believe in God used to say, to recognize and celebrate His greatness.'

'Do you mean like "Long live the Party"?' I asked.

'God is not the same as the Party,' my father explained. 'Allahu-akbar is what people of Muslim faith would have spoken in prayers. You know about different religious beliefs because teacher Nora explained it to you in the moral education class,' he said. '"Allah" meant God in Arabic.'

'Do we know any people who were Muslim in the olden days?'

'We are Muslim,' my mother replied, pulling out of her bag a handkerchief to clean off the mud she had just spotted on my shoes. 'We *were* Muslim,' my father corrected her. 'Most people in Albania were Muslim.'

I asked if Muslims believed in the afterlife. My mother nodded while still bent down, scrubbing the tops of my shoes.

'Then they were just as silly as all the other people who believed in a different God,' I said, wriggling out of my mother's hold, to cycle at full speed ahead.

Whenever I passed by the Party's headquarters on my way back from school, I thought about the man who had been shouting 'Allahu-akbar!' from the fifth-floor window. How bizarre, I thought, that all these religious zealots disagreed with one another about what exactly God looked like, and yet all believed that parts of us will survive after we die. If there was one thing that could convince us children of the irrationality of religion, of the ridiculous nature of belief in the existence of God, it was the idea that there could be a life after the one we had. In school we were taught to think about development and decay in evolutionary terms. We studied nature with the eyes of Darwin and history with the eyes of Marx. We distinguished between science and myth, reason and prejudice, healthy doubt and dogmatic superstition. We were taught to believe that the right ideas and aspirations survive as a result of all our collective efforts, but that the lives of individuals must always come to an end, like the lives of insects, birds and other animals. To think that people deserve a different fate from the rest of nature was to be a slave to myth and dogma at the expense of science and reason. Science and reason were all that mattered. Only with their help could we find out about nature and the world. And the more we knew, the more we could explain and control that which at first seemed mysterious.

'Do you understand?' I remember saying to Nini amidst the tears, on the day Enver Hoxha died. 'Uncle Enver doesn't live any more. His work will live for ever. But my wish to meet him will never be granted.'

My grandmother urged me to eat lunch. She kept praising the byrek she had made. 'I tried it myself,' she said. 'It's delicious.'

I wondered how she could eat on such a day. How could one even think about food? I was not hungry. I was too sad. Uncle Enver was gone for ever. All his books, which I loved, would remain unsigned. We didn't even have a photo of him in our living room. I would miss him terribly. 'I am going to cut a photo from the book he has written for his pioneer friends and frame it,' I announced. 'I will put it by my bedside.'

Nini stopped insisting about lunch. 'You're right,' she said. 'I'm not hungry either, I only tried one bite.' She was, however, determined to prevent me from cutting out the photo. 'We don't vandalize books in this house.'

The funeral took place a couple of days later. There was a lazy rain, after a long spell of sunshine. We stared at the television screen which showed thousands of people lined up on both sides of Tirana's main boulevard to watch the funeral procession: soldiers in tears, old women wailing and scratching their faces in despair, university students staring with an empty gaze. The images were accompanied by a symphonic march. The news reporter said little and spoke slowly, like a wretched Sisyphus who has been tasked to comment while rolling his boulder up the hill. '*Even Nature mourns the loss of one of the greatest revolutionaries of our time*,' he said. A long pause followed. Only the notes of the funeral march could be heard. '*Whenever Comrade Enver appeared on the tribune on 1 May, the weather changed, the sun came out from behind the clouds. Today, even the skies cry. The rain mixes with people's tears.*'

My family watched in silence.

'*The country mourns the loss of its most eminent son, the founding father of the modern Albanian nation, the clever strategist who organized the resistance against Italian fascism, the brilliant general who defeated the Nazis, the revolutionary thinker who steered clear of both opportunism and sectarianism, the proud statesman who resisted Yugoslav revisionist attempts to annex our beloved nation, the politician who never fell for Anglo-American imperialist plots, and who never surrendered to Soviet and Chinese revisionist pressure.*' The camera focused on the coffin, covered by a large Albanian flag, then on the grief-stricken faces of members of the Politburo, then on the new General Secretary of the Party, who was about to give a speech. The music continued. After another pause, the commentator recovered his strength and spoke again. '*Comrade Enver worked both for the nation and for international proletarian solidarity. He knew that the only way forward is national self-determination, coupled with a relentless fight against the internal and external enemies of socialism. Comrade Enver has now left us to continue the struggle without him. We will miss his brilliant guidance, his wise words, his revolutionary passion, his warm smile. We will miss him. The pain is great. We must learn to turn the pain into strength. We will do it tomorrow. Today the pain is simply too great.'*

'I know!' My mother suddenly broke the silence. 'I kept wondering about it. It's from Beethoven's Third Symphony. The funeral march. It's Beethoven.'

'No, it's not,' my father replied instantly, as if he had been waiting for her remarks all along. 'It's from that Albanian composer. I can't remember which one. But I have heard it before, it's not new,' he added, with the enthusiasm he manifested only when an opportunity to contradict my mother appeared.

'Zafo, you have no clue,' my mother said. 'You are completely tone deaf. When was the last time you even went to a classical music concert? The only music you listen to is the sound of the sports programme on the radio. The background music is from the second movement in Beethoven's Third Symphony; the "Eroica". It's called "Funeral March".'

He was about to contradict her again when Nini intervened to confirm that my mother was right. 'It's from the symphony Beethoven started to compose in honour of Napoleon. I recognize it too, Asllan was very fond of it.' Reference to my grandfather always settled family arguments.

'Will you really take me to pay my tribute at the grave?' I asked, with tears in my eyes, paralysed in front of the moving images on screen, and wondering why, instead of crying, my family was talking about music.

'This Sunday,' my grandmother replied, vaguely distracted.

'Will visitors be allowed as soon as this Sunday?'

'Not to Uncle Enver's grave, no,' Nini corrected herself. 'I thought you meant your grandfather's.'

'All the work collectives will pay tribute to Comrade Enver's grave in the coming weeks,' my father said. 'When it's my turn, I'll take you.'

For a few weeks, I looked forward to that visit. One afternoon, my father returned from work announcing that he had been to Tirana, to visit Uncle Enver's grave. 'You have been?' I asked with a mixture of anger and disappointment. 'You said you would take me. You broke your promise.'

'I tried,' my father replied apologetically. 'We left early in the morning, with the first train, and when I came to wake you up, you were sleeping, you didn't hear me. Nini tried to call you too, and you just stirred and turned over. It was late, and I had to leave. Don't worry, stuffed pepper. I'm sure there'll be another time.'

I was inconsolable. I sobbed and said that my parents clearly did not love Uncle Enver as much as I did, that they probably did not love him at all. It was a lie that they had called me that morning, I said, because, if they had told me the night before that we were about to visit his grave, I would not have slept at all and I would have jumped out of bed straight away. The truth was that they didn't care; they cared neither about visiting Uncle Enver's grave nor about keeping his photo in our living room. I had asked millions of times to have a photo of Uncle Enver framed, and they had never brought me one. All my friends had photos displayed on their bookshelves; my friend Besa even had a large photo of herself on Uncle Enver's lap during the last Congress, when she brought him a bouquet of red roses and recited a poem for the Party. I had never been to any Congress, and we had nothing.

My parents tried to reassure me. They loved the Party and Uncle Enver as much as I did, they said. The only reason his photo was missing from our living room was that we were waiting to have it enlarged. We needed a properly nice frame, my mother added, which would have to be tailor-made. The ordinary wooden frames one could find in the art shop were not worthy of Uncle Enver. 'We are working on it,' my father also emphasized. 'It was going to be a birthday surprise.'

I shook my head in disbelief. 'You won't do it for my birthday,' I said, wiping away my tears. 'I know it. You'll just forget. You don't love Uncle Enver. You clearly don't miss him, because if you missed him, you would already have a small photo, and you would also buy a large one.'

My parents seemed alarmed. They stared at each other. 'I'll tell you a secret,' Nini said. 'I have met Uncle Enver. I met him many, many years ago when your grandfather and I were still young. The two of them were friends. How could I not love him if we have been friends?' She promised that one day she would show me the letters they had exchanged. 'But,' she said, 'you must promise something in return: that you will never again say, to us or to anyone else, that we don't love or miss Uncle Enver. *Tu vas me donner ta parole d'honneur*, yes?'*

* 'You will give me your word, yes?'

5.

Coca Cola Cans

My family accepted that some rules were less important than others and that some promises could become
obsolete with time. In this they were no different from
other people, the rest of society or even the state. Part
of the challenge of growing up was finding out which
rules faded over time, which were trumped by other
more important obligations, and which ones remained
inflexible.

Take grocery shopping. There was always a queue. It
always formed before the distribution lorry arrived. You
were always expected to join, unless you had befriended
the shopkeeper. That was the general rule. But there
were also loopholes. Anyone was allowed to leave the
queue so long as they found an appropriate object to
replace them during their absence. It could be an old
shopping bag, a can, a brick or a stone. Then there was
another rule, eagerly endorsed and promptly enforced,
namely, that once the supplies arrived, the object left to
act as your representative immediately lost its representative function. It did not matter if you had left a bag, can,
brick or stone in your place. The bag was just a bag; it
could no longer be you.

Queues divided into those in which nothing happened and those in which there was always something

going on. In the first case, upholding social order could be delegated to objects. In the second case, queues were lively, noisy and boisterous; everyone had to be present and all limbs were in motion as people tried to catch sight of the counter, see how much was left of what had just arrived, and as the shopkeeper looked around for any friends in the queue they might need to prioritize.

During my training to navigate the queue system, I once asked why we had to leave a stone in the cheese queue so we could join the kerosene queue to leave a can there since nothing was happening in either of them. This was when I learned that queues could go on for an entire day, and sometimes the night, or several nights, and it was essential to let shopping bags, containers or appropriately sized stones take on some of the representative functions that would otherwise have to burden their owners. Objects in the queue were regularly monitored, and participants took turns to ensure that representative bags, cans or stones were not inadvertently removed or replaced by unauthorized items. In the very rare cases in which the system broke down, fights erupted and queues turned nasty, brutish and long. People fought bitterly over stones that looked similar, or net bags that had been cheekily replaced with sacks, or kerosene cans that had unexpectedly doubled in size.

Behaving respectfully in the queue, or joining forces to uphold queuing standards, could mark the beginning of lasting friendships. A neighbour you met in the queue or a friend you made while sharing supervisory duties would soon become someone to whom you turned in all kinds of adversity: if an elderly person in your household was unexpectedly ill and you needed childcare, or if you discovered you had run out of sugar in the middle of making a birthday cake, or if you needed someone with whom to swap food vouchers since you might have built up a stock of some items but run out of others. We relied on friends and neighbours for everything. Whenever the need arose, we simply knocked on their door, regardless of the time of day. If they did not have what we were looking for, or if they could not help with whatever we needed, they offered substitutions or recommended another family who might be able to help.

This subtle balance between following rules and breaking them also applied to other areas. It applied if you turned up to nursery or school wearing a uniform that seemed creased or, worse, had stains, or when the barber or your parents cut your hair in a style that might be thought imperialist, or if you grew your nails beyond the accepted length or varnished them with an unusual, revisionist colour such as very dark purple. The same principle, as I discovered later, also applied to more general questions such as whether men and women were effectively equals, whether the opinions of lower- and higher-ranking Party members carried the same weight, to what extent jokes about the Party and the state might have serious implications, and, as in my case, with whom it was appropriate to share observations about photos in your living room.

The trick always consisted in knowing which rule was relevant when and, ideally, whether it became looser as time passed, if it was ever meant quite as seriously as one thought, or if it was very demanding in some aspects but less so in others – and how one might know the difference so as to avoid finding out too late. The mastery of the subtle boundary between following rules and breaking them was, for us children, the true mark of growth, maturity and social integration.

For my part, I discovered one late evening in August 1985 that the promise I had made to my parents never to reveal their indifference to photographic memories of our leader was strictly binding, so strict that every other promise paled in its presence. It was at the end of a day I had spent mostly in the top of a fig tree, in the Papas' garden.

The Papas were our closest neighbours, a couple in their mid-sixties with children who had already left the house by the time I was born. My mother had made friends with the wife, Donika, when they had joined forces against a woman who they believed wanted to take their place in the kerosene queue. Like my mother, Donika had a tendency to mistrust people, and the first impression one got from her was of hostility. She was short, round, often quarrelled with neighbours and had a bad reputation with children, although with me she was unusually sweet. Before retiring, Donika had been a post-office worker. She had spent a lot of her life shouting, 'Alo, alo!' over broken telephone lines and, as a result, she had developed a tendency to turn every vowel into an A and to pronounce the end of each word in an elongated way, as if she were ringing an alarm bell: ALAA, ALAA, ALAA. Or if she was calling my mother, Doli: DALAA, DALAA, DALAA.

Donika's husband, Mihal, was a highly respected local Party official with a thick moustache that looked a bit like Stalin's. Mihal had fought in the war, destroyed many enemies, and collected a dozen medals which I was more delighted to play with than he seemed proud to own. I was fascinated by the story of a Nazi soldier he had killed, a blond man called Hans, to whom Mihal had offered water to wash the blood from his mouth while he was on his last breath. Hans had refused, continuing to mutter 'Heil Hitler' instead. I asked Mihal to describe how he had killed Hans, but he preferred to talk about the last thing he remembered of him: his thin moustache, a moustache that had not fully grown yet, he said. 'My own moustache had not grown either,' he added, and I was puzzled by how he described Hans almost with affection, as if he were describing a long-lost friend with whom he'd shared fond memories, rather than a mortal foe whose life he had taken.

The Papas lent us money regularly, looked after me when my parents and grandmother were gone and held a spare key to our house. I spent long summer evenings in their garden, eating grapes off their vines, before joining them for dinner, where Mihal would give me a little taste of his raki and let me jump off the table wearing his old partisan cap. There was a spectacular view on to the sea from their garden, and there was a gigantic fig tree with delicious fruit. Mihal had told me that by climbing that tree one could watch the sunset and count the boats entering and leaving the harbour. But I was always reluctant, because I kept thinking about the little girl whose grave was next to my grandfather's who had died after falling from a tree.

That day at the end of August 1985, however, I summoned the courage to climb the tree. But it was not to watch the sunset or count the boats in the harbour that I pushed myself to reach the top. It was in protest. That whole summer, my family and the Papas had not spoken to each other. In late June, my mother and Donika had had a falling-out, one which escalated into a fight that involved everyone else, and by the end of which I was the only member of my family with whom the Papas still spoke.

The reason for the falling-out was a Coca Cola can. One day in mid-June, my mother had bought an empty can from another teacher in her school, for the equivalent of what you would shell out for a painting of our national hero Skanderbeg in the tourist shop. She spent the afternoon deliberating with my grandmother where to put it, and since it was empty, whether to adorn it with a fresh rose from the garden. They had decided that though the rose was an original idea, it would distract from the aesthetic value of the can, and so they had left it bare, on top of our best embroidered cloth.

A few days after this discussion, the can disappeared. Then it reappeared on top of the Papas' television.

The Papas had access to our house, knew about my grandfather's old coat, in whose pocket all our money was kept, and helped us obtain permission from the Party for the private construction of our house. I had the impression they knew a lot of things about our biography too, but I never asked them what, since I did not quite understand what biography meant and did not want to embarrass myself. Mihal, who was still active in local Party circles, always helped my parents sort out administrative issues and defended them both in Party meetings and those of the local council.

Participation in the local council was compulsory for everyone in the neighbourhood, but membership of the Party was selective, open only to people with good biographies. My parents were not allowed to be members, but Mihal was a veteran, and his views on the merits of different candidates carried a lot of weight. He once almost blocked another neighbour, Vera, from joining because in one of the council meetings she had alleged that my family were reactionaries making excuses about cleaning on Sundays. Sunday cleaning was in theory optional, but in practice it was one of those cases where the norm meant the opposite of how it was announced. When my parents were new to the neighbourhood, they had struggled to interpret the recommendation in the right way. They soon learned.

My family and the Papas spent a lot of time with each other: they cleaned the street together on Sundays and helped out other neighbours when a wedding or funeral had to be organized. Weddings were usually held in people's gardens, with hundreds invited. Everyone mobilized to help make dinner, to bring benches and tables from the local schools, or to arrange the place where the orchestra would play music into the night. Our two families always carried the benches together and sat next to each other during the dinner and celebrations. The children stayed up till dawn, singing and dancing, and when the festivities reached their peak, the guests would make their way close to the bride, waving a one-hundred-lek note, which they would lick and slap on her forehead, as custom required. Mihal always slapped leks on my forehead too, saying I danced better and was more intelligent than the bride.

In late summer my mother and Mihal would often pool resources to make raki together. During those long days distilling fermented grapes, waiting for the alcohol to drip from the spout and testing how strong or weak the raki was, they would talk about the old times. I once overheard my mother mention the port of our town in the thirties, and say to Mihal that the largest boat her family had owned was still being used for exports. I was confused and later asked Mihal what it meant. But he said they had been talking about *arka* and not *varka* (crates rather than boats), then asked if I wanted to dance on the table, where he was eating meze.

I mention all this to emphasize that my mother would have never dreamed of accusing the Papas of theft, had it not been for the fact that the stolen object was a Coca Cola can. At the time, these were an extremely rare sight. Even rarer was the knowledge of their function. They were markers of social status: if people happened to own a can, they would show it off by exhibiting it in their living rooms, usually on an embroidered tablecloth over the television or the radio, often right next to the photo of Enver Hoxha. Without the Coca Cola can, our houses looked the same. They were painted the same colour; they had the same furniture. With the Coca Cola can, something changed, and not just visually. Envy came between us. Doubts started to emerge. Trust was broken.

'My can!', my mother exclaimed when she went to return the rolling pin that Donika had lent her and saw the red object standing on top of the Papas' television. 'What is my can doing here?' Donika squinted as if she couldn't see my mother's index finger pointing at the can, or as if she couldn't believe what she was seeing. 'It's mine,' she replied proudly. 'I bought it recently.' '*I* bought it recently,' my mother repeated, 'and look where it's ended up.' 'Are you saying I stole my can?' Donika demanded, confronting her. 'I am saying that *your* can is actually *my* can,' my mother replied.

That day, she and Donika argued like never before. They started in front of the television but came out on the road, screaming insults and waving rolling pins while everyone stood watching. Donika shouted that my mother was nothing but a bourgeois dressed in teacher's clothes, and my mother shouted back that Donika was nothing but a peasant dressed as a post-office worker. After a while, a witness was brought in: a neighbour who worked at the nearby cigarette factory confirmed that she had sold the empty can to Donika a day after my mother had bought hers.

At that point, my mother offered a formal apology. Donika and Mihal were so offended that they did not accept it. They turned their backs and walked to their house, and stopped calling out of the window to invite my parents for morning coffee. When they overlapped in the shopping queue, they ignored each other, and once Donika even pretended not to recognize the excellent large stone my mother used as her representative when she left the queue, even though it had come from the Papas' garden. We never discovered who was responsible for stealing our Coca Cola can, but we concluded it was unsafe to buy another, however much it improved our living room. I seized the opportunity to request a photo of Uncle Enver to replace the Coca Cola can on top of our television – a request my parents again ignored.

During that summer, the Papas still let me climb their trees in the garden, but they no longer invited me for dinner. When I asked Mihal if I could play with his medals and partisan cap, he said we would do it another time.

'It's about dignity; they trampled on our dignity,' I over-heard him say to Donika one day. I started to suspect that the Papas were not really peeved about my parents' accusations related to the Coca Cola cans but were upset about something else, something more important, the sort of thing my parents could never replace or make amends for. I was heartbroken. I hated to see Donika walk past my mother in silence at the cheese queue, and I missed her reedy, thin voice calling my mother from the window when she made coffee: Dalaaaa, Dalaaaa, Kaaafaaaa, Kafaaaaa. My parents were heartbroken too, only they did not know what else to say to apologize.

After a couple of weeks like that, I thought I would take matters into my own hands. I decided to hide in the Papas' garden, pretending to be lost so that my parents would go searching for me. I figured that if the Papas saw how the whole neighbourhood mobilized to look for me, and how upset my parents were to have lost their precious first child, perhaps they would join the search, and perhaps our families would be close again, just as they were when they shared cleaning tasks or sat on the same table at weddings.

The strategy worked. After hours of looking every-where – except for the branches of the fig tree, where they thought I would never go – my grandmother was in despair. My father roamed the street, shaking, his asthma pump in his hand, and even my mother – who never cried – was almost in tears. When the Papas saw her, they forgot all about Coca Cola cans. Donika hugged my mother, who never accepted being hugged, and told her that it would all be fine, that they would soon find me again. It was at that point, observing everything from the top of the tree, that I decided our two families were now reconciled. I climbed down the tree carefully but still getting cuts and scratches on my knees, and when I showed up with blood dripping from my legs, and tears flowing from my eyes, to reveal the details of my plan, everyone was moved beyond measure. I explained that I had climbed the fig tree and had got lost on purpose. I could no longer bear to see how my family and the Papas ignored each other in the queues. I said I wanted to sit next to them again at the weddings, and to play with Mihal's cap, and jump off their table on to their sofa. The Papas then declared, 'Never mind, all is forgiven and forgotten,' and even my grandmother nodded, she who always resolved disputes by declaring in French, '*Pardonner oui, oublier jamais*': forgive, but never forget.

That evening my parents invited the Papas for meze again. They drank raki and laughed heartily at how silly they had been to let Coca Cola cans come between them. Mihal licked a one-hundred-lek note and stuck it on my forehead. I had been very clever and brave, he said, to go to the top of the fig tree. He also noted later that Coca Cola cans were produced in imperialist countries, and they might have reached Albania as corrupting devices, introduced surreptitiously by our enemies to break the bonds of trust and solidarity. At the point in the evening when he mentioned this, it was no longer clear if he was serious, but I remember everyone laughed, drank more raki, toasted the end of imperialism and laughed some more.

Donika, however, was extremely serious when she offered my mother her own Coca Cola can. She said that they could take turns in displaying it, keeping it for two weeks on top of one television and two weeks on the other. My mother refused, insisting we absolutely did not deserve such kindness. On the contrary, my mother said, if we still had our own Coca Cola can, *she* would offer it to Donika, so that Donika could use hers for salt and my mother's for pepper, just like those sets that sometimes appeared in *Dynasty*. Donika replied that there would be no need, that Coca Cola cans had started to become a bit too common after all; it was the white-and-orange cans that were really sought after now, though she could not remember what they were called, something to do with 'fantasy' or 'fantastic'. Then she praised the cloth on top of which the can had stood, saying it looked much nicer without anything, that my mother had embroidered the tulip so beautifully it would have been a shame to cover it.

'We were going to have a photo of Uncle Enver on that one,' I interrupted cheerily amidst the noise. 'But they never want anything to do with Uncle Enver – they keep promising to put a photo there, and they never do it. I don't think they like Uncle Enver,' I said, playing with the hundred-lek note Mihal had just given me, emboldened by his remarks about how clever I had been.

That changed the mood in our living room. Everyone froze. My mother, who had been laughing with Donika, and saying nice things about how much she missed the baklava Donika made, stopped speaking and looked intently at her, as if trying to guess her thoughts. Nini, who was in the little kitchen extension preparing more food, came out holding a bowl of washed cucumbers. Her hands were trembling. My father, who'd been helping himself to more olives and cheese from the shared platter, dropped the fork. For a short while, only the mosquitoes dancing around the lamp in our living room could be heard.

Mihal frowned. He then turned to me with an extremely serious, even severe look on his face. 'Come here,' he said, breaking the silence, urging me to sit on his lap. 'I thought you were a clever girl. I just praised you for how clever you were today. What you just said is not what clever girls say. It was a very stupid thing to say, the most stupid thing I have ever heard from you.' I blushed and felt the heat burning my cheeks. 'Your parents love Uncle Enver. They love the Party. You must never again say these stupid things to anyone. Otherwise, you don't deserve to play with my medals.'

I nodded. I had started to shake and was about to burst into tears. Mihal must have felt the motion of my body on his knees, and regretted his tone. He softened his voice. 'Now, don't start crying,' he said. 'You're not a baby. You're a brave girl. You will fight for your country, and for the Party, when you grow up. Your parents sometimes make mistakes, like with the Coca Cola can, but they are good, hard-working people and they are bringing you up well. They have grown up under socialism, and they love the Party and Uncle Enver too. Do you understand? You must never repeat what you said.'

I nodded again. The rest were still silent. 'Come,' Mihal said. 'Let's raise another toast. To your future without Coca Cola divisions.' He picked up his glass, but before drinking, he interrupted himself, as if something else, something very important, had occurred to him. 'You must promise me that if you ever again have silly ideas like that about your family, you will come and tell me. Me – nobody else, not even Auntie Donika. Do you understand?'

6.

Comrade Mamuazel

'Comrade Mamuazel, halt immediately, you're under arrest!'

Flamur stood in front of me with his arms and legs wide, holding a cane about three times as long as he was tall in his left hand, and with his right clutching something small I could not see.

'Give me your Juicy Fruit,' he ordered.

'Let me check,' I replied, removing the silky red ribbon that held up my hair, then reaching for my school bag. 'Let me check. But I'm not sure I have Juicy Fruit. I might have Wrigley Spearmint or Hubba Bubba.'

'You do,' he said. 'I saw Marsida give it to you yesterday.'

'I don't have Juicy Fruit,' I insisted. 'I can give you Hubba Bubba. They look similar.' I picked up another flattened piece of coloured wrapping paper from the pocket of my dress, and held it under my nose for a few seconds to demonstrate how fresh it was. The paper smelled better than the usual blend of rubber and sweat; you could almost be reminded of the real thing. Flamur let go of the cane he was holding and opened his right fist, displaying his own collection of wrappers, checking what was available.

'It's really fresh,' I insisted. He grabbed my paper and smelled it.

'It's goooood,' he said. 'How old do you think it is?'

'I'm not sure,' I replied. 'But not more than three months. Maybe four. Depends on how many people have had it before and also –'

'Well, yeah, that's obvious,' he interrupted me aggressively. 'Do you think you only know this stuff because you can speak French?'

I had learned not to answer such provocations. I continued to stare at him, a supplicating look on my face. I was about to burst out crying, but if there was one thing that Flamur loathed more than girls with ribbons, it was 'cry-babies'. I knew that if I cried, I would lose my entire wrapping-paper collection.

'You'll be released from arrest once you tell me the password,' Flamur said, snatching the Hubba Bubba. 'Don't think, Mamuazel, I didn't see you take off that ribbon.'

'The password,' I whispered. 'The password is "Death to fascism, freedom to the people".'

This is one of my earliest memories. Perhaps I remember the scene with such precision because it played out in more or less the same form almost every day. Flamur was the second-most-dangerous bully in the neighbourhood. The most dangerous one, Arian, who was a few years older than us, rarely appeared on the street when we played. When he did, it was to confiscate someone's jumping rope, or to interrupt a game of hopscotch with instructions for the children to return to their houses because it was getting dark, or to order us to switch games from Fight-ball to Fascists and Partisans. Once everyone complied, he went back inside. We, on the other hand, continued to do as we had been told.

Nobody knew what would happen if we did not follow his commands. Nobody had ever tried to find out.

Flamur was a different sort of bully. He was always on the street, patrolling up and down from the end of school until late after dark. He was the youngest child in a family of five, and the only boy. His three older sisters lived at home and worked in the nearby cigarette factory. They all had different surnames starting with B: Bariu, Bilbili, Balli. Flamur was the only one whose surname did not start with B and was the same as his mother's: Meku. Flamur claimed that his father was away, fighting the Romans and the Ottomans. When Marsida once had the temerity to suggest that we had stopped fighting these empires a long time ago, he cut her ponytail off with his scissors.

When Flamur was alone, he would sit on the steps outside someone's door, beating pans and belting out melancholic gypsy love songs until the other children came out of their houses and gathered in the common play area. He decided which games we would start with, who was allowed to have the first go, who would have to sit out a particular round because they had been caught cheating, and what exemptions had to be made to accommodate younger siblings – whom he also terrorized, by wearing an old brown sack with holes over his eyes to make him look like a ghost and unexpectedly grabbing them. He generally wore an oversized yellow-and-green top with Brazil's flag on it and roamed the streets accompanied by a group of stray dogs whom he had named after famous players from Brazil's national football team: Sócrates, Zico, Rivellino and, his favourite dog, Pelé, who was half blind and had some kind of skin disease. He hated cats, and, if he found a stray kitten, he was very likely to dump it on the rubbish pile at the end of the road and burn it. He also hated girls with ribbons. He was the one who taught everyone else to call me Comrade Mamuazel and ask for the password.

One of Flamur's older sisters had once been summoned by the Party in the local council offices because she hit Flamur so hard on his back with a chair that the chair broke. When my grandmother learned the news, she yelled, almost beside herself with anger, that violence against children was no different from the violence of the state.

When I was growing up, I knew something about me was different but could not say what it was. My family, unlike Flamur's, never smacked me. My mother usually stayed out of things: she disciplined with invisible authority. To my father, disciplining meant sending me for a few hours of 'reflection' in their bedroom – or, as I called it, with childish exaggeration, the 'prison', because it had no toys. Occasionally, I was allowed to take a book with me, and in those moments of wounded anger I would choose a novel that featured orphans, like *Les Misérables*, *Alone in the World* or *David Copperfield*. But I never let the suffering of the main characters distract me from my own anguish or minimize the injustice of which I thought I was a victim. These stories fuelled wild fantasies about my family and, after a few hours of being lost in the lives of other children, I had even more questions about who I really was. Like the characters I read about, I dreamed about a change of fortune, the unexpected intervention of a benevolent stranger, or finding solace in the discovery of a distant relative.

From my parents' bedroom, I wrote long letters to

Cocotte, one of my grandmother's first cousins, who lived alone in the capital, Tirana, and often spent the winter with us. I called them 'the prison letters': I had numbered them, and often divided them by topic. In my letters, I complained about my parents' harshness, how they spoke French to me on the street, without concern that my friends could hear, and how they always expected me to outperform everyone in school, including in subjects like PE, where I had no talent at all.

Cocotte's official name was Shyqyri, but she disliked it. She said it sounded too ordinary. Everyone in my grandmother's family had a real name and a French nickname. She and my grandmother had grown up together in Salonica. They were Arnauts, as Ottoman Turks called Albanian minorities in the empire, but they spoke French to each other, as Nini did to me. Whenever Cocotte came to visit, she shared a room with us. She and my grandmother chatted late into the night, evoking remote places and their people: a pasha in Istanbul, émigrés from St Petersburg, passports in Zagreb, food markets in Skopje, fighters in Madrid, boats in Trieste, bank accounts in Athens, ski resorts in the Alps, dogs in Belgrade, rallies in Paris and opera stalls in Milan.

During those frozen winter evenings, our tiny bedroom became a continent, a continent of shifting borders, forgotten heroes of armies that no longer existed, deadly fires, exuberant balls, property feuds, weddings, deaths and new births. I felt the urge to understand, to connect my childhood to that of Nini and Cocotte, to picture their world, to rearrange years that seemed without time, to remember characters I had never known, or to ascribe meaning to events I had never witnessed. I felt confused and sometimes frightened by the sheer chaos of the things I heard about, adults who had lost track of each other, boats that never sailed, children that never lived. But just when I thought my efforts to understand were about to yield results, Nini and Cocotte stopped speaking in French and suddenly switched to Greek.

They were enormously fond of each other, but they could not have been more different. They had first travelled to Albania as adults, Nini to work for the government and Cocotte to find a husband. Cocotte didn't like the Greeks or the Turks, and she didn't like Jewish men – although she admitted reluctantly that the latter were 'the last intelligent people left in Salonica'. It turned out she didn't like Albanians either, or at least her parents continued to object that so-and-so was uncultured, or insufficiently wealthy, or politically unreliable, and as a result she never married. She had an imaginary husband called Rexhep or, in French, Rémy. 'Unlike your grandfather,' she used to say in my grandmother's presence, 'Rémy never brought me any trouble.'

The weeks when Cocotte visited were the only times I spoke French without reluctance. Otherwise, I hated it. It was not my language. My grandmother was not French. I did not understand why it was inflicted on me, why they taught me to speak French first, and then Albanian. I hated it when the children on the street were mobilized by Flamur to make fun of my broken Albanian, like when I called the slices of apple that we ate as a snack *des morceaux de pommes*. Their parents were usually more supportive, but even they seemed perplexed when my grandmother called me home at the end of the day and they heard me give a summary of our activities in a language they could not understand. 'Why French?' I heard one of them ask my grandmother one day. 'Why not Russian, or English, or Greek? There are so many possibilities.' 'I don't like the Greeks,' my grandmother said. 'And I don't speak Russian or English,' she added, perhaps to indicate her hostility to imperialism.

The time I hated French most of all was when I had to appear before a special educational committee to prove I was ready to start school. One did not normally have to take a test to go to school – an education was compulsory and began between the ages of six and seven. A few weeks before the start of the academic year, teachers would divide into teams of three or four and walk around town, knocking on each door to make sure all the children had been enrolled. The Party took pride in having abolished illiteracy at record speed, and there were often reports on television of how old women from remote villages in the north were now able to read, and to sign documents with their names rather than a simple X. There was much excitement in the weeks before the start of the academic year; happy children queued in the pioneers' shop and parents gossiped with one another in the classrooms where textbooks were sold. On the first day, everyone wore shiny, bright uniforms and showed off their new haircuts and flocked to the streets carrying bouquets of flowers. As our teacher Nora said: 'In imperialist countries we tend to observe this enthusiasm only during the sales period.' Nobody knew what a 'sale' was, but it felt like a stupid question to ask.

At the end of the summer of 1985, I was keen to start school. My mother had taught me to read and write, partly as a way to improve my Albanian, which was still broken because everyone spoke French to me, and partly so that I would no longer need help reading an old book of translated Russian fairy tales that had once belonged to her. My sixth birthday fell a week after the official start of the year, and my parents bought me a red leather rucksack. I liked it at first, until I realized that all the other children had been given brown or black school bags, mostly to be carried by hand. Only a few went over shoulders. The brown and black bags were sold in the pioneers' shop shortly before the beginning of each school year, alongside black uniforms, red scarves and all the usual paraphernalia: notebooks, pens, pencils, rulers, compasses, protractors, PE kits. The red rucksacks were in limited supply. They appeared in the warehouses for only a couple of days, and usually sold out before reaching the shops. Mine became yet another thing I had to explain about myself: things like the embroidered dresses with lace hems I wore on May Day or for Sunday walks; the white leather shoes, handmade to measure by Marsida's father, who was a shoemaker; or my hand-knitted coat, which had been designed after a model found on the torn pages of a children's fashion magazine smuggled from somewhere in the West.

When I realized the red rucksack would open a new front of bullying, I became reluctant to go to school. For a few days, fortune was on my side. No school in town was prepared to bend the rules to allow me to join early. My family insisted. They thought I was ready, and that I would be bored at nursery. They were advised to obtain special authorization from the educational section of the Central Party Committee. One evening in late August, at the end of the Committee's official business, we appeared in front of a panel of Party officials to make our case.

My parents had been preparing for the meeting for several days. They had rehearsed what they would say, tried to anticipate the questions they would face, and told me to repeat all the poems I knew about the Party and Uncle Enver, as well as the new partisan songs I had learned in nursery. I remember all of us advancing nervously towards the Central Party Committee building, my parents leading the way and my grandmother holding my hand while we walked a few metres behind. I wore a bright red dress, and held tight under my right arm a brown folder that contained the book with which I had learned to read, plus another with numbers and exercises in elementary maths. At one point, halfway through our march, my mother turned to see how far behind we were lagging, and suddenly emitted a loud sound between a howl and a shriek. 'White!' she said. 'It is white!' Her face filled with horror, she pointed to the ribbon that held up my ponytail. My father said nothing but, without waiting for further instruction, turned around and sprinted back to the house. A quarter of an hour later, he was back, breathless, holding a red ribbon in one hand and his asthma pump in the other. He was told there was no time for pumps. We all walked up the flight of stairs that led to the office of the education section, and I was scolded for whistling the tune of the new partisan song I had learned earlier that day.

In the meeting, my father gave the opening speech. He did not say that it would have been unreasonable to keep me from school for a whole year simply because my birthday fell a week after the registration date. He said he knew that a communist society valued education more than anything, and that the Party would be loyally served by such a keen representative of the younger generation of revolutionaries, so keen she had expressed several times the desire to start school as soon as possible. Of course, he said, he was aware that the final decision rested with the Party, and that the Party would decide fairly in any case. However, my parents had the presumption to believe that my enthusiasm at least deserved a hearing.

He said all this as he looked straight at the portrait of Uncle Enver on the wall, as if he had been talking to our leader rather than the people in the room. One member of the panel tapped his fingers on the desk while staring into the void, a second took notes while occasionally glancing at my mother's linen dress, a third looked at my grandmother as if he had already seen her somewhere. The fourth, a woman with short hair and an austere charcoal-grey suit, kept her gaze fixed on the red flag that sat on the desk, with a mysterious half-smile stamped on her face.

At the end of all the speeches, the reading and maths tests, and after the poem recital, the panel looked sceptical. They sighed, rolled their eyes, raised their eyebrows, then regarded each other. The man who had been gently tapping on the table with only three fingers now started to tap faster with both hands, making a noise that sounded like rain. It did not go unnoticed. The man who had been alternating note-taking with glancing at my mother's dress dropped his pen and started to stare at him instead.

It was my grandmother who decided to break the silence. With her eyes on the third panel member, who she also seemed finally to recognize, she said:

'Comrade Mehmet speaks French. Lea can read in French too. Perhaps you would like to give her something to read in French?'

'We can't test that,' the woman who had been smiling replied. 'We don't have any books for children here. Certainly, no books for children *en français*,' she added half-mockingly.

'Perhaps she can read from one of the works of Comrade Enver,' Nini volunteered. 'I can see a translation of selected works on the shelf,' she added, while the man called Mehmet nodded. A book was brought down, opened at random and I read out loud a few lines. Then I stumbled on one word, the only word I can still remember: 'collectivization'. I kept struggling to pronounce it.

'Collevization,' I said. 'Collectivation,' I corrected. 'Collectiviz—', I could no longer finish the word. I felt completely stuck, and my eyes filled with tears.

At that point, the panel started clapping, spontaneously, all at once. 'You are very bright!' Comrade Mehmet exclaimed. 'This is very difficult to read, even in Albanian. You can teach your friends. You can even teach them how to read in French. Did you know that Uncle Enver used to be a French teacher in school when he was young? Are you going to be like him?'

I nodded. 'I have read all the books that Uncle Enver has written for children,' I said, licking the tears and snot on my lips. 'I know what *collectism* means, it means that we all work better when we share things, I just can't pronounce it.'

That evening the panel approved the decision to lift the age restriction for starting school and sent us away with a letter explaining the exceptional circumstances under which it had been taken. My parents walked home ecstatic, with animated talk of how lucky we had been to stumble on Comrade Mehmet, to whom my grandmother had given French lessons many years ago in Kavajë, the little town where my father's family lived before I was born. They tried to buy beers to celebrate, but the week's supplies in the shop had run out, so they turned to the home-made raki we kept, inviting the Papas over for meze. They raised toasts, not to the Party, but to my education, and gulped one shot of raki after another, joking and laughing out loud until well past midnight.

For my part, I felt a mixture of pride and embarrassment: pride because I would soon start school, and embarrassment because I was still unable to pronounce 'collectivization'. I had kept trying since we left the Central Committee building, and kept on getting it wrong. When Mihal asked me to sing a song in French, instead of complying, as everybody expected, I declared how much I hated the language. I had hated it, I said, from the first day I was in the crèche, when the other nursery children insisted that I was not like them because I spoke only French. My fear now when I started school was that the same thing would happen, that I would not be able to make new friends *because* I spoke French. Besides, I did not understand why we had to speak a language nobody else understood, the language of a country we had never visited, and where nobody we knew lived.

'Did you hear what the comrade on the education panel said?' Nini asked, trying to convince me. 'Uncle

Enver also spoke French. He studied in France for many years. He also taught it to children like you. French is an important language, the language of the great writers and philosophers of the Enlightenment, and France is the country of the French Revolution, which spread the ideals of freedom, equality and fraternity, about which you will learn in school.' I shook my head in protest.

'You already know about the French Revolution. You watched *Cosette* at the puppet theatre, and you said how much you liked it, remember?' Nini insisted.

I was still thinking about the nursery, but her mention of *Cosette* made me resolve to confess all the details I had not yet dared reveal: how children lifted up my dress, pulled my ribbons and called me Comrade Mamuazel, how they scorned the way I walked and teased me for the expressions I adopted, all because of my French. For the second time that day, I burst into tears.

'You must not speak French if it makes you unhappy,' Nini said. Our neighbours nodded in approval.

From that day, and with the exception of the weeks during which Cocotte visited us, French was officially abolished. My grandmother spoke it to me only in one of three cases: when I played late with a friend and she wanted to discreetly encourage me to stop; if she herself was furious and wanted to let off steam; and as a way of scolding.

7.

They Smell of Sun Cream

I still associate all our efforts to learn from the outside world with Dajti, the name of the isolated mountain range that surrounded our capital and dominated its landscape as if it had captured it and was holding it hostage. Dajti was physically remote but always with us. I never visited it. I still don't know what 'receiving from Dajti' meant; who received what, from whom, or how. I suspect there was a satellite or TV receiver up there. Dajti was in every house, in every conversation, in everyone's thoughts. 'I saw it last night through Dajti' meant: 'I was alive. I broke a law. I was thinking.' For five minutes. For an hour. For a whole day. For however long Dajti would be there.

When my father became frustrated with the programmes on Albanian television he would declare: 'I am going to see if we can get Dajti.' He would then climb up on to the roof, twist our antenna this way and that and shout through the window: 'How is it now, is it better?' To which I would answer: 'Same as before.' A couple of minutes later he would shout again: 'What about now?' And I would shout back: 'Gone! It's completely gone! It was better before.' Then I would hear him swear, followed by metallic sounds that suggested he was still fiddling with the antenna. The more impatient he became, the less likely the signal was to return.

In the summer the situation improved, at least in theory. With good weather, we had two options: Dajti and Direkti. Direkti, the direct signal, could be picked up from Italy, thanks to our proximity to the Adriatic. In my mind, Dajti was the god of the mountains and Direkti was the god of the sea. But Direkti was much more whimsical than Dajti. With Dajti, once you got the antenna right, you knew that the signal would be lost only at the time of the *telegiornale*, the Italian news programme. Direkti was deceptive. When things worked out, even the *telegiornale* was accessible, from beginning to end. On other days, Direkti went from being 'a looking glass', as my father called it to indicate his satisfaction with the visibility, to absolutely nothing, a grey screen occupied by shaking spiderwebs. This meant that when there were important football matches on television, such as Juventus playing at the end of the Serie A season, my father had to face a dilemma: either go with Dajti and expect the signal to be reliable but not ideal, or take his chances with the fickle 'looking glass' of Direkti. He often fell for the latter, but having to own the consequences of a potentially misleading decision made him extremely anxious. On such days, he climbed the roof with sadness, like someone about to confront an adversary whose superiority was known. 'I'm going up to look at the antenna,' he would say, with resignation in his voice and occasionally a touch of despair. On the relation between my father and the antenna – the psychological dramas, the dynamic of attraction and repulsion it fostered, the subtle balance between triumph and defeat – depended every vital piece of information from abroad that my family received, from the attempted assassination of Pope John Paul II to rumours of a break-up between Albano and Romina Power after the latest Sanremo festival.

Without Dajti and Direkti there was little to watch on television. On weekdays, the 6 p.m. story time and the animated film that followed were both a struggle. They coincided with Yugoslav basketball, and the only form of compromise with my father was to switch channels every five minutes. There was more on Sundays: puppet theatre at 10 a.m., with a children's film immediately after, then *Maya the Bee* on Macedonian TV. Then you just had to accept whatever luck brought: a programme of folk songs and dances from different regions of the country, a report about cooperatives that had exceeded the five-year-plan target, a swimming tournament, the weather forecast.

Things got better when *Foreign Languages at Home* began to be broadcast at 5 p.m. The programme played daily on Albanian television and was therefore immune to the arbitrary power the antenna exercised on our lives. In addition to English, there was French, Italian, and also 'Gymnastics under Home Conditions'. I never tried the latter. We had plenty of exercise every morning at the start of classes, when the whole cohort of teachers and pupils gathered in the school yard to practise toe-touching, arm rotations and quad stretches, followed by swearing loyalty to the Party. But I watched all the language programmes with great enthusiasm, especially the Italian one. Imagine how much more I would enjoy the cartoons on Rai Uno, I told myself, if I could figure out what they were about.

Foreign Languages at Home was the subject of intense

discussion in the playground. There was always something to learn, not only about foreign languages but also about foreign cultures. I remember an intense discussion about shopping in England, as revealed in a supermarket scene where a mother read out a grocery list and her children had to identify the matching items on the shelves. Pasta, check. Bread, check. Toothpaste, check. Soft drinks, check. Beer, check.

And so we discovered that there was no need to queue. That anyone could choose any food they liked. That the shelves were overflowing with goods, but customers in the shop bought so much they could not even carry it. That people presented no food vouchers and seemed to have no limits on what they could buy, and in what quantity. We wondered why, if people could purchase food any time they wanted, they chose to stockpile it.

Most puzzling of all was how each food item had its own label. Instead of displaying a generic name, like 'toothpaste', 'pasta', or 'beer', it contained what looked like the name or surname of a person: Barilla pasta, Heineken beer or Colgate toothpaste. This also seemed to apply to the supermarket itself. Why couldn't a shop simply be called *Bread shop*, *Meat shop*, *Clothes shop* or *Coffee shop*?

'Imagine,' Besa said, 'having a shop called *Ypi's Meat* or *Marsida's Coffee* or *Besa's Bread*.'

'Probably the names of the people who made them,' I pointed out. 'You know, like we have plastic produced by the First of May brigade.'

Others contested that interpretation. Teacher Nora had explained that, outside Albania, people never knew the names of those who made things, the names of the workers. She told us that in the West one knew only the names of the factories where they were made, the people who owned them, their children, and their children's children. Like *Dombey and Son*.

The next perplexing topic was the function of shopping trolleys.

'The trolley was to carry children,' I said.

'Food,' Marsida corrected me.

'Children,' I insisted.

'Well, it was clearly used for both,' Besa said. 'Did you see what the children smuggled into the shopping trolley?' she added, with the air of someone who can distinguish the relevant from the trivial detail. 'The mother only discovered it at the end, when she had to pay. I think it was a Coca Cola can.'

'Yes, it was,' Marsida said. 'She still went ahead and bought it for the children. They said they were thirsty. Maybe the shop didn't have any water. Maybe they don't have everything after all.'

'I think it's a drink,' I almost whispered, as if I were revealing a secret. 'Those cans you sometimes see on top of people's shelves, they're to hold drinks.'

Then Flamur, who was feeding leftover bones to his favourite dog, Pelé, interrupted us. 'Blah blah blah,' he mocked. 'Of course Coca Cola is a drink, everyone knows it. I've tasted it before. I once saw a tourist kid drop a can in the bin, and I collected it. It was still half full so I tried it. It's a bit like the red aranxhata they sell on the beach, but for tourists.'

Everyone looked at him with suspicion.

'Then he saw me. He looked at me with angry, flashing eyes,' Flamur continued. He slightly raised his voice, the same way he did when he started a story about his dad fighting the Ottomans. 'He was angry. Very angry,' Flamur repeated. 'But he didn't hit me. Instead, he started crying and I returned the can, I returned it immediately. He cried even more, kicked it, jumped on it and ruined it. I left it there. It was useless, wouldn't even stand on a shelf.'

We wondered if it had really happened. Teacher Nora had said that most of the tourist children who visited Albania were from the bourgeois class. They were famously nasty, so nasty that the nastiness of Flamur, and even Arian, paled beside it. Who knew what they were capable of doing to a can?

'Do you think Flamur really took a can from a tourist child?' Marsida asked after Flamur had left.

'It's hard to say,' Besa replied. 'He does spend a lot of time rummaging in bins to find leftovers for his dogs. He didn't steal it. The child had dropped it in the bin.'

'I don't think it's a true story,' I said. 'I've never met any tourist children.'

In school we were told not to interact with people who did not look like us. We were advised to change our route if we stumbled on tourists, and to never, under any circumstances, accept anything they might offer, especially chewing-gum. 'Above all, beware of the tourist carrying chewing-gum,' teacher Nora insisted.

Sometimes, from a distance we saw the tourist children who visited the beach in summer, next to the Adriatik, the hotel for foreigners. A long trench in the sand separated the local beach from the foreigners' one, but there were no trenches in the water. On those occasions, my cousins and I would swim near the tourist beach and practise diving or water jumps or somersaults to grab their attention. Sometimes we would sing an English nursery rhyme we knew, 'Baa Baa Black Sheep': 'Ban ban backship, eni eni you.' They would stare back, with a look between the confused and the frightened, and my cousins would then urge me to say hello in French. I refused, at first. I refused not because teacher Nora had told us not to speak to tourists – I didn't think the restriction applied in shallow water, where no chewing-gum could be traded – but because I still hated speaking French. If it was so great to speak French, I thought, I shouldn't be teased for it. I shouldn't be asked to speak it only when tourists were involved.

'I don't want to say hello,' I protested. 'We don't know them. They're not going to answer. Plus, how do you know they speak French? They could speak something else.' But my cousins called me a wimp and a coward, and to show them I was not a coward I said a reluctant '*Ça va?*' The tourist children kept staring. I changed to: '*Ciao!*' They rolled their eyes. I added the only sentence I knew in German: '*Woher kommen Sie?*': 'Where do you come from?' I should have said, 'Where are you going?' because that was the point at which they left. My cousins then said: 'See, you scared them. You should have smiled.' 'Please come back,' I muttered to myself, seeing the children disappear behind large multicoloured towels. I hated to see them disappear. I hated them for not answering. The only thing I hated more was that I had succumbed to the pressure.

The tourist children had bright, unusual toys that looked so different from ours that we sometimes wondered if they were toys at all. They splashed around on floating mattresses displaying characters we had never seen, had strangely shaped buckets and spades and exotic plastic material we had no word for. They smelled different, a smell that was enticing in an addictive way, one that made you want to follow them, to go and hug them so you could smell it some more. We always knew when there were tourist children nearby because the beach smelled weird, a hybrid of flowers and butter.

I asked my grandmother what it was. She explained that they smelled of sun cream, a thick white liquid used to protect people from the sun. 'We don't have it,' she said. 'We use olive oil. It's healthier.'

From that day on, I had a name for the smell. 'They smell of sun cream,' I said to my cousins one day at the beach. 'I can smell it now,' one of them replied. 'I can smell sun cream. They went that way. Let's go. Let's follow them.'

We followed them until they disappeared with their parents, on to a tour bus or into a restaurant we had no permission to enter. Then only questions were left. What do they read? Do they enjoy *Alice in Wonderland, Jim Button and Luke the Engine-driver* or *The Adventures of Cipollino*? Do they also have to collect chamomile flowers to help factories make medical herbs? Do they challenge each other on who knows more names of Greek gods? On who can remember more sites of ancient Roman battles? Are they inspired by Spartacus? Do they compete in Maths Olympiads? Do they want to conquer space? Do they like baklava?

I thought about foreign children with curiosity, occasionally envy, but often also pity. I felt especially sorry for them on Children's Day, 1 June, when I received presents from my parents and we went to eat ice-cream by the beach and to visit the funfair. On that occasion, they also gave me a yearly subscription to several children's magazines. It was through these magazines that I learned about the fate of other children around the world. The magazine *Little Stars* was for children from six to eight years old, and on Children's Day it ran a cartoon called 'Our 1 June and theirs'. On one side there was a fat capitalist wearing a fat top hat buying ice-cream for his fat son, and on the floor next to the shop's entrance two ragged children and a caption: '1 June never comes for us.' On the other side, there were socialist flags, happy children carrying flowers and presents, holding their parents' hands, waiting to buy ice-cream in front of a shop. 'We love 1 June,' their caption read. The queue was very short.

In the late eighties, I also started to receive *The Horizon*, for teenagers. I was still young for it, but my father loved it because it featured a maths and physics challenges section, as well as a regular column about scientific and astronomic curiosities. Occasionally, he had to be reminded that he had bought the magazine for me, and needed to pass it on. *The Horizon* depicted Western children frequently; never in such detail as to exhaust all possible questions about their lives, but enough to provide a sense of how different they were. Unlike my world, theirs was divided: between the rich and the poor, the bourgeois and the proletarian, the hopeful and the hopeless, the free and the shackled. There were privileged, entitled children who, like their bourgeois parents, had everything they wanted but never shared it with the less fortunate, whose hardship they ignored. There were also poor and oppressed children who had to sleep rough, whose parents could not afford to pay the bills at the end of the month, who had to beg for food in restaurants and train stations, who could not attend school regularly because they were forced to work, who dug diamonds in mines and lived in shanty towns. There were regular reports about the fate of children in places like Africa and South America, and reviews of books about the segregation of black children in the United States and about apartheid.

We knew we would never meet these poor children, humiliated and oppressed by the capitalists, because they could never travel. We sympathized with their predicament but did not think we shared their fate. We knew it was difficult for us to travel abroad because we were surrounded by enemies. Moreover, our holidays were subsidized by the Party. Perhaps one day the Party would be powerful enough to have defeated all our enemies, and would pay for everyone to travel abroad too. In any case, we were already in the best place. They had nothing. We knew we did not have everything. But we had enough, we all had the same things, and we had what mattered most: real freedom.

In capitalism, people claimed to be free and equal, but this was only on paper because only the rich could take advantage of the rights available. Capitalists had made their money by stealing land and plundering resources all over the world, and by selling black people as slaves. 'Do you remember *Black Boy*?' teacher Nora asked when we read Richard Wright's autobiography in school. 'In the dictatorship of the bourgeoisie, a poor black person cannot be free. The police are after him. The law works against him.'

We had freedom for all, not just for the exploiters. We worked, not for the capitalists but for ourselves, and we shared the products of our work. We didn't know greed, or have to feel envy. Everyone's needs were satisfied, and the Party helped us develop our talents. If you were particularly gifted in maths, or dancing, or poetry or whatever, you could go to the House of the Pioneers and find a science club, or a dancing group, or a literary circle in which to practise your skills.

'Can you imagine, if your parents lived in capitalism, they would have to pay for all these things,' teacher Nora would say. 'People work like dogs, and the capitalist doesn't even give them what they deserve because, otherwise, how would he make a profit? Which means that part of the time they work for nothing, like the slaves in ancient Rome. For the other part, they receive a salary, and if they wanted their children to develop their talents, they would have to pay for private lessons, which of course they can't afford. What freedom is that?'

The tourists, however, could afford everything. When they visited, they found all they needed in the 'valuta' shop, where only foreign currency could be used. The valuta shop was the place where dreams came true. Although – according to teacher Nora – they were not dreams but mere capitalist aspirations. The valuta shop was right next to the Museum for Heroes of the Resistance. Elona and I went to take a look at it each time we visited the museum with our school: on 11 January for the Anniversary of the Republic, on 10 February to commemorate the Youth Resistance to the Fascists, on 22 April for Lenin's birthday, on 1 May, on 5 May, on 10 July, when we celebrated the founding of the People's

Army, on 16 October for Enver Hoxha's birthday, on 8 November for the Anniversary of the Party, and on 28 and 29 November for Independence. We called the woman who sat by the counter 'the Medusa' because she had curly, unruly hair and a hostile look that made you freeze on the doorstep and think twice before entering. The Medusa always kept *Zëri i Popullit* on the counter, open to the same page, and stared at the entrance while munching sunflower seeds. She had an uneaten pile of seeds on the left side of the newspaper, and the shells of the seeds she had already eaten on the right side. She peeled and ate the seeds without looking, her eyes never leaving the entrance to the shop.

When we went inside, she said nothing, but she stopped munching. She stared at us in silence for a few minutes. Then, if it was winter, she would say: 'What do you want here? Have you got any dollars? No. Then off you go. Close the door. It's cold.' If it was summer, she would say: 'What do you want here? Have you got any dollars? No. Then off you go. Leave the door open. It's hot.' She then returned to munching her sunflower seeds.

We never left immediately. We stared at the objects on display. Coca Cola cans to fill entire bookshelves, even after stripping them of all their books to make space. Roasted salted peanuts, which must have been like roasted salted sunflower seeds but even tastier, otherwise why would you only be able to buy them with dollars? A Philips colour television, which looked exactly like the one that belonged to the Meta family, the only people in my neighbourhood who had a colour television. 'Have you got tickets?' they joked each year on New Year's Day when around forty children sat in front of their Philips television to watch the Turkish version of *Snow White and the Seven Dwarfs*. There was a black MZ motorbike, magnificently displayed at the centre of the shop; it occupied most of the space and forced you to walk around it to reach the counter, in the same way you would have had to walk around Lenin's tomb in Moscow to reach the mausoleum exit. There was also a red bra with which Elona had fallen in love, even though she didn't have grown-up breasts. I liked the sun hat.

Some of the goods in the valuta shop resembled those that lorry drivers or sailors brought back from their journeys abroad as souvenirs for their wives and children, or for the wives and children of relatives and neighbours: Bic pens, Lux soap and nylon stockings. In rarer cases, they brought more expensive goods: T-shirts, shorts and swimwear, paraded on the beach in the summer, making the human models who wore them stand out because of the name of the brands they carried: 'the green Speedo man' or the 'red Dolphin girl'. 'You look like a tourist,' people would say to their friends. Mostly, it was meant as a compliment. Sometimes, it came as a warning. Very rarely, it might be a threat.

A tourist did not look like one of us. A tourist could not *be* one of us. A tourist appeared rarely but was easy to spot. A tourist dressed differently. A tourist had their hair styled in an unusual way, cut in strange shapes, or not cut at all, or recently cut at the border on behalf of our state – a modest price paid by world travellers to visit a country whose own citizens travelled the world only in thought.

Tourists visited in the summer months. They roamed the streets in the siesta hour, accompanied by the chirping sound of crickets and the hazy look of locals rushing home to catch the last of their afternoon nap. They carried multicoloured rucksacks filled with small plastic water bottles which turned out to be too small once they discovered the extreme heat, a heat that suffocated all lingering associations with the Soviet Union and reminded them of the Middle East. They were interested in everything: the Roman amphitheatre, the Venetian tower, the harbour, the old city walls, the tobacco factory, the rubber-making factory, the schools, the Party headquarters, the dry-cleaning shops, the piles of rubbish awaiting collection, the queues, the street rats, the weddings, the funerals, the things that happened, the things that did not happen, the things that may or may not have happened. Tourists held Nikon cameras, intent on capturing our past greatness and our present misery, or our present greatness and the misery of our past, depending on their point of view. Tourists knew that the success of their cameras in capturing anything at all depended mostly on the benevolence of local guides, who, unbeknownst to them, were often secret service recruits. Tourists did not know just how entirely it was in the guides' hands.

A tourist never came alone; instead, they always appeared as part of a group. Years later, I discovered that the groups were of two kinds: the realists and the dreamers. The dreamers belonged to fringe Marxist-Leninist groups. They mostly came from Scandinavia and were furious with the social wreckage that was called social democracy. They brought sweets to offer locals, who rarely accepted. They worshipped our country as the only one in the world that had managed to build a principled, uncompromising socialist society. They admired everything about us: the clarity of our slogans, the order in our factories, the purity of our children, the discipline of the horses who pulled our carriages, and the conviction of the peasants who travelled in them. Even our mosquitoes had something unique and heroic – the ways of their bloodsucking, which spared no one, including the tourists themselves. These tourist groups were our international comrades. They wondered how our model could be exported. They always waved and smiled, even from a distance. They believed in world revolution.

Then there was the second group, the restless Westerners, bored of the beaches on Lake Balaton and in Bali, moaning about how Mexico and Moscow had been invaded by tourists. They had joined niche clubs, and exclusive tour operators now sold them the ultimate exotic adventure: a place in the heart of Europe, just over one hour by plane from Rome and two hours from Paris. A place nevertheless so remote, with its hostile mountains, its dreamy beaches, its inaccessible people, its confusing history and its complicated politics, that only the most spirited traveller would dare to make the trip. They came to crack the code, to discover the truth. But it was a truth they had already agreed upon. They had talked about it while sipping cocktails in Bali and downing shots of vodka in Moscow. The truth was political. They had no political views but one: socialism was contrary to human nature, anywhere and in any form. They had always suspected it. Now they knew it. They waved, too, sometimes. They did not smile so often. They also carried sweets and wanted to talk. Sometimes they managed it. The next time they tried, nobody returned the wave, nobody was interested in sweets. They would never be able to guess if the locals who shared their views with them were random passers-by or secret service agents. It could have been either. They knew it would be hard to tell. But they always tried.

I don't know which of these two groups gave rise to the tourists I met when I joined my mother for a school trip to the island of Lezhë. It was an unusually hot day in the autumn of 1988, and I was trying to cross the street when I heard several voices say, in French: '*Attention! Petite fille, attention!*' '*Ça va,*' I answered instinctively, slightly resentful because I had seen their bus about to park and did not need to be told how to cross our streets, which, unlike Western streets, were not invaded by cars. Within minutes I was surrounded by more than a dozen humans who looked at me as if they had finally spotted their favourite animal at the zoo. I could smell sun cream everywhere. It was unbearable. I no longer wanted to follow them, or to hug them.

How come I spoke French? they asked. How old was I? Where did I live? We're French, they said. Did I know where France was? I nodded. Did I know anything about France? That made me smile. Then I felt offended. How could they even ask that question? How could they insinuate that I didn't know where France was? I didn't want to speak to them. But I wanted to show that I knew more than they thought. I sang one of my grandmother's favourite songs:

> '*Je suis tombé par terre,*
> *C'est la faute à Voltaire,*
> *Le nez dans le ruisseau,*
> *C'est la faute à Rousseau.*'

'I have fallen to the earth
It's the fault of Voltaire
With my rose in the gutter
It's the fault of Rousseau.'

'Gavroche!' one of them exclaimed. 'You know Gavroche's song! You know *Les Misérables*!' The others looked perplexed, as if they'd never heard of Gavroche or the barricades, or as if they could not believe what they had just witnessed.

I shrugged. They pulled out sweets from their bags. 'Do you want sweets?' they asked. I shook my head. A woman pulled out a postcard. 'Do you know this?' she asked. It was a colour postcard of the Eiffel Tower, a night scene. I was hesitant. 'Take it,' they said. '*Un petit souvenir de Paris,*' they added, as if to persuade me. I thought about it. I thought about my grandmother. Would she be happy if I brought back from the island of Lezhë a postcard of Paris? My mother called me. I ran back to our bus. As we left the island, I stared at the group from the bus window. I saw the woman who had offered the postcard. She saw me, too. She smiled again. She was still holding the card and waved the Eiffel Tower as if she were waving a handkerchief.

8.

Brigatista

When I returned home after the excursion to the island of Lezhë, I was no longer upset. I had been singing Gavroche's song in my head, but mixed up with 'Hello, oh Enver Hoxha, as great as our mountains, and as sharp as our cliffs', which my mother's students had been belting out on the bus's back seats. The more I thought about the encounter with the tourists, the less resentful I became. The part of me that had been offended at the idea that they knew far less about us than we knew about them found that same detail amusing – empowering, even. It had felt like a test that I was now increasingly confident I had passed.

We all gathered in the kitchen for dinner, and I recounted the episode to my family. Despite the relief I remember, I must have sounded troubled, because my grandmother stood up and left the room without saying anything. She returned a few minutes later, carrying a dusty transparent plastic bag full of faded photos. Then she pulled out a black-and-white postcard showing an image of the Eiffel Tower and passed it to me. On the other side it read: 'Congratulations! October 1934.' There was something else scribbled on the card, a signature perhaps, but it was no longer legible. It almost looked as if someone had made an effort to delete it.

'There,' my grandmother said, 'we've already got the Eiffel Tower. No need to worry about it.'

My mother was setting out the dinner plates, and as she glanced at the image in my hand she said:

'These tourists who come to visit, they're about as useful as the top of the Eiffel Tower.'

I was intrigued. It had never occurred to me that the tourists who visited us could be useful for anything. All they wanted was to test your knowledge of their country.

'What is the use of the top of the Eiffel Tower?' I asked.

'Nothing,' she replied. 'That's the point.'

'Perhaps to look at the view.' My father spoke.

'Exactly,' my mother said. 'Like the tourists.'

'Did you tell the tourists you sometimes look like Gavroche?' my father asked, changing the topic.

I shook my head with a smile. He often called me Gavroche. It was one of the two nicknames he'd given me when he'd withdrawn the title of 'stuffed pepper' because I no longer ate enough to deserve it. 'What games did you join to end up like Gavroche on the barricades?' he would ask when I returned home at the end of a day's playing outside, bright red in the face, panting, covered in sweat, still recovering from hours sprinting to catch fascists, battling with canes to defend against Roman conquests, and climbing trees to observe Ottoman sieges. Later, when I entered my teens, and wanted to make my views count, I would cut my hair short to eliminate ribbons from my life once and for all. I would also swap my handmade lace dresses for slightly oversized boys' clothes and a Phrygian cap. Then it would no longer be mentioned as a question; it became the expression of certainty. 'Still looking like Gavroche, I see,' my father would remark, in a tone that made it difficult to tell whether he intended it as criticism or praise.

I had my gaze fixed on the postcard my grandmother had shown me. 'You can keep it,' she said. 'So long as you keep it safe.'

I clutched the card in my hand and could feel myself sweating. 'Did tourists give it to you when you were little?' I asked.

Nini smiled. My grandfather had received it, she explained. He had studied in France, at a place called La Sorbonne. His best friend gave it to him when he graduated, a friend who was no longer with us.

'In France! He studied in France! Like Uncle Enver! Did he study natural sciences too? You told me they were friends! Did they meet there?'

'No, your grandfather studied law,' Nini replied. 'He and Enver already knew each other at school. They were friends at the French Lycée in Korçë. But yes, they met in France, many times. They were both part of the Popular Front.'

'What is the Popular Front?'

'The Front of the Fools,' my mother intervened. My father looked up with a frown. My grandmother continued as if she hadn't heard her. She explained that the Popular Front was a large organization devoted to the fight against fascism. They held meetings and protests and tried to build a large European resistance movement. There was a war in Spain, and there were international brigades volunteering to help the republican groups that fought the fascists, and my grandfather had wanted to be involved.

'He was in a big group of anti-fascists with Uncle Enver?!' I asked, with hardly concealed excitement. 'You never told me! You never told me my grandfather fought the fascists! I could bring his photos to school on 5 May! Do we have photos? Do we have letters? What can I bring to show my friends?'

'Well, he didn't make it to Spain,' my grandmother continued. 'His father discovered that your grandfather was at the border, ready to join the international brigades, so he wrote a letter to the Albanian ambassador asking to have him repatriated.'

'Why did his father do that?' I was puzzled.

My grandmother seemed not to hear my question, or wanted to ignore it. 'He came back to Albania, and brought anti-fascist leaflets, and tried to organize more meetings. But the police discovered it,' she continued.

'Why did his father not want him to fight the fascists?' I could not understand why anyone would object to fighting the fascists, in Spain, France, Albania — anywhere. I was annoyed that my grandfather's father not only had the same name and surname as our former prime minister, but had been a fascist just like him.

'Well, I don't know. I suppose he was a bit old-fashioned,' my grandmother replied with some hesitation. 'They had different views about politics.'

'Did he meet Uncle Enver again?'

My grandmother paused. She squinted, thought for a moment, then said: 'They . . . they . . . lost sight of each other. Anyway, we have an Eiffel Tower!' she exclaimed. 'That's what matters!'

'Is that when Grandpa went off to do his university research?' I asked, unwilling to let it go.

FREE

Nini seemed to become uncomfortable with the persistent questions. She looked at my father, as if to ask for help. But no help came.

'First he opened a shop selling alcohol,' she continued. 'He tried to practise law, but he was denied the licence because he was against the fascists and these were the years of King Zog. Research at university . . . hm, no, that was a few years later,' she added. 'When the war was over.'

'What did he do, then?'

'Oh, nothing special. He learned Russian and English, he worked on his languages, did translations, that sort of thing. Leushka,' she said to me, 'do you want to go and find some cutlery for dinner?'

'Babi, is that when he left the house for a very long time?' I asked, looking at my father. 'To do his research at university? Is that why Nini brought you up alone?'

'Yes,' my father answered. 'He translated Voltaire's *Candide.*'

'Voltaire! Voltaire! I was wondering about who Voltaire and Rousseau are. I mean, I don't know anything about them, I just know they helped with the French Revolution.'

My grandmother nodded enthusiastically. She seemed relieved that the subject had been changed. Perhaps she did not like the idea of my grandfather having left the family like that, to go off somewhere and spend so many years just studying languages and doing translations.

'That's all you need,' she continued. Her mood brightened whenever the French Revolution came up. She could go on talking about it tirelessly. She had told me everything she knew about it, how it started, who was involved, what happened to Louis XVI, to Marie Antoinette, and even to the poor Dauphin. She liked to repeat the bit of Robespierre's speech that said that the secret of freedom is in educating people, while the secret of tyranny is in keeping them ignorant. She described the famous battles of Napoleon and knew the names of all the generals who had been involved. She had tried to teach me, too, but I had found it impossible to remember all of them. She spoke about the characters involved in the French Revolution, from the meeting of the Estates General to the end of the Napoleonic Wars, with vivid detail and great precision, as if they were family relatives: the winners, the losers and everyone in between.

'Your grandmother thinks the French Revolution brought freedom to the world,' my father said, commenting on my grandmother's enthusiasm, 'but it was a nice idea that never really took hold.'

'Voltaire and Rousseau were philosophers of the Enlightenment,' my grandmother continued. 'That's why Gavroche says it's their fault. They first explained the ideas that people fought for during the Revolution. They thought everyone is born free, and equal, and people can think for themselves and have to make their own decisions. They were against ignorance, superstition and being controlled by more powerful people.'

'Right. Like Marx and Hangel. Did Voltaire and Rousseau also use the guillotine?' I asked.

'No,' my grandmother said. 'That came after.'

'Did Marx and Hangel use it?'

'Hegel,' Nini corrected. 'Or do you mean Marx and Engels? Marx and Engels, well . . . No, not really, they didn't. They wrote books, organized meetings, that sort of thing. They also thought everyone is born free, and equal, and they thought . . . Well, you know what Marx thought.'

'He thought there's no freedom in capitalism because the workers are not allowed to do all the things that the capitalists can do,' I added, content with my contribution.

'Exactly,' my father said. 'He was right. In socialism . . .' He paused, thought for a moment and started a different sentence. 'In capitalism,' he said, 'it's not that the poor are not allowed to do all the things that the rich can do. It's that they can't do them, even if they are allowed. For example, they're allowed to go on holiday, but they need to keep working because, otherwise, they don't make any money. And if you have no money in capitalism, you can't go on holiday. You need a revolution.'

'To go on holiday?'

'To change the way things are.'

When my father spoke of the revolution in general, he got as excited as my grandmother did when she spoke about the French Revolution in particular. In my family, everyone had a favourite revolution, just as everyone had a favourite summer fruit. My mother's favourite fruit was watermelon, and her favourite revolution was the English one. Mine were figs and Russian. My father emphasized that he was sympathetic to all our revolutions but his favourite was the one that had yet to take place. As to his favourite fruit, it was quince – but it could choke you when it wasn't fully ripe, so he was often reluctant to indulge. Dates were my grandmother's favourite fruit: they were hard to find, but she had enjoyed them when she was little. Her favourite revolution was of course the

French one, and this annoyed my father no end. 'The French Revolution has achieved nothing,' he said now. 'Some people are still extremely rich and make all the decisions, and others are very poor and can't change their lives.' He shook his head. 'They are trapped, like this fly,' he went on, pointing at a fly buzzing noisily against the glass in our kitchen window. Then he thought some more about it, and added something he always added, as if it had only just occurred to him, even though he said it every time to explain why his favourite revolution did not exist: 'Just look at the world, brigatista, look at the world.'

Even if my father did not have a favourite revolution, he had favourite revolutionaries. They were called 'brigatisti'. 'Brigatista' was the other nickname I'd received when he'd stopped calling me 'stuffed pepper'. I didn't understand its meaning until I was much older, but I remember that it tended to come up if I had broken some kind of rule. Over time, I had come to guess that it was equivalent to 'troublemaker', a term used for a person who challenged established authority. My father would say things like 'Come here, brigatista, look what you've done,' or 'You're late, brigatista,' or 'Brigatista, what are we going to do with you? You still haven't done your homework.'

I also thought the term had something to do with violence. This is because the only time my father applied the label to children other than me was when I told him I had refused to assist in the execution of a cat that had stolen the food intended for Flamur's stray dogs. Flamur had appeared in the common play-area on the street holding the cat and had tied a rope around its neck and ordered the other children to pull it until the cat could no longer breathe. When I reported the incident to my father, and told him I had not wanted to pull the rope, he said, 'So you are not really a brigatista after all,' in a way that made it clear that in that instance 'brigatista' was not intended as a compliment.

The other time my father mentioned the brigatisti, and included himself under this description, was during our regular visits to the cemetery, when we often stumbled on a beggar called Ziku. Ziku was a middle-aged gypsy with no legs who always wore shorts so that one could see the two long rows of stitches where his thighs ended and his legs had been cut. He dragged himself on the ground, and whenever he saw my father from a distance, he crawled faster and faster until he reached us. Then he blocked the way, and I remember thinking that Ziku was even shorter than me. 'Comrades, comrades!' he called. 'Have you got anything today?' My father always emptied his pockets. Literally. He gave everything he had. After meeting Ziku, we sometimes passed by a patisserie and I would pull my father's sleeve to indicate that a queue had started to form, which meant there was hope that ice-cream might soon appear. He would turn the inside of his pockets out to show that they were empty, and then say to me: 'I don't have anything left.' Then he would add: 'You saw Ziku, didn't you? Come, now, don't be upset, don't be stingy like your mum. Are we or are we not brigatisti?'

From this exchange I had inferred that a brigatista was someone who wanted to share all their money, and that my father identified with them because he didn't mind sharing what he had. When I was with Nini and we saw Ziku, she gave him some spare change too, but not as much as my father. She kept a few coins to buy me ice-cream and, while we waited in the queue, my grand-mother said: 'Poor Ziku, you see, he probably didn't like going to school and now he has to ask other people for money because he had no education. He should have done his homework, and read books, like you.'

My mother never gave Ziku anything. She said: 'Ziku needs to work!' I replied: 'But he has no legs!' She retorted: 'He has arms!' I objected: 'But he has no education!' 'It's his fault!' she answered back. 'He should have learned. People who want to learn, learn. Nobody gave me their spare change when I was growing up.'

When I asked my father why we must give all our spare change to Ziku since it was his fault that he did not go to school or like to learn, he said not everything is someone's fault. He explained that though gypsy children were now required to go to school and live in apartment blocks, that was probably not the case when Ziku had grown up in some nomad camp who knows where. He also said: 'Don't listen to your mother; she wouldn't give Ziku anything even if he had a doctorate. She wants to save everything.'

My father always liked to poke fun at my mother's desire to save everything. 'How would you like to proceed with this investment?' he would say to her ironically, as if she were a capitalist, when they discussed purchases, such as whether it was appropriate to buy a new winter coat. My mother never laughed at my father's jokes, not even the ones that were not at her expense. Nor did she protest. She shrugged, then imparted an order: 'Give me your old coat. I'll turn the collar upside down. It'll be as good as new.'

On my father's side, contempt for money was a mark

of distinction. Savings were seen as a burden to be relieved of, something that endangered one's status as a free human being. As soon as the family ended up with any spare money, however small the amount, my father and Nini started to panic. They wondered about what else they could buy or who they could give it to so as to prevent the disaster of building up a surplus. Birthdays were celebrated with extravagant expenditures. Everyone received at least one present, sometimes more. Being permanently in debt was a great relief, and the family had been indebted for as long as I had been around. In the rare cases in which they paid their monthly debts and also managed to cover basic expenditures, they started to think what other, more complex needs they might have, so that all savings could be redeployed.

At the end of each month, my grandmother stared at an empty cupboard and exclaimed, 'We've finished everything! There's nothing left! We'll have to wait until next month's vouchers!' There was some concern in her voice, but also a note of joy I never understood, as if alongside the upcoming challenge she was also announcing that we had reached some kind of target in which we ought to take pride. I assumed it ran in the family, because Cocotte once told me, while we were playing poker with beans, that in the old days she and my grandmother used to play poker with real money, and didn't mind losing quite a bit. I also overheard her say to Nini one night, while chatting late before going to sleep, that it was good that their grandfather, the Pasha, had encouraged spending most of the family fortune on jewellery, travel and balcony seats at the opera, since everything would have eventually disappeared anyway.

My mother and my father had radically different values, and fundamentally clashing attitudes to pretty much everything: how long it was appropriate to go on mending clothes before it was time to buy new ones, whether *Sacco and Vanzetti* was a superior film to *Gone with the Wind*, whether children rested better if they cried themselves to sleep, whether it was acceptable to drink milk that was slightly off, how late, if at all, one could turn up for meetings, and how many days one could recycle leftovers before accepting defeat. My father and Nini loathed money; my mother worshipped it; the former celebrated ancient codes of honour; the latter took pride in ignoring them. My father was deeply interested in politics, including the politics of faraway places; my mother cared only if it concerned her directly. It was a great irony that they had ended up marrying, because at different times and places they might have been in conflict. History had turned them into allies. Neither enjoyed the daily struggle that their interaction generated, but both had found strategies to cope with it. They were frank about the fact that they did not approve of each other's moral outlook. There had been no choice but to marry, they said. It all came down to 'biography'.

My father's contempt for money went far beyond his aversion to the frugal habits of my mother. It led to a hostile attitude towards the capitalist system, whose purpose, he said, was to keep buying and selling stuff for profit just to keep itself going. If you ended up with a lot of money, my mother said, it could be that you deserved it. My father insisted that there was no way one could make money without exploiting someone who lacked it. If you had a lot of money, you also had a lot of power and could influence important decisions, making it very difficult for people who didn't start off with the same amount as you to get to the same position. 'One has to do what one can, brigatista,' my father concluded, 'but in the end, to change things, you need a revolution, because nobody is going to give up their privileges without being forced.'

Years later, when I went to university, I was shocked to learn that my nickname came from the 'Red Brigades', the Italian far-left terrorist movement which resembled other guerrilla movements that had emerged in several countries of Western Europe during the seventies. My father had been finishing his degree at the university of Tirana in the summer of 1968, and he remembered the assassination of Martin Luther King in April, how de Gaulle had fled to Germany after the occupation of French universities in May, and how Soviet tanks had invaded Prague in August and Albania had abandoned the Warsaw Pact in protest. These events had been enough to convince him that unless all those who suffered from injustice everywhere in the world became free, no single, lasting victory could be achieved. For a moment that summer, he had thought that freedom was possible and required resisting authority in all its forms. But the student protests had failed, and the youngsters on the squares had become career politicians, converting their former ideals of freedom into some vague rhetoric of democracy. That was the point, he explained, when he realized that 'democracy' was just another name for the violence of the state, a violence that for the most part remains an abstract threat only to materialize when the powerful risk losing their privileges.

As a result of these events, which he only ever watched on Italian or Yugoslav television, my father had developed his fascination with revolutionary groups, those who rejected legal rights and parliamentary democracy altogether and believed that without the violence of the people one could never overcome the violence of the state. He was fascinated by Giangiacomo Feltrinelli, who'd set up a publishing company and whose stance he said he admired because it had catered neither to the family's capitalist interests nor to the democratic rhetoric of the liberal state. He told me the story of how Feltrinelli had died carrying his own explosives during an operation of the Gruppi di Azione Partigiana revolutionary group. He described his death with such narrative precision and refined psychological detail that you would almost think he had been present and had narrowly escaped. He told me the story before I could really understand what the operation was about, or why it was necessary to blow up electricity pylons to spark a revolution.

The Red Brigades were hardly mentioned on television in Albania in the seventies and eighties. My father had begun to follow them by listening to Italian radio in secret. Later in my life, I tried to make sense of this preoccupation with revolutionary violence. He must have drawn a parallel between the critique of the repressive state and his own predicament. Terrorist violence, he said, would not be necessary if revolutionary groups could fight the state with all the weapons available to a regular army. He hated all wars; he was a pacifist. But he romanticized revolutionary struggle. He was a free spirit stuck in a highly rigid political order, a man with a biography he had not chosen but which was enough to determine his place in the world. He must have sought ways of making sense of himself, trying to carry forward his moral commitments without someone or other interpreting them on his behalf, someone who tried to ascribe meaning to what seemed to me the altogether meaningless fact that his name happened to be the same as that of a former prime minister.

Yet when he tried to articulate all of this in a way that others might understand and relate to, when he tried to explain what it meant to achieve freedom away from the repressive machinery of the state and the exploitation of the market, he ran out of words. He knew what he was against but found it hard to defend what he stood for. Sentences, theories, ideals crowded in his head, and he struggled to find a way to order them, to explain his priorities and to share his views. Everything eventually exploded in thousands of fragments: what he knew, what he was, what he tried to be, what he wanted to see happen. Like the lives of the revolutionaries whose heroic deaths he admired, like his favourite revolution, the one that had never taken place.

9.

Ahmet Got His Degree

In late September 1989, a few weeks after the start of school, a new boy called Erion joined our class. His family had recently relocated from Kavajë, the town where my family lived before my birth. He was assigned the seat next to me and introduced himself. 'You're Lea!' he exclaimed with joy, when he discovered my name. 'Lea Ypi! My parents told me to look out for you. We're relatives. My grandfather is a cousin of your grandmother. They grew up together. I have a message to deliver. You must tell your grandmother that Ahmet got his degree. He's back. Ahmet is my grandfather. You can visit whenever you like.'

When I told my family that I had met a new cousin, they seemed surprised. 'A bit late for us to discover new relatives, don't you think?' my father joked. Then I delivered the message. 'Ahmet . . .' Nini muttered, absorbed in thought. 'Ahmet is back. He wants us to visit,' she mused. 'Should we go? Should we congratulate him on the degree? Should we bring a present?' My father nodded. My mother shook her head. 'We have to be careful,' she said. Ahmet's late wife, Sonia, had been a teacher, and Ahmet himself had no doubt already found a job. 'He is too old to work,' my father objected. Nini continued to stare blankly at the wall. 'Yes, it is late for him,' she said in the end. 'He's old now. But who knows?'

The discussion made no sense at all. Why couldn't we visit someone whose wife had been a teacher? Why shouldn't we congratulate a relative who had just graduated?

'I'd like to play with Erion,' I said. 'He's nice, I want to see him.' After a long discussion, the family decided to go ahead. A box of Turkish delight was bought, the visit was paid, the cousins reunited.

After that, Ahmet started to come to our house regularly. He tapped on our door with the cherrywood cane on which he leaned when walking. He brought little presents, like painted kites and cardboard hats, and sometimes he brought Erion along and we played Teachers with my dolls. Ahmet spoke slowly, almost with difficulty. He smelled of tobacco and carried a newspaper rolled up like a pipe; he used it to tickle me on my neck, just under my chin. When he picked up his coffee saucer, his hands trembled. The spoon in the cup made a tinkling noise which drew attention to his right hand, where the thumb was missing. His fingers were long and covered in a bright yellow colour, as if they had been painted, apparently from rolling tobacco.

When Ahmet's visits overlapped with Cocotte's stays at our house, everyone spoke French, just as they had done when they were children. I once asked if he wanted to play a bean poker game with us, but Cocotte said that poker was for bourgeois people. I didn't understand but didn't want to contradict her by telling Ahmet that we always played poker with beans, and nobody had ever suggested before that it was a bourgeois game. Ahmet then sat on the sofa next to my grandmother and talked about how much things had changed in the time he had been away. 'There is so much good stuff around,' he said. 'There is abundance everywhere. The shops are full. The people are happy. Everything feels so calm and precious.' Nini nodded quietly.

A few months later, my father received notification from work that he would be transferred from his office a few miles from the city centre to a different unit, in the remote village of Rrushkull. He would have to wake up much earlier and travel in the dark to reach the village, first catching a bus, then walking for a long time or, if he was lucky and met peasants on the way, getting a lift in a horse-drawn cart. Nini was concerned that in the winter his asthma would deteriorate. Everyone agreed it had been a mistake to congratulate Ahmet and to invite him for coffee. 'I knew it,' my mother said. 'I knew he had a job lined up. He was probably already working while studying. I told you we shouldn't make contact. His wife used to be a teacher. Many people took longer to gradu-ate because of her. One even dropped out.'

To me, the link between reuniting with Ahmet and my father's transfer seemed even more absurd than the discussion about whether to congratulate him for completing his degree. But the two events were regu-larly joined in family discussions. His visits meant that even the location of my mother's school was no longer deemed safe. 'We need to stop answering the door,' Nini declared at one point, 'or else Doli will be transferred before long.'

And so we did. When Ahmet and Erion came to visit, we pretended to be out. We switched off the radio and the television. For a few minutes, all went quiet. Sometimes Donika spotted them at the bottom of the slope and rushed to call my mother from the window: 'Dalaaaaa! Dalaaaa! He's coming. Your cousin is coming.' Ahmet tapped with his cane, and waited. Erion banged with his fist. I poked half of my head out of a corner of the window. They lingered a little longer, then picked up the bags with hats and kites they had left resting on the ground and turned away. Erion ran ahead, and Ahmet followed slowly. He dragged his feet as if they belonged to someone else, and his face had a vaguely detached expression, as if he were thinking someone else's thoughts. It made me sad to see them go. My father noticed I was upset. 'Don't worry, brigatista,' he tried to comfort me. 'Don't be sad. When you are older you will understand. Ahmet finished studying, but he's still working.'

My family had always taken a keen interest in people who finished university. It was one of our most frequent topics of conversation at birthday parties and extended family reunions. In the last few months before December 1990, it became the only subject deserving of attention. The less interested in politics my family appeared, the more enthusiastic their discussions about higher education. Each time a relative came to visit, coffee was brought out and the conversation went more or less like this: 'Did you hear Nazmi got his degree?' 'Oh, I thought he had already graduated.' 'No, it only happened recently.' Then they followed up by talking about drop-outs and excellent results, comparing how difficult it had been to go through university in the past, relative to the present: 'Back then, Isuf failed his degree, but when his wife enrolled, she did very well,' my grandmother would explain. 'Oh yes,' came the reply, 'she excelled; she stayed on to teach.' Some universities seemed to be much tougher to get through than others. 'Fatime ended up in B. and unfortunately she did not finish.' Or: 'Her husband had been at V. and then moved to T. There he passed exams without difficulty.' And again: 'Who knows what will happen now that the rector has changed?' Or else: 'Fewer people seem to be failing their degrees,' followed by a cautious reply: 'Yes, but who knows in what numbers they're enrolling?'

Several discussions involved comparisons between different subjects and the relative difficulty of completing each. For example: 'Josif studied international relations, but Bela was interested in philosophy.' Not only the universities one graduated from but also the contents of their study were classified based on how demanding they were. It was well known that if you went to university for international relations, for example, it would be impossible to graduate. But if you studied economics, you might finish relatively quickly. At other times, it sounded as though, if you efficiently earned a degree that was considered difficult to complete, you might be required to stay on to teach. This, for some reason, was viewed with suspicion. The reputation of teachers also varied: there were the strict ones, who inspired fear and who were to be avoided at all costs, and those whose teaching style was more relaxed and who were easier to approach.

The adults never mentioned the names of the universities, only the first letter. For example, they would say things like 'Avni graduated from B.,' or 'Emine began her studies at S. but was then transferred to M.' From the low table in our living room where I played with my dolls in silence, I tried to match the single letter I had just heard with the names of different university towns. When I thought I'd guessed it correctly, I would ask: 'Did you mean S. for the university of Shkodra?' At that point the grown-ups noticed I was listening and sent me to play in my room.

I found it especially confusing when we spoke about my grandfather's research. Some relatives said that perhaps he wouldn't have had to study for such a long time if his father, the man who was named like our former prime minister, had not been involved. Others said the two biographies were unrelated, that my grandfather would have gone to university no matter what, because he was an 'intellectual' and most intellectuals had to study. When I discovered that my grandfather had finished his first degree in Paris, I was curious to know where he had gone to conduct his later research, during the period in which he had learned English and Russian, and translated Voltaire's *Candide*, which took fifteen years to complete. But this second degree was surrounded by mystery. I was told: 'He studied in B. then went to S.' 'What are B. and S.?' I asked. 'Literature,' they replied. 'He studied literature.' 'I don't mean *what* did he study,' I insisted, 'I meant *where* did he study it.' 'Oh, well, here and there,' came the reply, 'not too far from here.' 'But where's here, and why there?' I asked one last time. 'Why? Well, biography,' they repeated. 'It was part of his biography.'

Of the many conversations that I absorbed over the years, the one I remember most clearly involved an old teacher of my grandfather whose name was Haki. Many of my relatives who had been to the same university as my grandfather knew Haki. They all reported that if you ended up in Haki's courses, there was an extremely high chance that you would never complete your degree; in fact, you were very likely to be expelled. The announcement that someone had been ousted was usually made in a whisper, accompanied by dark looks and trembling voices. 'I'm so sorry,' the receiver of the news would say, 'that is terrible. I'm so, so sorry to hear that.' The only thing that provoked an even more dramatic reaction than reports of failing a degree was the news that someone had dropped out, that they had voluntarily given up. 'It was Haki,' I would then hear. 'She couldn't take Haki.' And the comment: 'No, not just Haki, the whole degree.' 'Yes, but without Haki she might have made it.' Haki had a reputation for being highly committed to education. Haki was one of the most severe teachers, renowned both for the harsh penalties he inflicted and for the humiliation they provoked.

One story that involved Haki, and which I heard discussed many times, took place at the end of my grandfather's literature degree. It was the summer of 1964. My grandfather, Asllan, had come out of university and was unemployed. He knocked on many doors in search of work but found it more challenging than he had anticipated. His biography stood in the way. He resolved to write a letter to an old friend from school, someone very high up in Party circles. A copy of that letter is still with us, in the same dusty plastic bag that contains the faded postcards, including the one with the Eiffel Tower. 'Dear Comrade Enver,' the first line reads. It continues like the opening of some kind of constitutional document: 'Human dignity is inviolable. The foundation of socialism is the dignity conferred by work.' The next paragraph expresses gratitude for the further education received over the past year and congratulates the Party for the excellent progress made by the country under socialist rule. Then comes the request for a job, ideally one matching his skills.

A few days after Asllan sent his letter, a reply arrived from Party headquarters. A position as a lawyer had opened up. The next Monday, Asllan wore his only suit and went to work. It was a black pinstripe suit, the same one he had worn the day he'd left university, the one he would wear at my parents' wedding, and on the day I came out of the maternity hospital, as well as when he was buried. A few months into his new job, Haki knocked on his office door to request a legalized certificate.

At first, he did not recognize Asllan dressed in a suit.

'I need this signed,' he said, pointing at the piece of paper he was carrying.

'Please take a seat,' Asllan replied. 'May I offer you a cigarette?'

Haki then realized that he had met my grandfather before, and became uncomfortable. 'I don't think you recognize me,' he said. Asllan continued to smile. 'Welcome, Haki. What a pleasure to see you.'

Haki hesitated. 'I can come back another day,' he said. 'Don't worry,' my grandfather answered. 'We'll sort it out in no time.'

Haki sat in the office, smoking in silence, while Asllan completed the paperwork. In the end, Haki tried to pay, but my grandfather declined. 'You have already done so much, Haki,' he said. 'This one is on me.' Haki thanked him profusely and, when he left, the two men shook hands.

Of all the different stories about universities, this one stuck with me, not because of the number of times it was repeated over the years, but because both the tone in which it was reported and its reception differed with each iteration. 'Good on Asllan,' some relatives who had met Haki said when they heard. Others wondered: how could Asllan shake hands with Haki? Had he forgotten that Haki was responsible for his best friend dropping out? Later on, I discovered this friend was the same one who had sent the congratulatory postcard with the Eiffel Tower on it. 'Haki was just a teacher. He didn't make the rules he was asked to enforce,' Nini explained, trying to justify her husband's actions. 'Then it would be impossible to blame anyone,' our relatives retorted. 'A teacher always has some discretion not to be as harsh as the role requires. It's easy to just move up the chain of command, and blame the Ministry of Education or the minister himself for anything that goes wrong. But the truth is, a lot of people work together to apply the rules.' There is discretion at every level, they would say, at each point in time. Haki did not have to be so harsh. His cruelty should not have been rewarded with a handshake.

I often wondered why my grandmother repeated the story each time a relative visited and reminisced about their time at the university of B., where Haki had taught. I could not understand the importance of analysing at length how my grandfather offered Haki a cigarette after they had met at university. Why was it a big deal that my grandfather had treated him like an old friend? Once I heard my grandmother repeat a sentence of

Robespierre's: 'To punish the oppressors of humanity is clemency, but to pardon them is barbarism.' Haki's name was floated in the same context. It seemed exaggerated to treat Haki as an oppressor of humanity. But what did my grandfather learn at university? And why were my relatives so obsessed with who was responsible for making amends?

When I reflect on all the unsolved mysteries of my childhood and revisit the stories of Ahmet and Haki that made such an impression on me, I think of them as part of a truth that was always there, waiting to be discovered, if only I'd known where to look. Nobody had concealed anything from me; everything was within reach. And yet I'd needed to be told.

I had never thought to ask my family not *where* exactly the universities of B., S. or M. were located but *what* a university represented. I had no access to the right answers because I didn't know how to ask the right questions. But how could it be otherwise? I loved my family. I trusted them. I accepted everything they offered to satisfy my curiosity. In my search for certainty, I relied on them to help me make sense of the world. It had never occurred to me before that day in December 1990, after the encounter with Stalin in the rain, that my family was the source not only of all certainty but also of all doubt.

10.

The End of History

A few months before the day I hugged Stalin, I had seen his portraits paraded on the streets of the capital to commemorate 1 May, Workers' Day. It was the usual yearly parade. Television programmes started earlier and there was no sport to watch on Yugoslav television, which meant no clash with my father about who would have access to the screen. You could instead follow the parade, then watch a puppet show, then a children's film, then head out for a walk wearing new clothes, buy ice-cream and, finally, have a picture taken by the only photographer in town, who usually stood by the fountain near the Palace of Culture.

The first of May 1990, the last May Day we ever celebrated, was the happiest. Or perhaps it just seems that way because it was the last. Objectively, it could not have been the happiest. The queues for basic necessities were getting longer, and the shelves in the shops looked increasingly empty. But I did not mind. I had been picky with food in the past, but now that I was growing up I was no longer fussy about cheap feta as opposed to the more desirable yellow cheese, or about eating old jam rather than honey. 'First comes morality, then comes food,' my grandmother said cheerfully, and I had learned to agree.

On 5 May 1990, Toto Cutugno won the Eurovision Song Contest in Zagreb with 'Insieme: 1992'. I had made enough progress with *Foreign Languages at Home* to be able to understand the lyrics and sing the chorus in my head: *Sempre più liberi noi/Non è più un sogno e non siamo più soli/ Sempre più uniti noi/Dammi una mano e vedrai che voli/Insieme . . . unite, unite Europe.** It was not until a couple of years later that I discovered that a song I had always assumed celebrated freedom and unity in the spread of socialist ideals around Europe was actually about the Maastricht Treaty, which would soon consolidate the liberal market.

Meanwhile, Europe continued to be in the grip of all kinds of 'hooligans' who were undermining public order. Earlier in the year, Poland had withdrawn from the Warsaw Pact. The communist parties in Bulgaria and Yugoslavia voted to renounce their monopoly on power. Lithuania and Latvia declared independence from the Soviet Union. Soviet troops entered Baku to suppress Azeri protests. I overheard my parents talk about 'free' elections in East Germany, and asked my father: 'What do you elect in unfree elections?' He seemed to dislike the question, and tried to change topic. 'Aren't you happy,' he said, 'that Nelson Mandela has been released from prison?'

The number of visitors to our house doubled; they came even when there were no football matches or song festivals to watch on Direkti. My parents started sending me to bed early. Through the cloud of smoke

---

* 'We are ever more free/It's no longer a dream, and we are no longer alone/We are ever more united/Give me your hand, and you'll see how you'll fly/Together . . . unite, unite Europe.'

that cloaked our living room in the evening, the people rolling cigarettes from loose tobacco began to look like shadows.

I had noticed consternation in the hushed voices with which visitors were greeted as they came in, but there were no traces of threat. Everyone continued to smile and pat me on my shoulders, asking how I was doing in school, if anyone had performed better than me in my class, and if I continued to make the Party proud of my achievements. I nodded and delivered the good news.

I had just become a pioneer, one year ahead of my cohort. I had been selected to represent my school in laying wreaths on the tombs of Second World War heroes and was also now in charge of pronouncing the oath with which we swore allegiance to the Party. I stood in front of the entire school before the beginning of classes and declared solemnly: 'Pioneers of Enver! In the name of the cause of the Party, are you ready to fight?' 'Always ready!' the pioneers thundered. My parents were proud and, to reward me for my achievements, we went on a holiday to the beach.

Later that summer, I spent two weeks at a Pioneers' camp. Every day, the bell rang at 7 a.m. to wake us up. The bread rolls that we were served for breakfast tasted like rubber, but the women who distributed them in the canteen were unusually kind, even affectionate. We spent the rest of the morning at the beach, where we sunbathed, swam and played football. At lunchtime, we lined up to receive bowls of rice, yoghurt and grapes, then were sent to our rooms to sleep, or pretend to sleep, during the siesta hour, and the bell rang again at 5 p.m. In the afternoon we played ping-pong or chess, then separated into different educational groups: maths, natural science, music, art and creative writing. For dinner, we gulped down vegetable soup, then rushed outside to take our seats in the open-air cinema. At night, we chatted late and made new friends. The bravest and oldest fell in love.

During the day, we competed. We competed over who was best at making their bed, who finished their meals fastest, who could swim the longest distance, who knew the most capitals of the world, who had read the most novels, who could solve complex cubic equations, and who played the most musical instruments. The socialist bonds of solidarity that our teachers worked hard to inculcate during the year all but disappeared during those two weeks. After the first few days, competition was no longer discouraged but regulated from the top, and adjusted by age group. Races, mock Olympiads and poetry prizes were now centrally organized, and they had become such a fundamental feature of life at camp that only petit bourgeois, reactionary elements would have refused to participate. At the end of the two weeks, very few children returned home without at least a red star, a small flag, a recognition certificate or a medal, if not as an individual then at least as part of a team. I had one of each.

My two weeks at the Pioneers' camp were the last of their kind. The red Pioneer scarf I worked impossibly hard to earn and which I proudly wore every day to school, would soon turn into a rag with which we wiped the dust off our bookshelves. The stars, medals and certificates, and the very title of 'Pioneer', would soon become museum relics, memories from a different era, fragments of a past life that someone had lived, somewhere.

Our earlier holiday by the beach was the first and the last we spent as a family. It was the last time the state granted holiday packages. 1 May was the last time the working classes paraded to celebrate freedom and democracy.

On 12 December 1990, my country was officially declared a multi-party state, one in which free elections would be held. It was almost twelve months after Ceauşescu had been shot in Romania while singing 'The Internationale'. The Gulf War had already started. Small pieces of the Wall were already being sold in the souvenir kiosks of recently unified Berlin. For more than a year, these events had left my country untouched, or almost. The owl of Minerva had taken flight and, as usual, seemed to have forgotten us. But then she remembered and returned.

Why had socialism come to an end? Only a few months before, in our moral education class, teacher Nora had explained that socialism was not perfect, it was not like communism would be when it arrived. Socialism was a dictatorship, she said, the dictatorship of the proletariat. This was different, and certainly better, than the dictatorship of the bourgeoisie that ruled in Western imperialist states. In socialism, the state was controlled by the workers, rather than by capital, and the law served the workers' interests, not the interests of those who wanted to increase their profits. But she made it clear that socialism had problems too. Class struggle was not over. We had many external enemies, like the Soviet Union, which had long ago given up on the ideal of communism and turned into a repressive imperialist state that sent tanks to crush smaller countries. We also had many internal enemies. The people who had once been rich and had lost all their privileges and property kept plotting to undermine the rule of the workers and deserved to be punished. Still, with time, the proletarian struggle would prevail. When people grow up in a humane system, and children are educated in the right ideas, teacher Nora said, they internalize them. Class enemies become fewer in number, and class struggle first softens, then disappears. That is when communism really starts, and why it is superior to socialism: it does not need the law to punish anyone, and it liberates human beings once and for all. Contrary to what our enemies' propaganda suggested, communism was not the repression of the individual but the first time in the history of humanity in which we could be fully free.

I'd always thought there was nothing better than communism. Every morning of my life I woke up wanting to do something to make it happen faster. But in December 1990, the same human beings who had been marching to celebrate socialism and the advance towards communism took to the streets to demand its end. The representatives of the people declared that the only things they had ever known under socialism were not freedom and democracy but tyranny and coercion.

What would I grow up into? How would we realize communism now that socialism was no longer there? As I stared incredulously at the television screen, where the Secretary of the Politburo was announcing that political pluralism was no longer a punishable offence, my parents declared that they had never supported the Party I had always seen them elect, that they had never believed in its authority. They had simply mastered the slogans, and gone on reciting them, just like everyone else, just like I did when I swore my oath of loyalty in school every morning. But there was a difference between us. I believed. I knew nothing else. Now I had nothing left, except for all the small, mysterious fragments of the past, like the solitary notes of a long-lost opera.

In the following days, the first opposition party was founded and my parents revealed the truth, their truth. They said that my country had been an open-air prison for almost half a century. That the universities which had haunted my family were, yes, educational institutions, but of a peculiar kind. That when my family spoke of the graduation of relatives, what they really meant was their recent release from prison. That completing a degree was coded language for completing a sentence. That what had been referred to as the initials of university towns were actually the initials of various prison and deportation sites: B. for Burrel, M. for Maliq, S. for Spaç. That the different subjects of study corresponded to different official charges: to study international relations meant to be charged with treason; literature stood for 'agitation and propaganda'; and a degree in economics entailed a more minor crime such as 'hiding gold'. That students who became teachers were former prisoners who converted to being spies, like our cousin Ahmet and his late wife, Sonia. That a harsh professor was an official at whose hands many people had lost their lives, like Haki, with whom my grandfather had shaken hands after serving his sentence. That if someone had achieved excellent results, it meant the stint had been brief and straightforward; but being expelled meant a death sentence; and dropping out voluntarily, like my grand-father's best friend in Paris, meant committing suicide.

I learned that the former prime minister whom I had grown up despising, and whose name my father bore, did not have the same name and surname by coincidence. He *was* my great-grandfather. For his entire life, the weight of that name had crushed my father's hopes. He could not study what he wanted. He had to explain his biography. He had to make amends for a wrong he had never committed and to apologize for views he did not share. My grandfather, who disagreed with his own father so much that he had wanted to join the republicans in Spain on the opposite side of the struggle, had paid for the blood relationship with fifteen years in prison. I would have paid too, who knows how, my parents said. I would have paid, had my family not lied to keep the secret.

'But I was a Pioneer,' I objected. 'I became a Pioneer ahead of my cohort.'

'Everyone becomes a Pioneer,' my mother replied. 'You wouldn't have been allowed in the youth organiz-ation. You would have never been able to join the Party.'

'Were *you* stopped?' I asked.

'Me?' My mother laughed. 'I didn't try. A new col-league recommended me once; then he found out who I was.'

I would have paid for my mother's family too, I was told. I learned that the boats my mother had made paper models of with her uncle Hysen, and the land, factories and flats she had drawn as a child, had really belonged to her family before she was born, before the arrival of socialism, before they were expropriated. That her father had ended up cleaning gutters even though he

had graduated in economics at the University of Liège
before the end of the war. That the building that housed
the Party's headquarters, and in front of which she and
my father first explained to me what Islam was, had once
been her family's property too. 'Do you remember the
time we spoke about Islam when we were standing in
front of that building?' my mother asked. I nodded. She
reminded me of how whenever we went past that building she looked up to the fifth-floor window, the one
without the flowerpot. An alleged enemy of the people
had once stood there, shouting, 'Allahu-akbar!' before
throwing himself out. He had been trying to escape torture. The year was 1947. The man was her grandfather.

My grandmother also told me the full story of her
life, the same story I had tried to guess countless times
while eavesdropping on her conversations with Cocotte.
She was born in 1918 as the niece of a pasha, the second
daughter in a family of senior provincial governors of
the Ottoman empire. At thirteen, she was the only girl
at the Lycée Français de Salonique. At fifteen, she tasted
her first whisky and smoked her first cigar. At eighteen,
she won a gold medal for being the top performer in her
school. At nineteen, she visited Albania for the first time.
At twenty, she was an adviser to the prime minister, and
the first woman to work in the state administration. At
twenty-one, she met my grandfather at King Zog's wedding. They sipped champagne, danced the waltz, pitied
the bride and discovered that their shared antipathy to
royal weddings was surpassed only by the contempt in
which they held the monarchy. At twenty-three, she
married my grandfather. He was a socialist, but not
a revolutionary. She was vaguely progressive. Both

came from well-known conservative families who had been scattered across the Ottoman empire for several generations. At twenty-four, she became a mother. At twenty-five, the war ended, and she saw her relatives in Salonica for the last time. At twenty-six, she participated in the elections for the Constituent Assembly, the first elections in which women could vote as men's equals, and the last in which candidates from the non-communist left ran for office. At twenty-seven, those same candidates, most of whom were family friends, were arrested and executed. My grandfather suggested emigrating with help from departing British officers they had met during the war. She refused. Her mother, who had travelled to Albania from Greece to help with their toddler, had recently fallen ill, and she did not want to leave her. At twenty-eight, my grandfather was arrested, charged with agitation and propaganda and sentenced first to hanging, then life imprisonment, a charge later commuted to fifteen years. At twenty-nine, she lost her mother to cancer. At thirty, she was forced to leave the capital and move to a different city. At thirty-two, she started working in labour camps. By the time she was forty, many of her relatives had been executed or had committed suicide, and those who'd survived had ended up in mental hospitals, in exile or in prison. At fifty-five, she nearly died of pleurisy. At sixty-one, she became a grandmother, when I was born. The rest, I knew.

My grandmother explained that she had wanted to teach me French because it reminded her of life before, of how everyone had spoken French around her, and of the French Revolution. Addressing me in French was for her less a matter of identity than an act of rebellion,

Paternal grandparents skiing, Cortina D'Ampezzo, 1941

Maternal grandparents, Sarajevo, 1935

Mother's military training, Durrës, 1968

Family, Durrës, early 1980s

Lea and parents, Durrës, early 1980s

Lea and Nini, early 1980s

Lea and brother Lani, *c.* 1989

At the seaside, Durrës, 1986

First year as a pioneer, 1989

Pioneers celebrating Enver Hoxha

Communist magazines

Communist posters

a small gesture of non-compliance which, she thought, I would treasure later on. I could think about it when she would no longer be there to remind me of where I came from, of the odd politics in my family, of how people had paid a price for who they were, regardless of what they wanted to be. I could then reflect on how life could toss you one way, then another, and how you could be born with everything, then lose it all.

My grandmother was not nostalgic for her past. She had no desire to return to a world in which her aristocratic family spoke French and visited the opera while the servants who prepared her meals and cleaned her clothes could not read or write. She had never been a communist, she said, but nor did she long for the *ancien régime*. She was aware of the privilege in which she had grown up and suspicious of the rhetoric that had justified it. She did not think class consciousness and class belonging were the same thing. She insisted that we do not inherit our political views but freely choose them, and we choose the ones that sound right, not those that are most convenient or best serve our interest. 'We lost everything,' she said. 'But we did not lose ourselves. We did not lose our dignity, because dignity has nothing to do with money, honours or titles. I am the same person I always was,' she insisted. 'And I still like whisky.'

She explained all this calmly, clearly separating each phase of her life from the next, at pains to distinguish them, occasionally checking to make sure I was following. She wanted me to remember her trajectory, and to understand that she was the author of her life: that despite all the obstacles she had encountered on the way, she had remained in control of her fate. She had never ceased to be responsible. Freedom, she said, is being conscious of necessity.

I tried to understand and retain everything my grandmother and my parents said during those weeks, and we revisited those conversations many times thereafter. I felt confused. I could not understand if our family was the rule or the exception, if what I had just discovered about myself would make me more similar to other children or still more of an outlier. I had often heard friends speak about things they did not grasp, trying to decode meetings between grown-ups that were not easy to follow. Perhaps they also talked about socialism, and about the Party in the evenings, when Dajti or Direkti showed images of life elsewhere, and maybe they also exchanged views on universities that turned out to be prisons. Or perhaps their relatives were more like Haki, a true believer, as my grandmother said, who had no sense of when to be strict in the application of the rules and when to exercise discretion.

I learned the truth when it was no longer dangerous but also at a time when I was old enough to wonder why my family had lied to me for so long. Perhaps they didn't trust me. But if they didn't, why should I trust them? In a society where politics and education pervaded all aspects of life, I was a product of both my family and my country. When the conflict between the two was brought to light, I was dazzled. I didn't know where to look, who to believe. Sometimes, I thought our laws were unjust and our rulers were cruel. At other times, I wondered if my family deserved the punishments inflicted on them. After all, if they cared about freedom, they should not have had servants. And if they cared about equality, they should not have been so rich. But my grandmother said that they had wanted things to change too. My grandfather was a socialist; he resented the privileges his family enjoyed. 'Then why did he go to prison?' I insisted. 'He must have done something. Nobody goes to prison for nothing.' 'Class struggle,' my grandmother said. 'Class struggle is always bloody. It doesn't matter what you believe.'

For the Party, the sacrifice of individual preferences was a matter of historical necessity, the cost of the transition to a future better condition. Every revolution, we learned in school, goes through a stage of terror. For my family, there was nothing to explain, to contextualize, or to defend; there was only the pointless destruction of their lives. Perhaps the terror was over when I was born. Or perhaps it had not yet started. Was I saved by the new circumstances, or somehow still cursed because I never made my own discoveries?

I wondered if my family would ever have disclosed who we were, to prevent me from becoming something they did not want, or to protect me from believing in something they did not share. 'No, but you would have found out by yourself,' they replied.

'What if I hadn't?'

'You would have,' they insisted.

In the following weeks, I was assailed by doubts. I found it difficult to process the fact that everything my family had said and done up to that point had been a lie, a lie they continued to repeat so that I would continue to believe what I was told by others. They had encouraged me to be a good citizen when they knew full well that, because of my biography, I was only ever going to be a class enemy. If their efforts had been successful, I would have identified with the system. Would they have accepted my transformation? Perhaps I would have become like Ahmet, just another suspicious relative who had turned to the other side, out of fear, or conviction, or the influence of prison education, or some other motive, equally mysterious. Or perhaps, if I wasn't allowed to join the Party, I would have felt resentful. I would have discovered the truth and become hostile to everything the Party stood for; yet another silent enemy.

One afternoon, my mother brought home *Rilindja Demokratike*, the first issue of the first opposition newspaper. Its motto was: 'The freedom of each must guarantee the freedom of all.' For days there had been rumours that it was in print and would reach the bookshops – the only places that sold newspapers – early one morning. People waited, clutching empty bottles so that if they were questioned by the Sigurimi, the secret service, they could argue that they were only queuing for milk. My father read the editorial out loud. It was titled: 'The first word'. The newspaper promised to defend freedom of speech and of thought, and to always speak the truth. 'Only the truth is free, and only then does freedom become true,' he read.

More changes occurred in December 1990 than in all the previous years of my life combined. For some, those were the days in which history came to an end. It did not feel like the end. Nor did it feel like a new beginning, at least not immediately. More like the rise of a discredited prophet who had foretold calamities that all dreaded but no one believed. We had spent decades preparing for assault, planning for nuclear war, designing bunkers, suppressing dissent, anticipating the words of counter-revolution, imagining the contours of its face. We strove to grasp the power of our enemies, to reverse their rhetoric, resist their efforts to corrupt us and match their weapons. But when the enemy eventually materialized, it looked too much like ourselves. We had no categories to describe what occurred, no definitions to capture what we had lost, and what we gained in its place.

We had been warned that the dictatorship of the proletariat was always under threat by the dictatorship of the bourgeoisie. What we did not anticipate was that the first victim of that conflict, the clearest sign of victory, would be the disappearance of those very terms: *dictatorship, proletariat, bourgeoisie.* They were no longer part of our vocabulary. Before the withering away of the state, the language with which to articulate that aspiration itself withered away. Socialism, the society we lived under, was gone. Communism, the society we aspired to create, where class conflict would disappear and the free abilities of each would be fully developed, was gone too. It was gone not only as an ideal, not only as a system of rule, but also as a category of thought.

Only one word was left: *freedom.* It featured in every speech on television, in every slogan barked out in rage on the streets. When freedom finally arrived, it was like a dish served frozen. We chewed little, swallowed fast and remained hungry. Some wondered if we had been given leftovers. Others noted they were simply cold starters.

In the days and months leading up to December 1990, I walked to school, sat in my classroom, played on the street, shared meals with my family, listened to the radio and watched television, just as I had done every other day of my life. The same acts, and the desires and beliefs of those who undertook them, would later be remembered with radically different meanings. We would speak of courageous gestures, timely decisions and mature reactions to challenging circumstances. We could not bring ourselves to contemplate the possibility of accidents along the way; to imagine plans having gone amiss. Scenarios that would have been considered wild fantasies up to that point later acquired the features of strict necessity. We could not contemplate failure. Failure was the shore from which we sailed: it could not be the port where we arrived.

Yet all I remember from that time is fear, confusion, hesitation. We used the term *freedom* to talk about an ideal that had finally materialized, just as we had done in the past. But things changed so much that it would be difficult to say later if it was the same 'we'. For half a century, everyone had shared the same structure of cooperation and oppression, occupying social roles that would now all have to be different, while the men and women performing these roles remained the same. Relatives, neighbours, colleagues had both fought and supported one another, cultivated mutual suspicion while developing bonds of trust. The same people who had spied on each other had also provided protective cover. Prison guards had been prisoners; victims had been perpetrators.

I will never know if the working classes who paraded on 1 May were the same who protested in early December. I will never know who I would have been if I had posed different questions, or if my questions had been answered differently, or not answered at all.

Things were one way, and then they were another. I was someone, then I became someone else.

PART II

11.

Grey Socks

'Who will your family vote for?' Elona asked in school a few days before the end of the year, when free elections were announced.

'They will vote for freedom,' I replied. 'For freedom and democracy.'

'Yeah, my father too,' she said. 'He says the Party was wrong.'

'About what?'

'About everything. Do you think the Party was wrong about God?'

I hesitated. I knew why she was keen to know and did not want to upset her. In the end, I could not bring myself to lie. After a short silence, I told her I did not believe God existed. Then I regretted my words. 'I don't know,' I corrected myself. 'The Party was clearly wrong about a lot of things. That's why we have pluralism now. It means there are many different parties, and there are free elections where people choose which party to vote for, to find out who is right. My dad explained it to me.'

'That's probably why teacher Nora said that religion is the *opinion* of the people,' Elona said. 'The Party wasn't wrong about that one.'

'I don't remember her saying that. I only remember the bit about it being the heart of a heartless world.

I asked Nini about God again, but she says she doesn't know about God; she only trusts her conscience. Whatever that means.'

'Maybe it means that when there is pluralism, some parties say God exists, and some others say he doesn't exist, and whoever wins the election decides what is right,' Elona mused.

'Well, they can't change it like that all the time. Otherwise, what stops parties from trying to win an election by convincing people that Zeus or Athena or whatever are real, and that we have to make human sacrifices to gods, like the ancient Greeks.'

'Nothing stops them,' Elona said. 'That's the point. We're free now. Everyone can say what they like.'

I shook my head in disbelief. 'Then they would have to cancel and reinstate things like Christmas and New Year's Eve, depending on who wins the elections. They must have some facts. In socialism, we relied on science, we didn't just make things up. Science is real because you can make experiments and test theories. I don't know how you can test God.'

'I still believe in God, a little bit,' said Elona. 'I mean, I definitely believe in science too, but I also believe in God. Don't you?' she pressed.

'I don't know,' I repeated. 'I'm not sure what to think. I used to believe in socialism, and I was looking forward to communism. I thought we were right to fight exploitation and to give power to the working class. My parents now say our family was on the wrong side of the class struggle.'

'Nobody believes in socialism any more. Not even the working classes,' Elona said.

'Does your dad believe in it?' I asked. 'Which side of the class struggle is your family on?'

'My dad.' Elona thought for a moment. 'I don't think so. I mean, he's a bus driver; he's in the working class. He always paraded with his collective on 1 May. Now he swears at the television every time he sees a Party Secretary. He is very irritable these days. He drinks a lot more. It's hard to calm him down. Mimi, my sister, is still in the orphanage. He had promised to bring her home after six months, but he now says we can't afford it. He used to be a happy drunk, now he's just angry all the time. I don't think he ever believed in socialism.'

'My parents have changed too. They never used to get angry with power cuts and now they just lose their temper over nothing. They start yelling, "Bastards, bastards!" But if I'm late home from school, only my grandmother notices. At least she's always the same, she hasn't changed at all.'

'My grandfather says he always believed in God, a little bit,' Elona continued. 'He celebrated Christmas secretly, even when religion was abolished. He was a partisan. He says the Party did some good things, like making sure everyone could read and write, building hospitals, bringing electricity, that kind of thing. But it did terrible things too, like destroying churches and killing people. He says he is a socialist, and a Christian, and that if you're a Christian it's very easy to be a socialist. He's still in the Party – he didn't leave it.'

'My grandfather was a socialist too,' I said. 'He spent fifteen years in prison. My parents had no chance in the Party.'

'That's so weird,' Elona said. 'My grandfather says

maybe the churches will be rebuilt now that we have political pluralism. He says Mum is in paradise, and he prays for her. I asked him to teach me how to pray too.'

'We're Muslim,' I said. 'We go to the mosque. I mean, we don't have mosques now, so I don't know if we would go if they are rebuilt. My mum says, in her family, people have always believed in God.'

'I don't care about Christmas or New Year's Eve,' Elona said. 'They can celebrate whichever. Whichever people vote for. The elections will be on a Sunday. They haven't changed that. Did you know Christians used to go to church on Sunday?'

I shrugged. 'We're Muslim,' I repeated. 'I'm not sure what we're supposed to do on Sundays. I guess we'll see what happens.'

What happened was that we had a lie-in. We spent the Sunday morning of the first free and fair elections burrowed in our beds. Every now and then, my father would rise to check the news in the kitchen. 'There's time,' he whispered when he came back, as if he feared that the sound of his voice would add power to the broad light that filtered through our dark curtains, undermining everyone's effort to remain in their place. He stood by the bedroom door in the same grave posture he adopted when he intended to convey an important message. In this case, the message was contained in a single word. Thirty.

Then he returned to his room. An hour later he repeated the action, checking the news in the kitchen and stopping by the door to inform us of the new figure. Forty, he said. Later: fifty. Each time, there was a sound from under the bedcovers, like a cheer that one tried to suppress. 'It's going up,' my grandmother whispered, pulling the duvet up slightly from the bed we shared, as if it were midnight. 'I don't think it will get to one hundred,' my father replied. At that point, the cheer became louder, and impossible to censor. 'We must go back to sleep,' my grandmother said.

It was not a deep sleep. Just a light doze of the kind that one can order oneself to fall into, sometimes in the hope of reviving a pleasant dream, sometimes to suppress the reality that awaits. That time, the dream mixed up with the news. It was a dream about electoral turnout.

We wanted it to go up. But it had to go up slowly, not all at once. More importantly, it had to stop short of ninety-nine per cent. A turnout of close to one hundred, declared early in the day, would have meant that elections were neither free nor fair, that they were just as they had always been. In the past, on election day, everybody in my family was up at five in the morning. By six, they were already queuing at the voting booth. By seven, they had voted. By nine, the results had been announced. 'Every vote of the people is a bullet to our enemy,' went the official slogan. My parents had figured that the earlier they showed up, the less likely they were to be suspected of reluctance to fire bullets.

Usually, we were among the first to arrive. The queue for voting was similar to that for milk; it started in the middle of the night, but with the difference that there were no bags, cans or stones placed the night before to substitute for potential voters. Everyone was present in person. There was no loud shouting, no attempt to identify people you knew, and it did not feel as if things were about to descend into chaos from one moment to the next. The orderliness and sense of calm anticipation displayed by the whole thing had led me to conclude that voting was intrinsically more rewarding than buying milk. The mood certainly seemed brighter. In my parents' case, it was so bright that the only way I thought I could match their enthusiasm for voting was to come up with something only I could do. Sometimes I recited a poem for the Party in front of the election panel, and sometimes I prepared a bouquet of flowers to place in front of the ballot box, right next to Uncle Enver's photo.

The last elections I remembered under socialism occurred in 1987. I wrote the poem I would read myself, because, if I was too young to vote, I thought the poem could be considered my bullet. But I agonized over what kind of missile I had come up with, and if it could be considered sufficiently powerful to destroy our enemies. My grandmother reassured me of the poem's quality, but my parents tried to moderate my expectations by explaining that they did not know if there would be time to recite it. It would depend on the queue, they said.

It had still been dark when we left the house. I felt anxious and tightened my grip on my father's right hand, which was sweaty, like mine. We waited in the queue outside the voting office, and when the booth opened and our turn came, a panel member handed my father a white sheet with a typed list of names from the Democratic Front, the only organization that was allowed to file candidates. Without looking, my father marked the sheet, folded it twice and dropped it into the red box. His eyes were fixed on the panel member who, in the meantime, was preparing a sheet for my mother, the next person in line. Then my father greeted him with a nod of the head. The man on the panel answered with a raised fist. I raised my fist too, as I always did if I saw another fist raised.

I don't have any memory of reading my poem. I must have changed my mind about its quality at the last minute, or maybe my parents found a cunning way to remove me from the premises without humiliating themselves even further.

Now, with free and fair elections, everything was different. We didn't have to wake up early. There would be no queue. Nobody would care if we voted or not. We had the whole day to vote and, if we did not feel like it, we could choose not to vote at all. Everyone lingered in bed, as if they were still deciding whether it was worth disrupting one's sleep to go to the polls and, if so, who to vote for.

The evening before, everyone had lined up the clothes they would wear. My grandmother, who I had only ever seen dressed in black because she was in mourning for my grandfather's death, pulled a blouse with white polka dots out of a wooden trunk. The last election she'd dressed up for was in 1946. She also wore a hat then, she said, and a pearl necklace. She joked that the hat was probably still hanging in the wardrobe of the National Film Studio, where most of the clothes confiscated from bourgeois families had ended up.

My parents debated whether to vote early or to wait. Nobody could predict how the elections would unfold. The 1946 elections kept coming up. They had not ended well. Shortly afterwards, both my grandfathers were arrested and the rest of the family was deported. Could history repeat itself?

'It was a different world then,' my father pointed out. 'The Soviets had won the war. Now they've lost it.' 'The Soviets, yes,' my mother replied, visibly irritated. 'The Soviets were finished this time last year. Where were you instead?' she asked. The question was rhetorical because she then adjusted her voice to deal the final blow: 'Preparing the 1 May parade.'

My father shook his head with mysterious conviction. 'Enver is finished. The Party is finished,' he insisted. 'We're not going back.'

A few weeks before, the statue of Enver Hoxha in the capital's main square had been toppled. Students had started a hunger strike to demand renaming the university, at that point still called 'Enver Hoxha'. As Party officials hesitated on the best way to respond, proposing a referendum of all the students, conflicts continued to escalate.

But the Party was not finished. From *the* Party, it would soon become *a* party. One of many. It would contest seats in parliament with other groups, each of which would have its own candidates, its own newspapers, its own programmes, its own list of names. Some of these names were of people who had once been members of the Party but had recently switched camp. Other people remained loyal. The fact that the Party could break up and multiply like that, that it could be considered both the cure and the disease, both the root of all evil and the source of all hope, gave it a mythical quality that would be considered for many years to come the cause of all misfortune, a dark spell cast to make freedom look like tyranny, and to give necessity the semblance of choice. Setting yourself free from its all-encompassing presence was like chewing on the rope you suddenly noticed between your teeth. The Party had gone, but it was still there. The Party was above us, but it was also deep inside. Everyone, everything, came from it. Its voice had changed, it had acquired a different shape and spoke a new language. But what was the colour of its soul? Had it ever become what it was always meant to be? Only history would tell, but at that point history had not yet been made. All we had were new elections.

'Voting is a duty,' Nini had said the night before the opening of the polls. 'If we don't vote, we let other people decide for us. It ends up being the same as before, the same as slipping a single list of candidates into the ballot box without reading it.'

I thought about her words on the morning of the election. Why did my parents hesitate to vote? Why did they not simply go out to savour the freedom they'd been longing for? The staged yawning, the theatrical sleep, the faux indecision and all gave the impression that what they had wanted all these years was not for concrete things to happen but for abstract possibilities to remain available. Now that *something* specific was within reach, my family feared losing control. Instead of exercising the freedom of choice that elections were assumed to bring, they tried to keep that choice free from contamination. Perhaps they wanted to avoid committing to a specific individual or policy that might turn out to disappoint. Or perhaps they worried that if the same results were brought about through the actions of millions of other voters, who had different principles and motives, their hopes would turn into illusion.

My brother and I waited a little longer and charged into my parents' room. We found them lying stubbornly in bed, stiff, wrapped in a blanket of refusal to face reality. Covered in white sheets from head to toe, they looked like hospital patients who'd just been drugged in preparation for surgery. We went closer, studying them with bewilderment. When they noticed we were there, they rolled over on to their other sides. Then a voice came from under the sheets: 'Go away. It's not time.'

We returned to our room, and I started listening to the radio. The news programme announced that groups of people in remote villages of the south had occupied the streets; they were holding photos of Enver Hoxha, shouting pro-communist slogans and warning voters that it would not be long before the country came to regret this day. Journalists labelled these nostalgic protests 'counter-protests', to distinguish them from the real protests against the government that had taken place in the weeks before. 'Peasants,' my grandmother commented. 'What do they know?'

The groups, composed of peasants, workers and members of the militant communist youth, were in fact officially called 'Volunteers for the defence of the memory of Enver Hoxha'. They had started to assemble a few weeks prior to the election, when Hoxha's statue had been destroyed. 'Busts may be removed, but the figure of Enver Hoxha cannot be toppled,' the Party headquarters had stated in response. But the counter-protesters could not halt the course of events. Like people hanging off cliffs, they clung on to the few remaining symbols of the country's communist legacy. They feared the future too, in part. But, unlike my family, many of them still identified with the past. The Party had always spoken in their name and acted on their behalf. My family was a victim of state violence. They had been the midwives.

The counter-protests would last only a few more months. What had started as a series of reforms was increasingly labelled as revolution. In any other revolution, there would have been oppressed and oppressors, winners and losers, victims and perpetrators. Here, the chain of responsibility was so intricate that there could be only one camp. Executing leaders, imprisoning spies or sanctioning former Party members, would have fuelled the conflicts even further, sharpening the desire for revenge, spilling more blood. It seemed more sensible to erase responsibility altogether, to pretend everyone had been innocent all along. The only wrongdoers it was legitimate to name were those who had already died; those who could neither explain nor absolve themselves. All the rest turned into victims. All the survivors were winners. With no perpetrators, only ideas were left to blame. Communism was considered a vision so hopeless for some, so murderous for others, that the sole mention of the word would be met with either scorn or hatred. This revolution, the velvet one, was a revolution of people against concepts.

When my family decided the time to vote had come, the polls were about to close. We rushed outside, where many people were greeting each other by raising two fingers in the shape of a V, the new symbol of freedom and democracy. My brother and I found it surprisingly easy to replace the fist with the two fingers. My mother had clearly practised before. My father seemed hesitant at first. My grandmother, whose upper-class demeanour had never really gone away, probably thought it all beneath her. Or perhaps, like the Allied Forces that had invented it, the V sign hadn't reached Albania in 1946.

Campaigners on the street handed us stickers with the logo of the opposition party, a blue P, which stood for Party, curled inside a D, which stood for Democratic, as if it had found shelter there. I had never seen stickers before. I carried several on my chest, and left some on the shop windows, creating a welcome optical illusion that the shops had something to sell. I also stuck one or two on the doors of the very few cars parked along the road. When we entered the voting room, my brother tried to place a sticker near the ballot box. That was met with disapproval so he had to content himself with surreptitiously glueing it under the table.

The results came the morning after. The opposition's defeat was crushing. The party emerged triumphant with more than sixty per cent of the vote. My mother declared that the elections had been neither free nor fair. The entire campaign, she said, had been organized by the Party. It was absurd to expect it to both regulate a competition between itself and other parties and try to win the election at the same time. The whole thing was a fraud.

That turned out to be harsh, or at least harsh by the standards of the tourists who had in the meantime descended on our country, armed with notepads and television cameras, and who now went by the name of the 'international community'. Their official explanation, which set a precedent for official explanations that were considered authoritative only if they came from the international community, was different. They argued that the opposition parties had had little time to prepare and had struggled to file candidates in rural areas, and that since the old dissidents had been jailed and only recently released, it had been too late for them to run for office.

The months that followed saw protests and unrest increase everywhere. In the north, unidentified shots during one of the many demonstrations killed four opposition activists. The transition to liberalism was now sealed with blood. Democracy had its martyrs. A few weeks later, mineworkers, organized in newly independent trade unions, called a hunger strike. The character of their demands was economic rather than political. Both the Party and the opposition now agreed on the need for reforms; they differed only on the mode of implementation. In place of the old socialist slogans, a new formula emerged, one whose purpose was to explain and reassure, to warn and prescribe, to rouse the spirits and soothe the injuries. That formula captured everything, from the tragic reality of food shortages and factory closures, to the perceived necessity of political reforms and market liberalism. It was made of two words: *shock therapy*.

It came from psychiatry: shock therapy involves sending electric currents through a patient's brain to relieve the symptoms of severe mental illness. In this case, our planned economy was considered to be the equivalent of madness. The cure was a transformative monetary policy: balancing budgets, liberalizing prices, eliminating government subsidies, privatizing the state sector and opening up the economy to foreign trade and direct investment. Market behaviour would then adjust itself, and the emerging capitalist institutions would become efficient without great need for central coordination. A crisis was foreseen, but people had spent a lifetime making sacrifices in the name of better days to come. This would be their last effort. With drastic measures and good will, the patient would soon recover from the shock and enjoy the benefits of the therapy. Speed was of the essence. Milton Friedman and Friedrich von Hayek replaced Karl Marx and Friedrich Engels almost overnight.

'Freedom works,' then US Secretary of State James Baker told a spontaneous crowd of more than 300,000 gathered in the capital to welcome the first state visit by an American official. The spirit of the new laws, Baker emphasized, announcing the support of the United States for the transition to freedom, mattered as much as their letter. Both his government and private American organizations would be involved to help get things right. They would help us construct 'democracy, markets, and a constitutional order'.

The new government did not last long. Pressure from the international community, increasing looting and violence on the streets and deteriorating economic conditions forced the Party to call new elections. Within a year, the country was again in campaign mode. This time, the forces advocating swift change had longer to prepare.

One afternoon, Bashkim Spahia, a local doctor and former Party member turned opposition candidate, knocked on our door, visibly agitated. He was wearing a charcoal-grey jacket cut in the style favoured by Leonid Brezhnev; under it he had on a purple T-shirt with pink writing across the middle, above matching purple trousers. The writing was in English. It read: 'Sweet dreams, my lovely friends'.

Bashkim asked if my father owned any grey socks he could borrow for a few months. He had been knocking on every door, he said. He explained that, for the election campaign, the US State Department had distributed brochures containing important advice on what aspiring members of parliament ought to wear. 'Apparently, only dark socks are acceptable, grey or black, but better grey,' he added, visibly distressed. 'I only have white socks. They also say I need a *sponsour* for my campaign. What *sponsour* are they asking about? I don't even have socks to wear!' he exclaimed in despair.

My parents invited him in for coffee. They tried to explain that the advice could not have come from the State Department; perhaps it came from the US embassy. Even then, the embassy might be flexible. Bashkim shook his head. He was inconsolable. His son had translated the leaflets, he insisted, and had assured him they bore the imprint of the Department of State. He would never be able to win his seat back from those dirty communist bastards without the right colour socks.

On the night in which his victory was announced, we spotted him in a television debate wearing the thick grey woollen socks my grandmother had knitted for my father. My family was particularly proud to have contributed to Bashkim's victory. They bore no grudges; they were happy to overlook the fact that his wife, Vera, had once complained to the local council that my parents were reluctant to clean the street on Sundays. Nor did they hold it against Bashkim that he never returned my father's socks. Within a short period of time, our local doctor went on to become not only a charismatic politician but also a highly successful businessman. He swapped 'Sweet dreams' for a Rolex watch, and replaced the Brezhnev jacket with Hugo Boss. I bet he started wearing silk socks too. We rarely saw him again, and even when we did, it was only from a distance, as he slammed the door of his dark, shiny Mercedes Benz, surrounded by mighty bodyguards. It would have been imprudent, as well as implausible, to get closer and accuse him of wrongfully appropriating my father's socks.

12.

A Letter from Athens

Sometime in January 1991, before the first free and fair election, my grandmother received a letter from Athens signed by someone she had never heard of, a woman called Katerina Stamatis. Before we opened it, we brought the envelope to show our neighbours. A small crowd gathered in the Papas' house. Donika, who had worked in the post office all her life, was handed the letter. She stood in the middle of her living room, surrounded by curious faces, their gazes fixed on the thin, creamy paper, where Greek characters written in ink lined up like hieroglyphs of the future.

I knew Donika could not read Greek. Only a few weeks before, she had asked my grandmother to translate the list of ingredients on the back of a bottle containing a yellow liquid. It was brought to her as a present by a cousin who had recently travelled to Athens. She had washed her hair with what she assumed was foreign lemon shampoo, then felt an unusual tingle which made her head itchy. My grandmother's translation revealed the cause to be an exotic, previously unknown substance called dishwasher liquid.

Donika studied the envelope quietly for several minutes, inspecting the front and back. Her solemn pose cast an expectant silence over the room. Only the sound of wood crackling and burning in the stove could be heard. She put the envelope under her nose and sniffed it in various places, each sniff followed by a deep breath out. She shook her head, then clicked her tongue with disapproval. Then she inserted her index finger under the flap, holding the outside part under her thumb. She dragged both fingers along the edges of the envelope, with a slow, sullen movement and a frown of concentration, as if the act of sliding caused her a pain which she was obliged to contain. Once the inspection had been concluded, she looked up with an expression of dismay that, as she began to speak, slowly converted to anger.

'It's been opened,' she announced, looking towards the door. 'They've opened it.'

The silence in the room transformed into a collective murmur.

'Bastards,' my mother finally came out with.

'They haven't just opened it once. Several times,' explained Donika.

'Yes, obviously,' her husband, Mihal, retorted. 'It's not like they've hired new people to work in the post office. They just do what they're used to doing.'

Some neighbours nodded. Others disagreed. 'Post-office workers should be instructed to stop opening letters,' Donika replied. 'Privacy,' my mother said. 'Privacy is so important. We never had any privacy before.' Then she suggested that nothing would happen before the post office was privatized. Only privatization could respect privacy.

Everyone agreed privacy was important. 'Not just important, it's your right. It's a right,' Donika explained, her voice charged with all the wisdom and authority she had accumulated during the many years spent opening envelopes.

After that, my grandmother was invited to read the letter out loud, translating it word for word. The sender, Katerina Stamatis, claimed to be the daughter of Nikos, a business associate of my great-grandfather. Nikos, she wrote, had been with my great-grandfather when he died in Salonica in the mid-fifties. The woman wondered if my grandmother would be interested in taking legal action to reclaim the properties and land that had belonged to her family in Greece, and offered help in pursuing the matter. My grandmother said the surname sounded vaguely familiar. It was no scam.

Nini had last seen her father at her wedding, in Tirana, in June 1941. After the war, 'the roads were closed', as she put it, and although she remembered receiving a telegram from Athens announcing her father's death, she had not been granted a passport to attend the funeral, nor did she know anything about the circumstances of his passing. She recalled how she had learned of the death almost forty years ago, at a time when she was working in the fields during the day and giving French lessons to the young son of a prominent Party official in the evening. On the day she received news about her father's death, they were going over possessives, and when asked to make a sentence using 'your', the little boy said: 'Your eyes look red.' That little boy later became a prominent Party official himself, the same Comrade Mehmet who was on the panel that gave me permission to start school early.

In her letter, Katerina wrote touchingly about the loyalty of her father, Nikos, to my great-grandfather. She recalled how she had promised Nikos on his deathbed to contact my grandmother, should circumstances in Albania ever change. The affair, she added less emotionally, would be very lucrative for both families. She was prepared to host my grandmother in Athens, accompany her to the relevant archives and assist her in contacting lawyers who would help investigate the matter.

My grandmother reacted to the news as if she had rehearsed for the part all her life, knowing that it was just that, a part that at some point she would be asked to play. Her mind turned to a different kind of financial consideration. Ever since obtaining permission from the Party to build a private house on the street where I grew up, my parents had been heavily in debt. They owed cash to everyone: my uncle, my mother's colleagues, and some distant relatives in other towns. That day, Nini and my parents sat down to discuss with the neighbours whether it was likely that my grandmother would get the visa, and to make various calculations: how much money my family still owed, what my parents had left over at the end of each month, what my grandmother's pension amounted to, and whether she could afford to make the journey to Greece. They laid out as much detailed information as they could, and it soon became clear that our savings barely sufficed to cover a day in Athens, let alone the cost of a visa application fee and travel expenses for two weeks.

In the past, my grandmother had shown me a document from when our country was still a kingdom, with a black-and-white photo of herself stapled on cardboard above a few lines with information about her height, hair and eye colour, place and date of birth, and birthmarks. The passport was kept in the same drawer that stored the Eiffel Tower postcard and my grandfather's letter to Enver Hoxha after his release from prison. My grandmother's face in the photograph had a serious expression which would have been considered pompous if she had looked more than seventeen years old. Her hair was cut extremely short, in a style intended to suppress the impression that it was any style at all. Her lips were tightly clenched in what seemed like a concerted attempt to suppress a smile. Her whole pose conveyed an effort to convince the viewer that the answer 'female', after the question concerning gender, was entirely coincidental, if not some kind of administrative error.

'This is what we need,' my grandmother had often said. 'This is called a passport.' Passports, she had explained, decided whether roads were open or closed. If you happened to have a passport, you could travel. If you did not, you were stuck. Only a few people in Albania could apply for a passport, usually to travel for work. And since the Party decided what counted as work, we simply had to wait. 'You can add a child's photograph to it,' she had said. 'If I ever receive one for a trip, I will take you with me.'

In December 1990, it became clear that what my family had been waiting for was not for the Party to authorize our passports, but for passports to survive the decline of the Party, just as they had survived the exile of the king. But when the letter from Athens arrived, and I overheard the grown-ups in Donika's living room make their patient calculations about whether my grandmother and I could afford the journey, a new feeling of confusion took hold of me. I discovered that being in possession of a passport had never been enough, that the passport was only the first and most immediate obstacle in a series that became increasingly abstract, and increasingly removed from us. For the roads to really open, we needed a visa, the issuing of which, it turned out, could not be guaranteed either by the old Party, which was on its last legs, or by the new parties that had recently formed. Yet more upsetting was the fact that, even if we succeeded in obtaining a passport and a visa, neither came with any funding for the trip. How were we then supposed to travel abroad? It took a surprisingly long time to reach the logical conclusion. We could not.

A few days passed, and the letter from Athens, carefully folded back into its envelope, found its place on the low table in our living room, next to a vase and a packet of cigarettes we kept there to offer guests. Nobody had the courage to put it in the drawer, since in that drawer only our past lived, and we liked to think of the letter from Athens not as the past but as the present, even the future, though a distant one. My mother looked after it like a recently domesticated animal that retains the capacity to bite. She cautiously wiped the dust off the table and ensured that no drops of water from the flower vase would fall on the letter, which we now called 'Keti', after its sender. The rest of us wouldn't go close. We tiptoed around it, occasionally gave it a furtive glance, but mostly we pretended to ignore its presence. Once or twice, it became the trigger of family arguments about what form the response should take so as not to immediately foreclose the possibility of future travel, the occasion of reprimands about what we could have done to better manage our finances in the past, and the source of speculations as to whether there was someone who might loan us money to whom we were not already in debt.

Just when we had abandoned hope, the solution came from my other grandmother, Nona Fozi. She had come to visit for my brother's birthday, and when she noticed Keti lying on the table she asked what had come of our preparations for the trip to Athens. Nini sighed.

'It's harder for us to go to Athens than it was for Gagarin to go into orbit,' my father joked.

'Comrade Stamatis has promised to pay for the ticket,' I interrupted to explain, anxiously. 'We managed to find money for the visa. But we can't travel all the way to Greece without any money as back-up, in case something goes wrong.'

'Mrs Stamatis,' my mother corrected me. 'Not comrade. She's not your comrade. The rest is true.' She then turned to her mother.

Nona Fozi left the house in haste, before she had time to finish her coffee or eat her portion of the birthday cake. She returned half an hour later with something tightly gripped in her right fist, which she waved from a distance like a communist salute. When she reached the table where Keti lay, she opened the palm of her hand, and, with immaculate precision and a proud look in her eyes, dropped five Napoleonic gold coins on to the envelope. They fell to the table with a tinkling sound, a far cry from the thud our leks made when they dropped on the floor, a sound as foreign and removed from us as the coins' possible source. Nobody had ever known that Nona Fozi still owned gold. My mother had sometimes wondered if her parents had hidden some gold before the family's belongings were expropriated. She doubted it, she said, since even when they were desperately hungry, the gold reserves were mentioned purely hypothetically, as if the mere idea sufficed to fill their stomachs. Nona Fozi said now that she had tried to save some gold from being confiscated, and had kept it safe for the day when the roads would open. 'There,' she told Nini, with the visible satisfaction of someone whose foresight has been proved right. 'Now you can travel. Inshallah your gold will multiply.'

My father took the coins to the bank to be converted into paper money. Soon after, he returned with a hundred-dollar bill he had received in exchange. Intense discussions followed about where to hide the note so that it would neither be spent nor get lost. At one point there were fifteen neighbours crammed into our living room, volunteering to lend us wallets of different periods and sizes, all of which, after careful inspection, were declared unsafe because 'everybody knows the West is full of pickpockets'. After ruling out various options – the bottom of the suitcase, the pages of a book, the inside of an amulet – a unanimous decision was reached to sew the bill into the hem of my grandmother's skirt, with the recommendation to take the skirt off only for sleeping and never to wash it.

On the day of our departure, the whole road came to bid us farewell, each family of neighbours contributing some item we might need for the journey: byrek wrapped in newspaper, garlic bulbs to bring good luck, the names (but not the addresses) of long-lost relatives to look up in case the Stamatis family failed to show up. In the car, my grandmother kept rearranging her skirt in order to ensure the one-hundred-dollar bill was still there. She did this with a dignified expression and a fake half-smile that said: 'I am fully aware that a lady doesn't walk into an airport fiddling with her skirt.' At one point, in the departures area, our greatest fear seemed to have materialized. 'I can't feel anything,' Nini said in a panicked voice. We rushed to the bathroom and, since she couldn't bend to look through the minuscule hole in the hem, I had to stretch out on the floor to see if the note was still there; it was, only slightly wrinkled, as if to manifest its disappointment about leaving the bank only to end up inside my grandmother's skirt.

The departure lounge in the airport was largely empty. There were only a few foreigners waiting for their flights and purchasing items from the small store located at the entrance, which looked similar to the valuta shop but with the difference that you could pick out items from the shelves yourself. My grandmother commented that the shop assistant smiled like a spy. 'How do spies smile?' I asked her. 'Like this,' she replied, making a grimace with her mouth without showing her teeth. 'It looks like a normal smile,' I said. 'Exactly,' my grandmother replied. 'That's the point.'

Scattered around the place were police officers in blue uniforms. One agent looked at the sticker on the passport, which I had learned was our visa, then stamped it. Others waited for us while we deposited our bag to be searched. 'Bastards!' I whispered, recalling my mother's reaction when she discovered the letter from Athens had been opened. Nini looked perplexed.

'Nobody cares about privacy in this country, do they?' I said after the control was finished. 'I guess they haven't hired new people to work at the airport.'

On the plane I saw a coloured plastic bag for the first time in my life. The air hostess asked if we were new to air travel, then handed it to me with instructions to use it if I needed to vomit. I spent the rest of the journey asking myself whether I was ready to throw up, and was concerned at the end that it hadn't happened. We were served lunch in plastic containers, but we had our own byreks to eat. We saved the lunch boxes in case we were hungry later, but also because the plastic cutlery and plates looked like nothing we had seen before and we wanted to bring them back home to use for special occasions. 'So pretty,' my grandmother commented. 'They didn't make them like this before the war. I don't remember this material.'

When we arrived in Athens, my grandmother encouraged me to start a diary. I made a list of all the new things I had discovered for the first time, and meticulously recorded them: the first time I felt air conditioning on the palm of my hands; the first time I tasted bananas; the first time I saw traffic lights; the first time I wore jeans; the first time I did not need to queue to enter a shop; the first time I encountered border control; the first time I saw queues made of cars instead of humans; the first time I sat down on a toilet instead of squatting; the first time I saw people following dogs on a leash instead of stray dogs following people; the first time I was given actual chewing-gum rather than just the wrapper; the first time I saw buildings made of different shops and shop-windows bursting with toys; the first time I saw crosses on graves; the first time I stared at walls covered by adverts rather than anti-imperialist slogans; the first time I admired the Acropolis, but only from the outside because we could not afford the entrance ticket. I also described at length my first encounter with tourist children as a tourist child myself, when I learned with surprise that they did not recognize the names of Athena and Ulysses, and they laughed because I did not recognize the image of an apparently famous mouse called Mickey.

Our hosts, Katerina and her husband, lived in a rooftop flat in Ekali, a wealthy suburb in northern Athens, where spacious gardens with neatly cut grass and swimming pools could be seen through the gates that separated their villas from the world outside. The Stamatis had no swimming pool, but they had something even more eccentric: five different-sized fridges, scattered in several rooms, not one of which was a Yugoslav Obodin. Two of the five contained only drinks, and one contained only soft drinks, including Coca Cola, which was not distributed simply in the cans I was familiar with, but also in plastic bottles. I developed a habit of waking in the night to open the fridge and drink Coca Cola, partly because I found the taste addictive but mostly because I could never decide if the drink in the can tasted exactly the same as that in the bottle, and, if so, why both were sold. Our hosts had encouraged us to help ourselves to food and drink whenever we felt like it, but my grandmother had severely prohibited me from doing so and instructed me never to ask for treats. She pinched my thigh under the table if she noticed I was about to request an extra banana or glass of soft drink; or if I was further away from her she muttered something in Albanian behind her teeth, clenched in a pretend smile adopted to mislead others about the nature of our exchange. Like a spy, I thought. As for her, she barely ate. This in turn prompted Katerina's husband, Yiorgos, the largest man I had ever seen, who owned a factory for making loofah sponges and who had acquired the shape of a loofah sponge himself, to regularly exclaim over meals: 'Forty-five years of Hoxha's rule have contracted your stomachs to the size of an olive!'

We visited Salonica and found the old French lycée where my grandmother had studied. The building now housed company offices. To me, it looked like a bank, similar to those I had seen in Western films. Nini remembered one by one the names of the most popular boys in her class; she had shared cigars with them during breaks. She also remembered her old teachers, in particular a certain Monsieur Bernard, who had forecast that her future would always be bright if she did not smile too much and kept her hair short. She had rigorously stuck to both pieces of advice, she said, but it turned out that Monsieur Bernard's prediction was a little off.

We visited her father's grave and she handled the pain she must have felt with a stoic dignity only she could muster. She was silent throughout. Only when she left did she bend to give a soft kiss to the photograph on the stone, encouraging me to do the same. I didn't feel like it; I had never met this man, and he had never met me. But I complied so as not to disappoint her. She insisted on finding the grave of her old nanny, Dafne, whom she had last seen at the end of the war. As she stood rigidly by the side of the white cross, she squinted and, clutching her handbag, looked pale and thin, as if the intervening years had dried out her flesh and left only the bones. A few tears rolled from her eyes on to the marble, where the winter sun quickly dried them. She noticed. 'You see?' She turned to me with a melancholic half-smile. 'Dafne always dried my tears. She still does.'

We found her old house in the Ottoman part of town, a large white building with a garden where fruit trees had started to blossom. One of Nini's first memories, as a two-year-old, was of the house catching fire. She recalled being carried outside in a rush, wrapped in scorching blankets. It was almost as if she could still hear the shrieks, she said; she remembered seeing flames in her mother's hair. Traces of the fire were still visible on the front of the house, and she would have liked to show me what it looked like inside. We went closer to the front door, and a woman appeared on the veranda, asking if she could help. My grandmother explained why we were there and asked to take a look inside. The woman replied that she wanted to believe us, but that she was there only to clean the house and could not take responsibility for letting in outsiders. My grandmother told her that she understood. 'Do neighbours also clean each other's house inside?' I asked. 'She's paid to clean,' Nini replied. She then turned again to the cleaner and, with an air of confident familiarity, as if she had met the woman before, shouted 'thank you' in Greek.

My grandmother knew she was unlikely to ever receive her properties back. She had agreed to the trip partly out of an obligation not to destroy the hopes of those who entertained them, and partly in the spirit of reconnecting with her past and introducing me to it. She was cordial and well disposed towards the people we met, though perhaps less interested in pursuing money than they might have expected. Different lawyers explained the difficulties associated with reclaiming ownership of the flats and land that had once belonged to her family, describing the population swaps after the collapse of the

Ottoman empire, emphasizing the changes in property law, the challenges in retrieving much of the required documentation, the fact that our two countries were technically still at war and had been since the forties, the legacy of the colonels' regime in Greece, and more. She nodded. We were driven around to many different offices for various appointments. The Stamatis always sat next to us and listened carefully, taking notes. Sometimes they responded with words I could not understand, and sometimes with agitated movements, waving their arms in the air, wagging their fingers, shaking their heads.

On the last day's appointment, Yiorgos became so furious with one of the lawyers that he started yelling something in Greek across the room and pointed his finger at me, as if to illustrate his argument. Then, continuing to raise his voice, he came closer, grabbed my arm and started waving it in the air just as he had done with his, all the while continuing to yell. I could not understand what he was saying. I looked at my grandmother. She kept nodding, both when the lawyer explained, and when Yiorgos replied. I decided it was wiser not to withdraw my arm.

'It was about a document called the will,' my grandmother told me that night, 'where people write down who they want to leave their belongings to after they die.'

'Have we got it?' I asked.

'The will?' My grandmother laughed. 'There were more important letters I couldn't save from confiscation by the police.'

In the fifty years my grandmother had spent outside the country, she had only ever spoken Greek with Cocotte, when she did not want me to understand their debates over politics. Our hosts in Athens, who some-times addressed me in broken French, much worse than mine, or broken English, much better than mine, observed that she had not lost her Greek at all. But she spoke it with an amusing upper-class accent that now sounded out of date, they said, and her tone of voice was much lower than what I discovered to be the Bal-kan average. When I saw her interact continually in a language impenetrable to me, it was almost as if I were travelling with two people: Nini, the person I trusted and admired most, and someone else, a mysterious woman from another time.

My grandmother had always insisted she had not changed. Prior to our trip to Athens, I believed her. I had found her words reassuring, her presence comfort-ing, especially in that winter of 1990, when everything around me was unstable, including my parents, whose reactions switched suddenly from anxiety to enthusi-asm with little in between. With my grandmother, it was different. She was always calm and consistent, able to adapt to the most challenging circumstances, overcom-ing difficulties with an ease that suggested the greatest obstacles are those that we create ourselves, that all that is needed is the will to succeed. She had convinced me that our present is always continuous with our past, and that in every set of apparently random circumstances one can observe rational characters and motives. Her very look, her posture, her way of speaking – all of it contributed to conveying that same impression.

During that trip to Athens something felt different. When we stared at old photographs of people who were long-dead and whom she had loved, I felt indifferent.

Those people, who were supposed to be my relatives and ancestors, meant little to me. One day Katerina gave my grandmother an old pipe that had belonged to my great-grandfather, and when I took it to play with, Nini suddenly lost her temper. She snatched it from my hands with a violence I had never seen before, and shouted: '*Ce n'est pas un jouet! Tu ne penses qu'à toi-même!*'* I could not understand the sacred reverence she showed towards that object, why its retrieval meant so much to her. 'Come on,' I said. 'It's just a pipe. You don't even smoke any more.'

Nini had always said that my brother and I were the most important things in her life. But we knew little of that life. When she let go, the way she did when standing in front of Dafne's grave, or when thinking of her schoolfriends, or when reminiscing about her father with our hosts, her reassurance did not ring true. I felt a sense of detachment, of alienation. I realized I was the product of events that had taken her away from her life, condemned her to years of hardship, isolation, loss and grief. If she had never left Salonica, she would never have met my grandfather. If she had never met my grandfather, my father would not have been born. If my father had not been born, I would not be here. These events were all part of a logical sequence. That's what she had always said. If I could understand the link between cause and effect the way she had explained things to me, I would accept that decisions have consequences. I would find continuity where others saw only rupture. I would be the product of freedom rather than necessity.

* 'This is not a toy! You only think about yourself!'

When we were in Greece, it was difficult to believe she had always owned the consequences of all the decisions she had made, that she had found a way of reconciling herself with all that followed her return to Albania. It was impossible to understand how she could have chosen not to emigrate when the opportunity presented itself at the end of the war. Perhaps she couldn't have known what was to come. But she must have felt, if not hatred, or desire for revenge, at least deep resentment. What new love could she experience, after having to cancel her past? In that foreign country, foreign to me but all too familiar to her, I associated myself not with the pride and affection she always said she felt for me, but with her loss. I wanted to leave. I wanted to go home. I wanted to feel safe.

13.

Everyone Wants to Leave

On my last evening in Athens, I prepared a plastic bag with half a Milka chocolate wrapped in tinfoil, a chewing-gum that looked like a fake cigarette and a loo-fah sponge in the shape of a strawberry from Yiorgos's factory. I had promised Elona I would bring her a present from my first trip abroad and was proud to have kept my word.

She was not there when I returned to class. I was told she had fallen ill and had to miss school for a few days. A whole week passed, but she did not come back. Then another week. Then it was spring break.

When classes started again at the end of April, Elona had still not returned. I decided to visit her, to check on her health. I had eaten the Milka chocolate but saved the cigarette-shaped chewing-gum and the sponge that looked like a strawberry. I knocked on her door. Her father opened it. 'I'm looking for Elona,' I said. 'I'm told she's ill. Can I see her?'

'Elona?' he asked, as if he did not recognize his daughter's name. 'Elona is a bad girl. A very bad girl.' He slammed the door in my face. I stood there for a few minutes, wondering what to do. He must have seen me from the window, or noticed I was still on the doorstep. He opened the door again. 'Can you give her this?' I said in a shaken voice, passing him the plastic bag, which trembled beneath my hand. He grabbed it, and flung it a few metres away, into the middle of the road, shouting: 'She's not here. Do you understand? She's not here.'

Not long after this conversation, Elona's name was taken off the school register. The teachers denied she had ever been ill; she had changed school, they said. In class, we speculated about her whereabouts. Some children said she had gone to live with her grandparents in a different part of town. Others that, like her sister, she had been sent to an orphanage, only one for older children. Others that she had left the country. When we ran out of guesses, she stopped being a topic of conversation. I asked my parents. They shrugged. 'Poor girl,' my grandmother commented. 'Her mother was such a good woman. Who knows where that poor girl has ended up?'

We learned the truth one day in late October of the same year, when Nini and I were returning from a walk. I recognized Elona's grandfather on the street. He had been to our class on 5 May the year before, to tell us about his heroic fighting as a partisan in the mountains near Greece. I could not remember his name. Elona had always called him 'Grandpa', so I shouted across the boulevard: 'Comrade! Comrade!' He did not turn. 'Sir! Sir!' my grandmother shouted, more loudly then I had. He stopped, and recognized me. I told him I missed Elona and wanted to know where she was. He took a deep breath, then sighed. 'Elona,' he said. 'That wretched child. We recently received a letter from her. Which way are you going?' He started to explain, walking by our side.

On the morning of 6 March 1991, Elona left her house

to go to school, wearing her uniform, carrying her bag, heavy with the textbooks and exercise books she needed for that day's lessons. During those weeks, she would take off earlier than usual, to meet with a boy she had got to know, a young fellow of about eighteen called Arian, he said.

I knew about Arian. He lived on my road. We hardly talked to him; even Flamur was afraid to go near him. Elona had mentioned once that she knew him, when we had gone to visit her sister at the orphanage. But I did not think they saw each other regularly. It turned out they met every morning in one of the secluded little alleyways off the main road that connected her house to the school. I knew the place; there was a sheltered area at the rear entrance to a small block of flats where couples could meet without being seen. Only 'bad girls' went there. It was odd to imagine Elona and Arian together. I wondered why she had never told me. She had recently turned thirteen, but I had always assumed she shared my complete indifference, even contempt, for older boys. Perhaps she had started seeing Arian while we were travelling to Greece.

On the morning of 6 March, her grandfather explained, the roads were teeming with people. Even the sheltered area where Elona and Arian met was crammed with families who spoke with strange accents and seemed to have spent the night there, in preparation for another trip. Locals also hurried on to the street, swarming in the direction of the port: youngsters, workers in factory uniforms, men and women carrying children wrapped in blankets.

Elona waited for Arian until she could hear the school

bell. She was about to leave when he finally showed up. 'The port is no longer guarded,' he said. 'All the container ships are full of people. Everyone's trying to leave. The soldiers don't shoot. They have joined the crowds on the boats. I'm going. You coming?'

'Coming where?' Elona asked.

'To Italy,' Arian replied. 'Or somewhere abroad – I don't know. Wherever the boat takes us. If we don't like it, we can come back.'

By then, it was too late to go to school. Elona followed Arian to the port, at first only to take a look. The closer they got to the area where the container ships were berthed, the denser the crowd on the street became. They wrestled their way to the mooring, close to one of the largest boats, a cargo ship called *Partizani*. A man shouted that *Partizani* was about to depart. Arian jumped inside, pulling Elona behind him. The boat's ladder went up.

The journey lasted seven hours, Elona wrote in her letter, but they had to wait for official authorization to disembark. The order came after twenty-four hours. At first, the new arrivals were accommodated in a local school turned refugee camp. A few days later, they were distributed around the country. Elona and Arian settled in the north of Italy. They lived in a tiny flat shared with some people they had met on the boat. She was too young to work, but Arian had found a job delivering refrigerators for a local shop. He did not make much money, she said, but they survived. As proof, she had put a few banknotes, worth 20,000 Italian lire, in the envelope. She had also written down her postal address but asked for letters to be directed to Arian, since she was pretending to be his sister.

It was hard to believe that my friend, who only a few

months before bought sunflower seeds and played dolls with me, and who had hardly ever travelled outside our town, could have found the courage to leave the country. How could she leave behind her home, the school, her family, even her sister?

'I tried to go myself,' Elona's grandfather said to my grandmother. 'I wanted to find her. To bring her back. I left in August. I was on the *Vlora*. We were treated like dogs.'

I remembered the day the *Vlora* departed. That morning, Flamur's mother had knocked desperately on every door of the street to ask if we had seen her son. He'd embarked on the boat without telling her. My friend Marsida and her parents left too. Her father was mending a pair of broken shoes when the customer stormed into the shop, asking for them to be returned immediately. She would wear them broken, she said. The port was open, there was no time to waste. Marsida's father left his sewing machine and ran to collect his daughter from school and to find his wife in the factory where she worked. They jumped on the *Vlora* too.

Tens of thousands of people were crowded into the port. The *Vlora* had just returned from a trip to Cuba, carrying a load of sugar. It was commandeered while sitting in the dock waiting for repairs to its primary motor. The crowds broke into it and forced the captain to sail to Italy. Fearing for his life, he decided to start the boat on a supplementary motor, but without radar. Although it had a capacity of only three thousand people, the *Vlora* carried nearly twenty thousand that day. It seemed an eternity until the boat reached the port of Brindisi, the same port where thousands of people had disembarked successfully in March. This time, though, the authorities instructed the captain to turn away, and set course instead for the port of Bari, some 110 kilometres from Brindisi. It took the boat another seven hours to complete the journey.

The images of the *Vlora*'s arrival in Bari are still fresh in my mind. On the screen of the small colour television that we had recently bought, I saw the dozens of men who had managed to climb to the top of the masts, half naked, with sweat dripping down their necks, their faces dirty and badly shaven, their hair grown long at the back, in mullet fashion. Standing there precariously, struggling to hold on to the mast, they looked like the self-proclaimed generals of an army that had lost its morale before the battle had even started. They waved their arms senselessly at the television cameras, shouting, 'Amico, let us exit!', 'Let us disembark!', 'We are hungry, amico!', 'We need water!' Above them hovered two or three helicopters. Under them, on the deck, there was a sea of people: thousands of men, women and children, scorched from the heat, injured from waiting in close quarters, pushing each other, wailing, desperately attempting to leave the boat. Squeezed inside the cabins, other passengers perched on the windows, gestured or shouted instructions to those on the deck, encouraging them to dive into the water. Some followed the advice and were arrested. Others managed to escape. The rest continued to scream: that they had consumed the last lumps of sugar from the cargo hold several hours before, that many people were severely dehydrated and were drinking sea water, that there were pregnant women on board.

The events that followed were first recounted by those

who lived them, to warn others against repeating their mistakes. A journey of about seven hours lasted thirty-six. When disembarkation orders finally arrived, the crowds were forced into buses and locked in a disused stadium, guarded by police. Those who tried to leave were arrested and beaten. Packaged food and bottles of water were dropped by helicopter. Inside, men, women and children fought to reach the supplies. Some people had brought knives with them and started to use them to butcher other people.

In the stadium, rumours spread that, since our country was technically no longer a communist state, requests for political asylum were likely to be rejected. Instead, the new arrivals would be considered economic migrants. This was a new, unfamiliar category. It applied to the same people, but with different, if slightly obscure, implications which became clear only some days later. After almost two weeks in the stadium, the crowds were shovelled into buses. They were told they would be sent to Rome, to sort out the paperwork. Soon they realized the buses were directed to the port. They were embarked on return ferries. Those who protested were beaten up.

'I didn't want to stay in Italy,' Elona's grandfather explained to Nini. 'I just wanted to find Elona and bring her back. But they didn't let anyone explain. I wanted to tell them that I did not need any papers to stay, that I was just trying to find my granddaughter. They didn't listen. They gave us 20,000 lire each and forced us back on to a boat. They would not listen to me,' he repeated.

'Perhaps you can try again with the embassy?' my grandmother said. 'Maybe you can apply for a visa?'

'A visa?' he snorted. 'Have you seen what it's like at

the embassy? You can't even get close to the door. It's a military zone. There are guards everywhere. There are five layers of protection. Inside. Outside. Everywhere.'

'Have you tried calling to make an appointment?' I asked. I remembered how we had made an appointment at the Greek embassy to receive our visa.

'Call?' he laughed. 'Call?' He laughed again, louder. 'You'd be better off waiting for death to call.'

'We went to Greece,' I said. 'We got a visa. We had made an appointment at the embassy.'

'When did you go?'

'Earlier this year,' my grandmother answered.

'Just before Elona left,' I added. 'I didn't see her when I came back.'

'That's it,' he replied. 'Now, they've closed the roads. All blocked. Can't go anywhere, unless it's for work.'

'Our government—' my grandmother began.

'No, not the government,' he said, interrupting her. 'Our government would be happy if everyone left. Perhaps they've even organized the boats themselves, just so they could get rid of people. Then they won't have to feed them, or find them jobs, now that all the factories are closing. I mean the embassies, the foreign states. They can't take any more immigrants, they say. But I'll try again. I'll find a way. I've thought about the south,' he explained. 'The land border. I'll try the land border with Greece. It's dangerous. You might be shot. I know the area. I fought there in the war. But I'm not as agile as I used to be. I'm not a partisan any more.'

He gave a faint smile.

'Some people managed to leave,' I said. 'Like Elona and Arian – they managed to get away.'

He shook his head, absorbed in thought. 'In March, they said we were all victims. They accepted us. In August, they looked at us as if we were some kind of menace; like we were about to eat their children.'

My grandmother nodded. I was thinking about how my parents had never considered leaving. When Marsida and her parents had stopped by our house to bid us farewell, before they sailed to Italy on that cargo boat, Nini had tried to persuade them not to take that risk. 'It's dangerous,' she warned. 'It's dangerous even if it works. I was born an immigrant. I know what life as an immigrant is like.'

'It was hard enough for her in the Ottoman empire, when the pashas and the beys of her family were running it,' my father teased. 'It can't be as bad as here,' said my mother, who would have liked to try. Nini kept shaking her head.

I did not want to leave either. I had enjoyed being in Athens at first, before it became difficult with my grandmother, but eventually, I started to miss home. I was frustrated by not being able to understand the language. I grew angry when people stared at me, pointing their fingers, and I couldn't understand their words. At least when tourists visited our country, it was reciprocal. They stared at us; we stared at them. Our worlds were divided. Now we were no longer divided. But we weren't equal.

'Maybe they'll open the roads again,' I said.

'I don't think so,' Elona's grandfather replied. He turned to my grandmother. 'They're trying to make it harder to cross. They've increased marine patrolling. They don't wait for you to be there. At first, they were unprepared. Now, they know what's coming. I tell you, they're not about to dismantle any controls, they're making them more efficient.'

He spoke like someone who understood the technicalities of border control, who could decipher them in the same way he had deciphered guerrilla strategies in his youth. 'If they discover you trying to cross the border, they put you in a camp. You can get stuck for ever.'

'You need money too,' my grandmother commented.

'When we went to Athens, everything was so expensive,' I said. 'We had no money. It was horrible. There was so much in the shops. There were no queues. But we couldn't buy anything.'

'Money,' he said, his mind more on his plan than our remarks. 'Yes, money is another way. Of course, if you have money, the roads are not closed. If you put it in a bank, and you make the bank issue some kind of statement that you have a deposit, then it's a lot easier.'

'I'm sure Elona is fine,' my grandmother said. 'If she has written to say she's well, she probably likes being in Italy. Teenagers. It helps one grow up to make big decisions like that. Back in my day, girls that age were sent to boarding school.'

'Or work,' said Elona's grandfather.

My grandmother nodded. 'She will come back to visit before long,' she tried to reassure him. 'She probably needs to sort out the paperwork. As long as she stays in touch . . .'

To me, it all sounded absurd. How, I thought, could someone be happier abroad than at home? I could not imagine how living with Arian might make you better off, even in Italy. The more I reflected on it, the more it seemed implausible.

'Everyone wants to leave,' I wrote in my diary, commenting on the events of March and August 1991. 'Everyone except us.' Most of our friends and relatives spent days, weeks, even months, planning how they would leave. There was a wide range of possibilities: falsifying documents, hijacking boats, crossing the land border, applying for a visa, finding a Westerner who could invite them and guarantee their stay, borrowing money. People hardly gave thought to the purpose. Knowing *how* you would get somewhere was more important than knowing *why*.

For some, leaving was a necessity that went under the official name of 'transition'. We were a society in transition, it was said, moving from socialism to liberalism, from one-party rule to pluralism, from one place to the other. Opportunities would never come to you, unless you went looking for them, like the half-cockerel in the old Albanian folk tale who travels far away, looking for his kismet, and in the end returns full of gold. For others, leaving the country was an adventure, a childhood dream come true or a way to please their parents. There were those who left and never returned. Those who went and came back soon after. Those who turned the organization of movement into a profession, who opened travel agencies or smuggled people on boats. Those who survived, and became rich. Those who survived, and continued to struggle. And those who died trying to cross the border.

In the past, one would have been arrested for wanting to leave. Now that nobody was stopping us from emigrating, we were no longer welcome on the other side. The only thing that had changed was the colour of the police uniforms. We risked being arrested not in the name of our own government but in the name of other states, those same governments who used to urge us to break free in the past. The West had spent decades criticizing the East for its closed borders, funding campaigns to demand freedom of movement, condemning the immorality of states committed to restricting the right to exit. Our exiles used to be received as heroes. Now they were treated like criminals.

Perhaps freedom of movement had never really mattered. It was easy to defend it when someone else was doing the dirty work of imprisonment. But what value does the right to exit have if there is no right to enter? Were borders and walls reprehensible only when they served to keep people in, as opposed to keeping them out? The border guards, the patrol boats, the detention and repression of immigrants that were pioneered in southern Europe for the first time in those years would become standard practice over the coming decades. The West, initially unprepared for the arrival of thousands of people wanting a different future, would soon perfect a system for excluding the most vulnerable and attracting the more skilled, all the while defending borders to 'protect our way of life'. And yet, those who sought to emigrate did so because they were attracted to that way of life. Far from posing a threat to the system, they were its most ardent supporters.

From our state's point of view, emigration was a short-term blessing and a long-term curse. It acted as an immediate safety valve to relieve the pressure of unemployment. But it also deprived the state of its youngest, most able and often more educated citizens, and tore families apart. In normal circumstances, it would have been more desirable for freedom of movement to include the freedom to stay in one's place. But these weren't normal circumstances. With thousands of factories, workshops and state enterprises facing closure and cuts, leaving was like taking voluntary redundancy when faced with the sack.

Yet not everyone tried. And not all who tried made it out. Of the people remaining, many had to ask themselves what a life without work was. My parents would soon be among those.

14.

Competitive Games

My father lost his job shortly after the first multi-party elections. He returned home one afternoon and announced that his office would close for good in a few weeks. Trained as a forest engineer, he had devoted the first half of his life to designing, planting and looking after new trees, especially laurels. Now the state had other priorities. Not only were new trees no longer planted; the existing ones were being chopped down. Power cuts and heating demands on the one hand and the brand-new cultivation of free individual initiative on the other meant that every night more trees disappeared from the forests. One might also have called it theft, except that an individual appropriating common resources constitutes the very foundation of private property. Bottom-up privatization would be a better description.

My father announced his office's closure in the same tone with which he had in the past announced other administrative changes to his work life, for example that he would be transferred from one village to another, or that a new director would replace the current one. He said that he would no longer need to provide his biography, the one where he explained the family's history. Nobody cared about that history now. All that one needed was a Latin text, called Curriculum Vitae, or CV for short.

'Who is going to write it in Latin?' I asked.

'We don't have to write it in Latin, brigatista,' he replied. 'Only the first line. But a version in English would be useful. Might be good for applications in the private sector.'

Everyone seemed relaxed about this news of the redundancy. They reacted as if there were dozens of much more desirable jobs lined up, like home-made biscuits cooking in the oven, waiting to be eaten – as soon as the CV was submitted.

'Will you start next week?' I asked, thinking about the timing of his transfers in the past.

'No!' my mother exclaimed, as if the mere insinuation insulted my father's dignity. 'Nobody gives you a job that easily!'

'We'll see,' he replied. 'This is capitalism. There's competition for work. But, for now, I am free!'

Because of the sense of confidence which lingered in the air from the moment his redundancy was announced I was confused, almost alarmed, when I returned from school one day and found him lying across the sofa. He had changed from his pyjamas into the oversized yellow-and-green tracksuit that my mother had recently bought for him at the second-hand market. He gripped the remote control of our small new Philips television with both his hands and, with an expression of intense concentration on his face, waved it in the air, as if he were directing the rotation of the planets in orbit.

'This is so depressing,' he said when he saw me, turning off the television, his focused expression now coated with sorrow. 'It's too sad. I can't bear this. I'm not sure what to do.'

'It will get better,' I replied vaguely, without knowing myself what I meant. 'I'm sure it will get better.'

He shook his head. 'I'm trying to watch the European championship, but I can't,' he added. 'It breaks my heart. Yugoslavia is about to win its fifth title. Last year they won the World Cup.'

'That's good news, no?'

'This may well be the last time they play together,' he said, a grim expression on his face. 'Slovenia's already declared independence. Croatia will soon be gone. It's like watching someone win a song contest with throat cancer. It's too sad. As far as I'm concerned, basketball is dead.'

My mother didn't technically lose her job. She was offered early retirement at the age of forty-six, and she accepted it. To mark the occasion, my father, who had just received his last salary, bought Amstel beers from a newly opened mini-market. It was a perfectly pleasant family evening until my mother made an announcement concerning how she was planning to keep herself occupied during retirement. She declared that she had joined the opposition party. On the day it was founded.

Nini and I froze. My father looked up from his plate with bewildered surprise, which I knew would soon turn into a full-blown explosion of rage. It was the look he gave my mother when she made important decisions without consulting him. What started with those bewildered looks turned into an inquisitive interrogation, reprimands, fury, mutual aggression and, after that, silence, a silence that could go on for weeks. As a next stage, there was only the threat of divorce.

It had happened twice before. The first was when my mother illegally bought fifty chicks from someone working on a collective farm, to raise in our garden so that we wouldn't have to queue for eggs. When she informed my father, he was livid. We would be arrested, he said. Our garden was small, and fifty chicks would be impossible to hide. My mother replied that we would store them in our bathroom, and that she was expecting a very low survival rate. At most, ten were likely to make it. The man from the cooperative had said it himself. Both he and my mother were right, it later turned out. But that detail only exacerbated the tension. If there was one thing my father could bear even less than the danger of being arrested, it was the grief caused by the mass extinction of the baby chickens. Every time he went into the bathroom and found a dead chick, he came out heartbroken, and felt even more bitterly towards my mother. A truce was reached only several months later, when the death rate declined and Nini threatened to go into a care home unless my parents reconciled.

The second time was when my mother encouraged me to sell loofah sponges alongside the Roma girls hawking lipsticks and hairclips on the pavement of the main boulevard. In Athens, Yiorgos had given us an extra bag full of them to distribute to family members and other relatives – it was unclear whether as presents or as adverts for his factory. My mother remembered how her own grandfather had built the family fortune by starting with something much more insignificant: chopping wood in the village where he lived, and bringing it to town to sell.

We could start our own business too, she said, but we had to move fast. Everyone would soon try to make profits by finding ways to buy and sell on the free market. But she felt it would be too awkward for her to sit next to the Roma girls herself; her pupils might pass by and recognize her, and that would undermine her authority in class. Instead, she wrote down a price list and instructed me to sit on the pavement and shout: 'Lovely Greek loofah sponges! Lots of colours, lots of shapes!', which is what I did. By the end of the afternoon, all the stock had run out.

I did not expect my father to become so angry when I brought home all the money I had earned. At first, he thought the idea had been mine. He was about to send me to my room to reflect on my actions when I explained I had only followed my mother's instructions. He then turned to her, his eyes flashing with anger. He yelled that, just because anyone could now go out and sell what they wanted, it didn't mean you were entitled to exploit your own child. My mother initially ignored him. Instead, she turned to me and asked: 'Didn't you want to go yourself?' I confirmed with a vigorous nod. My father shook with rage. 'Of course she did!' he shouted. 'It wouldn't be exploitation without consent. It would be violence.' My mother stayed calm. She explained that I was no longer a child, that I would soon be twelve, and that it was very normal for Western teenagers to be involved in flourishing family businesses. 'But we haven't got any family business!' my father screamed back. 'Neither failing nor flourishing!' 'And you never will,' my mother muttered back.

My father would probably have vetoed my involvement in the sponge trade even if my mother had requested his permission beforehand. But the fact that she hadn't so much as thought about consulting anyone strengthened his resentment. In general, my father's determination to make his views known matched my mother's resolve to ignore them. My parents argued all the time. But they almost always argued as equals. When my mother made decisions without asking my father the symmetry broke down, and my father felt hurt. My parents had built their relationship on heckling, and as the years went by, the boundary between the playful and the bitter exchanges became increasingly blurred. Their marriage was like a rocky mountain range; as experienced climbers, they knew how to ascend the dangerous peaks, and how to shrink back from the abysses into which many others had fallen. But there were times when I feared they too would fall. The third time was when my mother announced her decision to enter politics.

My father knew he would never be like many of his friends, those whose wives needed their husband's approval before they could even apply lipstick. My mother never wore lipstick, and her will was made of gun-metal. Every time his desire to be consulted encountered my mother's stubbornness, he faced a dilemma. He could pretend he exerted control over her actions, reacting as he would have been expected to, with outrage. Or he could admit defeat and go about it as if it didn't really matter. Only, he loved her too much for it not to matter. He couldn't let go without a fight. He never became violent with her; he channelled his anger by smashing crockery. But when his whole body shook with anger and his voice trembled with rage, one could scarcely be sure that the only casualties would be saucers and plates.

When my mother announced that she had joined the opposition movement, I assumed that the scene would play out as it had always done. I was wrong. My father gave my mother the bewildered look I was familiar with. But then he turned pale. He did not stand up. He did not move towards her, nor did he wave his finger threateningly. He did not shout. He continued to stare at her incredulously, a grimace frozen on his face, his body paralysed on the chair.

My mother noticed. She must have felt sorry somehow. She too reacted differently. She didn't just look straight past him, as she used to do, to indicate that my father's threats meant nothing to her. She felt compelled to explain. She said everything was still controlled by spies. There were former communists everywhere, both in the government and in the opposition. People with biographies like theirs had to be involved. Someone had to find the courage. Otherwise, things would never change. We would always be represented by the same people. We had to take matters into our own hands, to represent ourselves. It would have been better to take advice perhaps, to make a collective decision. She knew my father might be sceptical; his politics weren't the same as hers. But she had to do it. Now that he no longer had a job, they also needed the connections, to look for opportunities in the future. She seemed to have given some thought to this.

My father listened quietly. He kept his rage locked inside him. When I thought about this episode later, it dawned on me that perhaps he had cared about losing his job more than he let on. Perhaps, in his mind, there was a significant difference between being made redundant and taking early retirement. Perhaps, now that he was dependent on the pensions of two women, he felt like less of a man. He could no longer do what other men did: shout, threaten, shake with rage and throw crockery at the wall. Or perhaps everything around him had changed so much that all the usual responses felt inappropriate, as if they belonged to a different era, or could come only from a different person, an older version of himself that he no longer recognized. With all the familiar coordinates gone, he had lost his orientation. He had no explanation for his predicament. He had no solutions either. All that was left was quiet nodding, like the nodding he usually reserved for his bosses at work.

My mother did not stop working when she retired. She entered one of the busiest periods of her life. Shortly after joining the Democratic Party, she became one of the leaders of its national women's association. She attended party meetings, selected candidates for elections, organized rallies, ran reform campaigns, joined national committees, met foreign delegations. The time that was left she spent in the archives and in court, pursuing the restitution of family properties that had been confiscated in the past.

'You should stay at home a bit more, look after the children,' Nini said to her. 'I'm fine,' I usually replied, delighted that the once-per-term check on my maths had now slipped from my mother's agenda. 'Mami, you should get a driving licence,' I suggested as an alternative.

'We don't need a driving licence,' my father intervened, worrying that if he didn't oppose the prospect right away, his ongoing unemployment might promote him to family chauffeur. 'It's not good for the environment.'

That topic usually led to another argument. My mother would say: 'Everyone is buying a car. It's a necessity. Chernobyl was much worse for the environment!' 'What's Chernobyl got to do with the car?' my father would reply. My mother would continue, apparently unperturbed: 'The metallurgic factory the Chinese built for us, what good did that do to the environment? Our problem is not the environment, it's that we haven't got enough savings to buy a car!' 'Two wrongs don't make a right,' my father would point out.

Those seemingly innocent exchanges about whether or not we ought to buy a car typically led to wide-ranging world-historical disputes: from the damage to the environment done by the Industrial Revolution to the advances in knowledge enabled by the Space Race; from Euro-Communism to the responsibilities of China; from who had a right to pollute to who sold weapons where; from the Gulf War to the dissolution of the former Yugoslavia. 'It doesn't follow! It just doesn't follow!' my father would reply to my mother when he didn't know what else to say. She rarely changed her mind. 'Is that what you say to your crowds in the rallies?' he would ask, finally giving up. 'Is that how you prepare your speeches?'

My mother never prepared her speeches. She gave hundreds of them. As I was entering my teens, I was more likely to see her on the platform of a political rally waiting for her turn to speak than to meet her at home for dinner. She stood erect, high up on the stage, and spoke to tens of thousands of people, pausing frequently and modulating her voice, as circumstances dictated, sometimes forcing the audience into a terrifying silence, sometimes rousing the crowds to roaring applause. She always spoke without notes. She delivered her speeches as if she had written them in her head many years ago, as if she had rehearsed every day of her life the sentences that she would later utter. But her words didn't come across as if they had migrated from the past. They were new, if a little foreign-sounding: individual initiative, transition, liberalization, shock therapy, sacrifice, property, contract, Western democracy. Except for the word *freedom*; that one was old. But she pronounced it differently, always with an exclamation mark at the end. Then it sounded new.

When my mother was not in political meetings, she was either rummaging through the city archives to find her family's belongings, often consulting maps and boundary divisions, or she was in court, trying to recover ownership titles, leading her siblings' fight to reclaim the thousands of square miles of land, hundreds of flats and dozens of factories that had once belonged to their grandfather, a wood-chopper turned millionaire, shortly before the end of the war. My father and grandmother never took any interest, partly because they did not think the properties could be recovered, and partly because they doubted that they should be.

'Such a waste of time,' my grandmother would occasionally comment, shaking her head. It was often ambiguous whether she meant that politics was a waste of time, or the search for my mother's famed properties, or both. 'One should let bygones be bygones,' she once said to a foreign journalist who came to interview her about having been a dissident in the past, and asked about her own family properties. 'Everyone is a dissident now. The land in Greece? It's just mud.'

My mother, on the other hand, would never let go. It was not only the necessity to find sources of income but a matter of principle. The two were somehow combined. For her, the world was a place where the natural struggle for survival could be resolved only by regulating private property. Everyone, she believed, fought as a matter of course, men and women, young and old, current generations and future ones. Unlike my father, who thought that people were naturally good, she thought they were naturally evil. There was no point in trying to make them good; one simply had to channel that evil so as to limit the harm. That's why she was convinced that socialism could never work, even under the best circumstances. It was against human nature. People needed to know what belonged to them and to be able to do with it what they wanted. Then they would look after their assets and there wouldn't be fighting any more; it would be healthy competition. She believed that if only one could discover the truth about who was the first owner of anything, all the interactions that followed could be regulated so that not only our family but everyone else, too, would have the opportunity to become as rich as her ancestors had once been.

It was like resuming a chess tournament that had been interrupted halfway through, she said. All of the players had started from equal positions, and some had accumulated an advantage. Then they had been forced to play a different game. That was socialism. When the Cold War came to an end, the games could resume. But the old players had died, and in their place only their designated successors could return to the board. It would have been unfair, my mother thought, to start

197

a different game. All the new players had to do was retrace their ancestors' moves, keep to the same pieces, play by the same rules.

For her, finding the truth about family property was as much a matter of rectifying historic injustice as of regulating property rights. The only purpose of the state, as she saw it, was to facilitate such transactions, and to protect the contracts necessary to ensure that everyone could stick to what they had earned. Anything else, anything that went beyond that, encouraged the growth of parasites who wasted money and resources. It was socialism by another name. The state was like a chess tournament director, who enforced the rules and checked the clock every now and then. But he could never start giving tips to the players, or changing their moves, or returning pieces to the board, or bringing in a player who had been disqualified. That would have been a perversion of the role. In the end, there would be winners and losers. So what? Everyone knew that; everyone consented to the rules. It was in the nature of the game. It was a competition after all, even if healthy.

15.

I Always Carried a Knife

One day, in late summer 1992, a group of Frenchwomen from an organization partnered with the one led by my mother announced that they would visit our house. We prepared for their visit as if it were New Year's Eve. We repainted the walls, brought down the curtains to wash, put our mattresses out to air, scrubbed the insides of the cupboards, and took the dust off every book on the bookshelf. In the few hours prior to their arrival, the house turned into the battleground of a disciplined, highly organized military unit, armed with brushes, rags, sponges, tubs, buckets, mops and all the other domestic artillery needed for the operation. Like a general, my mother imparted loud, sharp orders to my father while running around tirelessly herself, turning tables and chairs upside down, monitoring what had been left undone, revealing areas of dirt unnoticed by previous rounds of cleaning. Once the house looked sparkling, she captured my brother and me in the fatal half-hour prior to the arrival of our visitors and brought us to the bathroom to be cleaned. She had no time to check the temperature of the water she poured on us, and scrubbed our faces with the same fervour as she had shown the floors. When that was done too, she went to prepare herself.

My mother consulted my grandmother on the dress code most appropriate for receiving representatives of an organization committed to the pursuit of women's causes. Nini advised a one-piece outfit, and my mother chose an item she had recently found in the second-hand market, a selection in part inspired by all the women she had seen on the soap adverts she associated with Western female emancipation, and in part because it read 'Gloria' on the back. (It denoted, she thought, a high-end luxury fashion brand.) A knee-length piece of dark red silk, it was adorned with black lace at the bottom, ribbons on the sleeves and a V-shaped neckline. At the time, it was common for Western items of nightwear that entered the local second-hand market to be confused with regular clothing and to be worn during the day. In the same period, several of my teachers came to class wearing nightdresses or dressing gowns. My mother had not done it before, not because she could tell the difference but because she wasn't normally attracted to frilly things. She wore trousers, despised make-up and brushed her hair without a mirror. The only ribbons and laces she knew were those she and Nini inflicted on me – as a public affirmation that fifty years of dictatorship of the proletariat were unable to crush their will to bring me up as the Balkan version of Velázquez's Infanta Margarita Theresa.

The five visitors turned up in dark professional suits – like a Maoist delegation, my father commented in the kitchen. We sat around them in our living room, and served coffee, raki and Turkish delight. Our visitors didn't bat an eyelid at my mother's nightdress; they must have assumed it was either an expression of our culture or of our newly acquired freedom. 'We were very impressed by the reaction to your speech in the meeting the other day,' one of them, called Madame Dessous, said to my mother. 'It was wonderful to hear such long applause from the audience. Obviously, we couldn't understand it in Albanian,' she added with an apologetic smile. 'We would be very interested to hear what you said about women's freedom.'

My grandmother, who was helping out with the French, translated Madame Dessous's words. My mother looked alarmed, like someone sitting an exam who suddenly realizes they have prepared for the wrong questions. 'What speech is she talking about?' she muttered to my grandmother in Albanian. 'I never said anything about women.' Then, slowly regaining control, she turned to the visitors and declared confidently: 'I think everyone should be free, not only women.'

'Doli believes this is a very complex issue,' Nini translated.

The visitors nodded. 'Ah, that is certain,' Madame Dessous agreed unreservedly. 'We know, under socialism, there was much rhetoric about women's equality,' she continued. 'But what was the reality? Did Albanian women experience *harassment*?'

There was a brief silence during which my grandmother hesitated again on the translation. The word stuck in my head, but I did not quite understand its meaning at the time. I remember the perplexed look on my mother's face, as she stopped stirring the sugar in her coffee and stared at her interlocutor, pondering the effects of what she was about to say. There was something comic, as well as distressing, about the sharp contrast between the playful sensuality of the dress she had on and the gravity of the pose she assumed. She rested the coffee cup on the table, but then, feeling nervous, reached out to pick up a piece of Turkish delight and stuffed it into her mouth. 'Sure,' she replied, while still chewing. Then she cleared her throat. 'I always carried a knife.'

Madame Dessous was startled. She receded into the sofa, as if to increase the space between my mother and herself. The rest of the women exchanged uncomfortable looks. 'Just a kitchen knife,' my mother hastened to add, noticing the reaction her confession had provoked, and determined to explain. 'Nothing fancy.' As the visitors seemed to shrink even further, she began to speak. Her words came out quickly and without breaks, like small stones rolling down a steep hill.

'I was young, no more than twenty-five. I had a daily commute to a remote school in a northern village. I had to rely on lifts from casual truck-drivers to get back home. In the winter, it gets dark early. You couldn't hitchhike without a knife. I only used it once. Not to kill or anything.' Then she smiled to herself, as if some hilarious detail had unexpectedly emerged from a neglected corner of her mind. 'Only a little tickle on his hand. You know, he was resting it on my thigh. It was uncomfortable.'

My grandmother translated word for word. My mother took a deep breath of relief, evidently satisfied with her own explanation, especially the lightness with which she had succeeded in summarizing what must have been a traumatic episode. But her words failed to achieve the intended effect. The visitors remained motionless. My mother looked at my father as if to ask for help. He had been silent up to that point but clearly knew the story already, and reacted as if each sentence gave him new reasons to be proud. Their eyes met, and he gave her a complicit smile, as if he'd handed her the knife himself. Then he turned to the visitors, confident in his abilities to achieve what my mother had failed to: 'This woman's got fire in her belly!' he said. 'She is one of a kind. Do help yourselves to some raki. Doli makes it herself.'

That intervention did not help either. The women reached for the glasses and made a timid noise of approval as they brought the liquor to their mouths, but carefully avoided swallowing. Assailed by new doubts, and feeling she had reached the limits of her capacity to elaborate, my mother stretched her arm and picked up another piece of Turkish delight. Halfway through the gesture, she changed her mind, returned the sweet to its container, and decided to try a different strategy.

'In the land of freedom,' she began, as if she were about to deliver one of her speeches, 'in the United States of America, people are allowed to carry guns. That obviously makes it easier to defend oneself. In Albania, our options were limited. Socialism did not authorize the personal use of firearms. We knew, of course, how to deploy them; we received mandatory military training in school from the age of sixteen. But we had no control over those weapons. Unlike the American people, we were not free to use them when we wanted.'

In general, if my mother could have trained the women in her organization to protect themselves from harassment by using knives, she would have done it. Failing that, she limited her leadership role to coordinating assistance for the visa applications of mothers who wanted to visit their emigrant children. She gathered names, made lists, raised funds for those who needed financial assistance, helped them fill out the forms and made appointments at the relevant embassies. Officially, the trips were to visit partner associations in various capitals of Europe: Athens, Rome, Vienna, Paris. In reality, the delegates dispersed to different towns as soon as they crossed the border. Only she and another colleague or two attended the planned meetings; the other women went to spend time with their children and grandchildren, and stayed with them for the duration of the trip. On the last day, they reconvened to visit food stalls and explore shopping centres. Not to buy anything, since even the cheapest items were prohibitively expensive. Only, as they put it, 'to open their eyes'.

My mother was aware of the cost of disclosing the real purpose of the trips. She had swiftly mastered the formulas she needed to repeat to get her through the visa interviews: effecting knowledge transfer, developing team synergies, working on training skills, crafting vision statements, understanding strategic planning, and so on. She once reported that in the course of an appointment a diplomat had asked whether the women's organization she directed would also be involved in feminist campaigns. 'I asked what "feminism" meant,' she reported. 'I didn't understand what he was talking about.' He replied with something about quotas and affirmative action. She had assured him that this was exactly why those visits to the West were invaluable: her organization had already finalized their action points, and hoped to learn more through knowledge exchange with more experienced partners. 'Quotas! Equality!' she snorted when she came home that day. 'I had to say yes to everything. It was the only way we would get the visas. I bet his wife has hired a cleaner to do her chores. I bet she grumbles about women's rights while out for a jog.'

When my mother recounted how the visa interviews had gone, large red spots developed on her cheeks and her neck. 'Affirmative action!' she yelled. 'Feminism! What about mothers and their children? My women haven't seen their children for years. Sanie, who's on the list for Rome, has no idea how her daughter lives. All she has is a street name, scribbled on a piece of paper. She told me she lies awake at night, worrying. Do you think she worries about quotas? If I said that to the embassy, they'd see me straight to the door. They'd say she can't receive a visa. She's unemployed, and there's no guarantee she will come back. They wouldn't even return her visa money. I'd like to see some *affirmation* of that. But no, letting these mothers see their children, that's not what they mean. It's about teaching us representation or participation or some other fantasy like that. Of course. That doesn't cost them anything.'

Then she turned to my father abruptly. 'How would you feel about affirmative action?'

He shrugged. 'Good,' he replied. 'I guess it depends on how it's done and by whom; it can be an excuse too, and it can stigmatize black people.' He tried to elaborate with reference to the only authority he recognized when it came to civil rights. 'I recently watched an interview with Muhammad Ali—'

My mother interrupted him. 'I'm talking about women, not black people. Did you hear what I said? These Western women, you know, they can't multitask, they're such losers. If they have to study and work, or work and look after children, or look after children and cook, they can't keep up. And they assume everybody here is like them, and somehow this should be the state's problem. So that another loser can come up with a silly list of criteria of how to give women a chance.'

'What's affirmative action?' I asked.

My mother started to explain, but her nerves got the better of her. 'Imagine someone bumps up your grades at school just because you're a girl,' she started. 'How would you feel about that? You would feel insulted, right?' With every question, her voice became louder. I tried to say something, but she answered herself. 'There would be no difference between you, who worked hard to get the best grades, and your friends, whose grades are bumped up only because they look like you, because they're girls too. How does that sound?'

I tried to imagine how I would feel. But my mother was not interested in my opinions. Her questions were rhetorical. She simply wanted to let off steam. 'Imagine if that applied to everything you did,' she said. 'How would you know what the difference is between someone who got the best grades on merit and someone who didn't? What would you do if people always assumed you got where you are with a little help from your friends?'

My mother despised affirmative action and gender quotas as much as she pitied those who advocated them. If anyone had dared to insinuate that whatever she had achieved was due to the fact that she was a woman rather than because she deserved it, her kitchen knife would have come out to perform a tickle. In the meetings she had with women from partner organizations, she often emphasized that there was only one thing to be proud of when assessing the legacy of the communist past. It was the way the Party had enforced strict equality between genders without making any concessions; the fact that everyone, male and female, was expected to work, and that not only was every job accessible to both groups, but both were actively encouraged to take it up. Even clothing restrictions were equally distributed. During the Cultural Revolution, when we were inspired by our Chinese allies, a Western trench coat would have got you into trouble, regardless of what gender you were.

She was right, but only in part. In the past, all women had been expected to work. They were expected to work everywhere. All my friends' mothers worked. Not one stayed at home. They were up at dawn to clean their houses and prepare their children for school, and then they went on to drive trains, dig for coal, fix electric cables, teach in schools or nurse in hospitals. Some travelled long hours to reach the offices, farms or factories in which they were employed. They returned home late and exhausted. They still had to prepare dinner, help the children do their homework and wash the dishes. They had to cook into the evening, preparing meals for the next day. During the night, they had to nurse their babies, or make love to their husbands. Or both.

At home, the men rested. They read newspapers and watched television, or they went out to see their friends. Many expected their shirts to be ironed and made sarcastic jokes if their coffee was served a little less than piping hot. If their wives left the house to see their friends too, their husbands had a right to know why. Sometimes they found the reasons given insufficiently compelling, or disapproved of the purpose of the visits. They issued orders for their wife to remain indoors, or to stop meeting this friend or that. They always did it out of love, they said. In their minds, loving women and controlling them were virtually indistinguishable. They had learned it from their fathers, who had learned this from their fathers, who had learned it from theirs. And as they learned it, they passed it on to their children.

Some wives were reluctant to follow instructions. Occasionally, the boundary between exercising control and losing it might become porous, like that between love and control. Then a scene might follow, featuring a broken wrist or a bleeding nose, with snotty-nosed children watching everything from a secret hiding place, then reporting with meticulous detail to their friends in school the next day. News would reach the teachers, and sometimes the Party would become involved. When the situation deteriorated, there would be a meeting in the workplace or in the neighbourhood council. Comrades would speak out to condemn the appearances of an act whose essence was attributed to the limitations of human nature, or community norms, or the legacy of religion. Socialism had succeeded in ripping the veil off women's heads, but not in the minds of their men. It had managed to tear chains carrying crosses from their wives' chests, but those chains still shackled their husbands' brains. There was little to do other than wait for the times to change or, as my mother saw it, to defend yourself.

My father wanted to be different, just as his father had attempted to be. In prison, my grandfather had translated Olympe de Gouges, then shown the Albanian text of *The Declaration of the Rights of Woman and of the Female Citizen* to Haki, who made him eat it. As to my great-grandfather the prime minister, his official contribution to the Albanian women's cause had been a law to legalize sex work, something the Party abrogated shortly after the end of the war. We don't know about his brain. It was blown apart by a bomb, and we weren't allowed to think about him, in any case. Still, my family's history suggested that, for several generations, the men had at least in theory acknowledged the existence of women as entities not entirely reducible to their own lives.

How well this translated into more mundane things, such as who cooked and cleaned, and who was in charge of doing the dishes, was a different matter. My father's relationship to domestic chores was like that of a child to cabbage. He knew they were good for him but, in the end, they made him sick. To his credit, he only ever invoked his asthma as an excuse, never his chromosomes. To release my mother, he often enlisted his own mother for help. But my grandmother was resentful in her own way; not because she thought chores should not be left to women, but because she had always seen them performed by servants. In the end, both my father and my grandmother relied on my mother to do the hard physical work. They were in charge of education.

It never occurred to my mother that things could have been different for her. When she saw a problem, she thought only about how she could solve it herself, not whether she could appeal to others. The charisma she possessed, and the authority she commanded, made her independent from other people, sometimes too much. The only weapon she could offer to other women was her own strength. The only defence she passed on to me was her example. I grew up seeing how people were deferential to her, as if intimidated by her – not just the pupils in her class, the children in our neighbourhood, and us, her own children, but also quite a few adults, including men. I wondered where her power came from, and thought that perhaps she instilled fear in others because she was never scared of anything herself. But when I tried to be like her, and sought to control my fears, even dominate them, I struggled. I realized that she was an impossible model to follow. My mother did not fight and conquer her fears. She never knew fear in the first place.

It was the same for all the women she sought to help. If men were intimidated by my mother, women could hardly consider her their equal. She would never admit to a shared weakness, the need for help, the call to rescue. The support she offered only ever came in the mode of charity, never solidarity. To her, moral dilemmas, reliance on other people and the pursuit with them of a common cause, were distractions, pointless hurdles to the achievement of her own goals. This was why she found it difficult to consult anyone. She had no trust in anyone but herself.

Most of all, she distrusted the state. She was allergic to abstract discussions about equality, or about the role of institutions in promoting justice. Asking yourself whether something ought to be this way or that way was the wrong place to start. You should never wonder what the state could do for you, she thought, only what you could do to reduce your reliance on the state. She suspected that all the discussions around affirmative action and women's quotas were distractions that gave more power of scrutiny to bureaucratic institutions, and more opportunities for parasitic individuals to be corrupted. She never saw the state as a vehicle of progress. She never believed in the power of collectives.

It was not until many years later that something new occurred to me: how lonely she must have been. What also occurred to me around the same time was that perhaps she didn't stand out after all, perhaps there were hundreds, even thousands, of other women like her. They would have conducted their lives unaware of one another's existence, content with their self-sufficiency, resentful at each other's lack of courage, or aspiration, or resolve to fight. It was either a failure of institutions or a lack of imagination that my mother lived all her life in a socialist state convinced that one can only ever fight against others, never alongside them. I would have offered my sympathy, if I hadn't thought she would feel insulted.

16.

It's All Part of Civil Society

One afternoon in October 1993, I returned home from school to find my grandmother on the doorstep, a troubled look on her face. She followed me silently around the house, waiting for me to put down my school bag and books, change into my house clothes, and eat the meatballs she had warmed up. She then pointed at the sofa in the living room, gesturing for me to sit and taking her usual place in the armchair opposite. Finally, she broke into a question that sounded as absurd as it was unexpected.

'Where did you learn what condoms are?'

'Where what?' I replied, so quickly that my grandmother took the speed of my response as evidence that I was denying the truth she was after. 'I have no idea what condoms are.'

'You do,' she insisted. 'Your father bumped into Kasem on the street. He warned him about you. His son was there when you said people should use condoms. There were about twenty boys in the room, apparently, all much older than you. Even they were embarrassed to hear a young woman from a good family talk like that in school. *Ton père est en colère*. Really very angry.'

'Oh, do you mean the French translation?' When I heard her speak French, it finally dawned on me what she was referring to. 'I didn't say it to anyone in particular, I was just translating the end of a French film.'

That made things worse.

'Why were you translating a film about condoms in school?' she asked, continuing the interrogation.

'The Mule asked me to,' I answered. 'I just looked up *préservatif* in the dictionary. I have no idea what it means.'

'The Mule' was a nickname for the former Marxism teacher in the secondary school I'd just started attending. When she walked, she looked as if she were trotting. She panted, and carried a heavy rucksack around her shoulders, as if she were carrying a human whom she was about to drop. My parents suspected she had been a Sigurimi agent in the past. Whenever they spotted her on the road, they would cross over to the opposite side. The Mule had recently joined civil society. She topped up her meagre school salary by helping out a couple of foreign NGOs that had opened branches in our town, often enlisting her pupils to help with event organization. The transition from when she'd organized evenings for the communist youth groups and put on shows to celebrate the birthday of Enver Hoxha had been seamless. My father joked that some skills were eminently transferable.

'Why does the Mule want you to translate a film about condoms when you don't even know what a condom is?' Nini's anger was slowly dissipating, replaced by puzzlement.

'She didn't ask me to translate the film, just the end of it,' I explained. 'It's about a young woman who dies of AIDS, a contagious and life-threatening condition. At the end of the film, she tells her story. I have to convey to the audience what she says. I have to stand in front of everyone and declare: "Please wear a condom." That's what that woman says. We don't show the whole film, just that bit; it's very effective, the woman has tears in her eyes, and everyone is moved by the scene. The Mule is now the head of a new NGO called Action Plus, and their mission is to raise awareness about AIDS, and we hold afternoon events in school every two months or so, and at the last event we showed the end of this French film as part of the awareness campaign, and different people were asked to do different things – Besa was asked to read the poem "If" by Rudyard Kipling, and another group was asked to perform "I Want to Break Free", which had been sung by Freddie Mercury, who died of AIDS, and I was asked to translate the end of this film because the Mule had found it very moving, though she didn't really understand it, and only I could speak French, and some Americans who help fund Action Plus came to watch the event, and afterwards they clapped and said our awareness campaign was *fantastically inspiring.*'

When I had finished my explanation, I was breathless. While I had succeeded in convincing my grandmother of my innocence, I had begun to suspect there was something dirty about Action Plus.

My grandmother said nothing. She moved from her armchair to sit next to me on the sofa and gave me my first lecture in sex education. She explained what a condom was and why it was needed. For my part, I told her about HIV and, together, we worked out how AIDS, of which she had never heard, was transmitted. I also told her about all the famous people who had died of

AIDS, like Rudolf Nureyev, whom she knew of because he had defected from the Soviet Union to the West in 1961, and Anthony Perkins, whom she didn't know but immediately recalled when I told her he had played Norman Bates in *Psycho*.

'Terrible,' she said, shaking her head in disbelief. 'Really terrible. I had never heard of it. But who knows, it may arrive here soon.' She promised to convince my father that Action Plus was an organization that was not only harmless but positively needed, and that there was no reason to censor my involvement with the Mule's activities. She would explain that even though there were no cases of AIDS in a country where well-brought-up women were unlikely to have intercourse before marriage, it might all happen soon. As with drugs and other Western perversions, it was safe to assume AIDS would eventually reach us, and that preventive measures were therefore not simply appropriate but mandatory.

'It's freedom,' my grandmother concluded. 'It's what too much freedom brings. There are good things, and bad things. It's impossible to keep people always under control. Impossible to stop everyone from contracting this virus. I suppose that's why we need these NGOs. To protect us from all these new diseases, all these upcoming disasters. We can't rely on the state to do it. That's why we need civil society.'

'Civil society' was the new term recently added to the political vocabulary, more or less as a substitute for 'Party'. It was known that civil society had brought the Velvet Revolution to Eastern Europe. It had accelerated the decline of socialism. In our case, the term became popular when the revolution was already complete, perhaps to give meaning to a sequence of events that at first seemed unlikely, then required a label to become meaningful. It joined other new keywords, such as 'liberalization', which replaced 'democratic centralism'; 'privatization', which replaced 'collectivization'; 'transparency', which replaced 'self-criticism'; 'transition', which stayed the same but now indicated the transition from socialism to liberalism instead of the transition from socialism to communism; and 'fighting corruption', which replaced 'anti-imperialist struggle'.

These new ideas were all about freedom, though no longer the freedom of the collective, which had in the meantime become a dirty word – but of the individual. There was this lingering suspicion, or perhaps residual cultural memory, that without social control greater individual freedom would entail the freedom of individuals to harm themselves. That social control, it was now assumed, could no longer be entrusted to the state. This gave greater urgency to the need to embrace civil society. Civil society was supposed to be outside the state but also something that might replace it; it was supposed to emerge organically, but also had to be stimulated; it was supposed to bring harmony while acknowledging that some differences could never be resolved. Civil society was made of many different community groups and organizations, which sprang up like friendships in a socialist queue, some as a result of local initiatives, but most with help from our foreign friends. One of the problems of our country, one often heard, was that we didn't have a functioning civil society. It wasn't clear if we had had it in the past and it had been captured by the Party, like Cronus swallowing his children at birth, or if we ought to create it from scratch. In any case, it felt safer to proceed as if both were required, getting Cronus to vomit his children back out and producing the vibrant social life that would enable individuals not just to organize spontaneously, exchange ideas, interact with one another and create spaces for both mutual learning and commercial exchanges, but also to protect themselves from the upcoming dangers.

My teenage years were years of hyper-activism in civil society. Like many others, I was not blind to the benefits. Those were both spiritual and material. With the debating teams of the Open Society Institute, for example, you could discuss such motions as: 'Capital punishment is justified' and learn about the Eighth Amendment of the US Constitution. Debating 'Open societies require open borders', you could learn about the function of the World Trade Organization. With the Action Plus information campaigns about AIDS, you could kill an afternoon eating free peanuts and drinking Coca Cola in the former ping-pong room of the Palace of Sports. With the Friends of Esperanto, there were promises of travelling to Paris. With the Red Cross, one could hang around when distributing groceries to families in need and get a free packet of rice. This was different from the rice we used to borrow from our neighbours; firstly, there was more of it; secondly, it came from the West; and thirdly, it contained a 'use-by' date which informed you of when you were supposed to eat it, usually the week before.

My friend Marsida started a Koran reading group. Her family had left Albania on the *Vlora* but been shipped back, like everyone else. When her father's shoe workshop was converted into a nightclub he lost his job and decided to train to become an imam, following in his father's footsteps. Marsida taught me the Surah Al-Ikhlas: *Bismillah Hir Rahman Nir Raheem/Que huwa Allahu ahad/Allahu assamad/Lam yalid walam yulad/Walam yakul-lahoo/kufuwan ahad.*[*] One of the best surahs to learn, she said, was the declaration of the attributes of God: unity, authority and eternity. It took twelve seconds to say it out loud but, according to the Prophet, reciting it was the equivalent of knowing one third of the Koran. When she translated it, and I learned that Allah is the one to whom we turn for support, I decided to join the mosque so I could hear more about the Muslim God.

'Did you pray for me to find a job?' my father joked, when I told him that the mosque had been added to the list of my civil society activities. 'It won't help,' I replied. 'You need to change the font on your CV. You need to switch from Times New Roman to Garamond.'

It worked. I don't know if it was the prayer or the change of font – or perhaps my mother's new political connections – but my father was offered a job around the time of my fourteenth birthday. He was hired to manage Plantex, a state company that had previously dealt with the export of medicinal plants but whose immediate target was the reduction of its huge debt.

My father accepted the job after receiving multiple reassurances that his predecessor had taken care of all

---

[*] In the name of Allah, the most gracious and the most merciful/Allah is One and Indivisible/Allah is the one to whom we all turn for support/ He has never had offspring, nor was he born/There is no one comparable to him.

redundancies. He was excited about the prospect and felt ready to take on the challenge.

His post-communist record in handling the finances of our family spoke for itself. A few weeks prior to his hire by Plantex, he had managed to pay back the money we had borrowed when Ronald Reagan defeated Jimmy Carter on 4 November 1980. I remember the date because this is how my family recorded the last loan my uncle had made.

When I think about it now, my father's professional transition from planting trees to raising money strikes me as a bit like sending Pinocchio to the Field of Wishes. But there was nothing especially arrogant or unusual about the confidence he felt; his attitude to finance was one the entire country shared.

We had no savings in 1993. Lending between relatives and neighbours was slowly disappearing, in part because there was now the possibility of travelling abroad, or of *spending* what one saved, which had seldom been the case in the past. And in part because people's incomes had started to differ sharply so there was a risk that knocking on someone's door to ask for help might single you out as a loser. What used to be called 'workplace lotteries', a form of credit pulled together through voluntary contributions from salaries to help colleagues buy a washing machine or a television set, were also disappearing. Personal transactions were anonymized; lending companies and insurance agencies were on the rise. My family didn't trust these companies enough to deposit any savings with them, or to rely on them for loans. 'Do you remember the chapter on bankruptcies in *César Birotteau*?', my grandmother would say, as if citing fictional characters from Balzac's *Comédie humaine* constituted definitive proof of the immorality of the credit system. My mother had more nuanced views on the topic. It would have been fine, she suggested, if we also owned real estate, like her family had done in the past. Later on, she changed her mind, but in the meantime, we continued to store the little money we saved in the inside pocket of my grandfather's old coat, 'to bring good luck'.

The coat was one of the few things that worked the same way under capitalism as it had under socialism. We kept ourselves afloat. My grandmother started giving children private French and Italian lessons. Word soon got around that she had not learned her languages with the help of songs and films, like everybody else, but had studied in a French lycée. As a result, there was soon more demand for her lessons than she could satisfy. Our bedroom was transformed into a classroom, complete with folding tables and chairs, an easel, chalk, and verbs that stayed permanently conjugated on the board, as if to immortalize the actions they described: *je viens d'oublier, tu viens d'oublier, il/elle vient d'oublier.* I felt as if I had taken up permanent residence in school. My father collected the cash at the end of each lesson, combining grace with authority in soliciting late payments, and managing our finances with a disciplined frugality one would have never in the past associated with him. My grandmother thought he had a natural talent for business, just as much as my mother. In reality, he was terrified of debt. He used to say that debt is like a beast who sleeps in socialism, like everything else, but stays awake in capitalism. We had to kill it, before it killed us. He gave himself no rest until we had repaid all the money we owed. Once he'd eliminated one species of beast, he felt ready to face the next. Hence his enthusiasm for the next heroic mission: saving Plantex.

My mother bought him a black tie decorated with tiny white elephants in the second-hand market, and mended my grandfather's jacket and trousers. On his first day of work, my grandmother, who had never before shown any religious inclination, made him kiss the Koran three times before leaving the house, 'just to be on the safe side'. Between our recent financial record, the elephants on the tie, the good-luck outfit he wore to the office and the respect paid to Allah, there was only one front left from which misfortune could strike: his lack of proficiency in English.

Initially, this seemed like a trivial worry. My father was fluent in five languages besides Albanian. He spoke French, which he had learned as a child, like everyone else in the family; he had mastered Italian by reading smuggled copies of Pirandello's *Novelle per un anno*; and he had won Russian competitions, back when our country still maintained good relations with Moscow. With the support of his Russian and visual help from Yugoslav television, he'd also taught himself Serbo-Croatian, and Macedonian, which he claimed was the same as Bulgarian. He could not have known that none of this would compensate for what he came to consider the greatest mistake he had ever made: failing to learn English. Not only did he take no comfort in his other languages, but he began to treat his fluency in them as the manipulative work of malevolent forces, who had turned him away from the only idiom he really should have learned: English. 'If only I'd watched *Foreign Languages at Home*,' he would often say to me, holding his head in his hands. 'If only I'd studied the *Essenshel*.'

'It's called *Essential English for Foreign Students*,' I pointed out, correcting him.

That upset him even more. 'You were lucky, brigatista. You started with English in school because we'd already split with the Soviets. I only did Russian.' English became his new demon; the nightmare that kept him awake. 'They will arrive before long,' he would say with a tremor in his voice, 'the foreign experts. They will be here soon and I won't be able to communicate.' Then again, later: 'I'll be sacked as soon as the government changes. I know it. I have no English.'

'But Zafo, you can learn it,' my grandmother gently answered him. 'And you have French – Brussels is important, you know, since we're about to join the European Union. There are a lot of people who learn French still.'

'Yeah, the French still learn it,' my mother mocked. 'They learn it twice. Once as a native language, and the second time as a foreign one.' She felt superior because she had some basic English, thanks to Nona Fozi, who had been to an American boarding school for wealthy girls before the war. 'But it's true, learn it!' my mother ordered. 'Don't waste your time worrying.'

My father didn't usually 'waste time' worrying. It was the opposite, it was floating from one set of worries to the next that helped him mark the passage of time, that structured events and shaped expectations. Worrying was the default condition of his existence, a predicament as natural as breathing and sleeping. He would have found a reason to feel anxious about his new job, even if something much less vital than English had been at stake. The problem with English was not that he worried, but that nobody could offer reassurance. Nobody could say it didn't matter.

At first, he confronted the challenge in the same way he'd done in the past: by getting himself a dictionary and picking a book to translate. This effort soon failed. Perhaps because he realized that he could not rely on the languages he knew to help him make progress. Or perhaps because the book in question was *The Complete Works of Shakespeare*, in a nineteenth-century luxury edition that seemed to have escaped the confiscation of family belongings only so as to humiliate my father half a century later.

After that, I tried to persuade him to join the afternoon English programme I had enrolled in. It was called the Cambridge School and offered free tuition. In return you had to write fifty or sixty letters to random addresses in the United Kingdom. Each participant in the course received a package with several photocopied pages from a telephone book and could select the recipients. In the letters, we introduced ourselves and our families, attached a photograph or two, expressed the desire to make friends abroad, and asked for money to sponsor the English course. I was assigned the letter F. I never found out what the next step would be after receiving a reply, since I never heard back. It was like throwing eye-drops into the ocean. There were rumours that some participants had found financial assistance and that others had been invited to visit or study in the United Kingdom. But nobody ever saw the evidence, since the people who received such invitations did not bring the letters to class, in case someone less lucky would 'steal the sponsor's address'. In my case, the benefits were restricted to improving my English. Each letter had to be different, and this helped me find a variety of formulations to express what were ultimately the same elementary facts. My father was enthusiastic too. But when he came to enrol, he was informed that the programme was limited to children and teenagers. It was unlikely, he was told, that anyone would reply to letters sent from middle-aged Albanian men. Needless to say, this dragged him even further down.

Hope came in the form of a fortuitous meeting on the bus home from work with a group of young Americans. Probably Marines, he said – that was how he'd heard them introduce themselves. One could see it in the discipline with which they carried their black rucksacks, in the tight-fitting trousers, the crisply ironed white shirts, the clean-shaven faces and the short, impeccably cut hair. The Marines had approached my father to ask for directions. He tried to explain that he did not understand a word, but he must have also conveyed the sadness with which he lived with that predicament. They wrote something on a piece of paper and slipped it into his pocket. They organized free English classes in the evening, they said, and he was welcome to enrol.

He joined the class at his first opportunity. He was extremely satisfied with the arrangement. He met people he knew, including our neighbour, Murat the shoemaker, now training to become an imam. Not only was my father making fast progress learning English from native speakers, the textbooks they used were also interesting in their own right. He learned about something called the Church of Latter-Day Saints, and about a new doctrine which he had never heard of before. Just like Islam, it permitted polygamy. The debates in class were always very profound, very substantial, my father reported, never about the kind of trivialities you would expect in an elementary English class. Several attendees defended the superiority of the Prophet Mohammed, who, unlike Jesus, had never had the temerity to suggest that he was the son of God; he was only one prophet among many, but with the advantage of being the last and therefore the most right. My father didn't take sides. He had read somewhere that matters of reason and matters of faith could not be adjudicated using the same criteria. But he enjoyed listening and arbitrating. Some of the people in the course could be quite aggressive in their critique of the Latter-Day Saints, he said. Murat invited the Marines to check out the old mosque, which had been converted back from being a youth centre, recently renovated with the help of Muslim friends from Saudi Arabia.

In fact, they were not actually called Marines, my father had learned. His English comprehension was so poor, he had misheard on the bus. They were called Mormons. They said they were missionaries, but there was some controversy in my family as to the exact nature of their mission. My father thought they only wanted to teach English; Nini insisted that, if they only wanted to teach English, they would call themselves not missionaries but teachers. Missionaries were called missionaries because their mission was to convert people to their religion. 'It's all part of civil society,' was my mother's contribution to the conversation, as if the mere mention of those two words could end all religious disputes.

'Poor boys,' my grandmother sighed.

'Poor boys indeed,' my father replied. 'It's very unfair to say they're trying to convert people. They're in the minority in that class, and always have to defend themselves. It's Murat and his friends who are trying to convert them to Islam.'

'That's what I mean,' my mother said. 'It's all part of the debate.'

'Poor boys,' Nini repeated.

From that day on, whenever my father attended his evening English class, she would say he'd gone to see 'those poor boys'.

17.

The Crocodile

My father also practised his English with 'the poor man', initially known as the Crocodile. His name was Vincent Van de Berg. Born in The Hague, he had lived abroad most of his life. He, too, was a missionary of sorts. He worked for the World Bank. He didn't walk around carrying the Bible in a rucksack; in its place, he had a pink newspaper called *The Financial Times*. He carried it in a small leather bag which also transported a fancy computer, the first computer I had ever seen. He had moved to Albania to advise the government on various privatization projects. He was an 'expert' – the kind of expert my father had rightly predicted we would soon come to meet, and for whom he felt the urgency of learning English.

Vincent was an expert on societies in transition. He also lived in his own kind of transition. He was always on the move from one transitional society to the next. He had been a resident of so many different countries that I remember only one question that embarrassed him even more than when we asked him how much he earned: where had he previously lived? He was unable to recall the names of all the different places he'd visited. He shrugged slightly, squinted and paused, staring into the void. He gazed at the horizon as if waiting for the clouds to gather in the shape of the globe, to form a map that would help him see all the countries he had crossed. He scratched his head, and almost blushed when he said with a mysterious half-smile, between the regretful and the apologetic: 'Oh many, many countries. So many. In Africa, in South America. In Eastern Europe. Now in the Balkans. Everywhere. I'm a citizen of the world.'

Vincent was largely bald, though he had some patches of short grey hair, and sported large spectacles with thin silver frames. He wore dark blue jeans and short-sleeved shirts that looked a bit like those of the US Marines, except that instead of a pocket they had a tiny crocodile. The crocodile was made of cloth, always stared in the same direction, and had a wide-open mouth and sharp teeth that seemed disproportionately large compared to the rest of the body. Van de Berg changed his shirts frequently, and wore a different colour every day, but the crocodile was a fixture. I joked that perhaps he was fond of crocodiles because they reminded him of all the exotic places he'd visited. My father replied that it was more likely to help people recognize Vincent. When Van de Berg came to live in our neighbourhood everyone called him the Crocodile, until something happened which earned him the nickname of 'the poor man'.

It was Flamur who brought Van de Berg to our road. The two met in the food market, where Flamur worked as a pickpocket. He had chosen this vocation when he had to drop out of school after his mother's factory had closed down and several attempts to leave the country had failed. He tried to steal Vincent's wallet before realizing what he was up against. Van de Berg was as much an expert in identifying objects shifting in his pocket as in managing transition. 'I left the wallet where it was,'

Flamur later reported, 'and, to distract him, I asked if he needed help in the market. I showed him around the various stalls. He'd just arrived and was looking for a place to rent. I offered our house.'

Van de Berg came to see the house and liked the look of it. He asked when he could move in, and Flamur replied that the current tenants had promised to leave very soon, at most within a week. During that week, we helped Flamur and his mother, Shpresa, pack up all their belongings and move to a room they had agreed to rent from their next-door neighbours, the Simoni family, whose house was empty after their emigration to Italy. With the money the family made from the difference in rent, and the fact that Shpresa offered her services as a cleaner and cook for Van de Berg, Flamur could return to school, where he reported in detail on the Dutchman's activities. The Crocodile leaves very early in the morning, he would say. The Crocodile only ever invites foreigners for dinner, never any Albanians. The Crocodile had salad for dinner in the garden with his friends. The Crocodile said it reminded him of Greek salad. The Crocodile dated a girl who worked for the Italian Catholic school, then her friend, who translated for the Soros Foundation. The Crocodile said his underwear had been stolen from the line last night. That sort of thing.

The Crocodile started to be called 'the poor man' a few weeks after he'd moved to Flamur's house; after the first dinner all the neighbours organized to welcome him to our road. He was not actually poor; at least, we assumed he wasn't. If he'd been really poor, he would have tried to leave our country, like everybody did; he would not have come to settle in it. On the contrary, everyone assumed Van de Berg was very rich, but also very stingy. He never offered anything when he met you on the street, not a stick of chewing-gum or a sweet, unlike all the tourists we encountered when we were little.

The dinner to welcome Vincent was a happy occasion, at first. We laid out tables and chairs in the Papas' garden, just as we used to do in the old days. There was the usual buzz, children ran back and forth to fetch cutlery and plates, dogs rummaged under the tables, and music played from loudspeakers. Several courses of meze were brought out from different houses, together with byrek, meatballs, stuffed peppers, roasted aubergines, olives, various yoghurt sauces, lamb on skewers, Turkish delight, baklava, kadaifi, beer, wine, slivovitz, grape raki, ouzo, Turkish coffee, espresso, mountain tea, Chinese tea, and many, many cans, not only of Coca Cola but of all the other soft drinks that had started to appear in the shops. Flamur assumed the role of DJ and sat at the top of the veranda, tirelessly swapping cassettes to satisfy all styles and tastes, and ordering younger children to fetch more cassettes if he felt the repertoire had a gap. The dance floor remained full throughout the evening: some people stood up to join the traditional line dancing, some jumped up only when they heard the Cossacks song, others emerged gracefully in already formed couples from behind the tables when 'The Blue Danube' was played and still others, like my father, would only consider dancing to Bill Haley and Elvis Presley. And when people didn't dance, they sang: from 'Ochi Chyornye' to 'Let It Be', from Al Bano and Romina Power's 'Felicità' to 'Luleborë', which was the only tune whose lyrics were sung with some resemblance to the actual text.

Van de Berg sat at the table in the centre of the garden, in the place that would have been reserved for the bride and groom if this had been a wedding. He did not sing or dance, but he seemed content as he tapped on the table, rhythmically shaking his head left and right, humming the songs he knew. It reminded him of parties in Ghana, he said. The men took turns introducing themselves, vigorously shaking his hand and slapping him on the back. 'Welcome, Vincent! One more shot of raki! I made this one,' someone would say. 'This round is for your health!' someone else would add. And again: 'It's the Netherlands you come from, didn't you say? This is for the friendship between Albania and the Netherlands!' Or also: 'Here, Vincent! Long live the World Bank! God save America!'

As the evening progressed, the women took over. They were not as loud as the men but were no less committed to ensuring that Van de Berg felt welcome, remained involved in the increasingly lively discussions and, most importantly, had enough to eat. 'Vincent, did you try the meat-and-onion byrek?' 'It's lovely,' Vincent replied. 'I've had samosa before, but that was spicier.' '*Samovar?* What is it? Russian, right? Here, have some meatballs with the tomato sauce, that's how you're supposed to eat them, no, not that one, Vincent; that sauce has gone cold, you should have it with this one here, or with the yoghurt sauce, this one, this is much better; Leushka, go and fetch the pestle and mortar, we forgot to grind some pepper, Vincent needs to try it with pepper . . .'

Halfway through the meal, Vincent looked tired. He

tapped less on the table and held his stomach with his hand as if he were in pain. People continued to ask him where he had lived, wanted to know how he found his work in Albania, and enquired about his family circumstances: 'You were born in The Hague, you said? I have a cousin who lives in The Hague. He left the country in the fifties, through the Yugoslav border. His name was Gjergji, Gjergji Maçi. I think he called himself Joris over there; ever come across him – Joris, Joris Maçi? Of course, he might be dead now . . .' Van de Berg shook his head. A frown had formed on his forehead, barely visible, and he smiled less, but nobody seemed to notice.

After a while he stood up and asked for directions to the bathroom. A group of men accompanied him inside the house, then accompanied him back out when he was finished. 'Vincent,' Donika asked when he returned to his seat, 'you're not married, you said? How come? You're not very old; how old did you say you were? Don't worry, maybe you'll meet a lovely Albanian girl. Albanian women are very pretty, and they work very hard! Here, have some baklava, I made the pastry myself, it's got walnuts in it.' 'Walnuts,' Vincent repeated, but he politely declined. 'I've had the one with peanuts, but not the one with walnuts, but I am now full, thank you.' 'Full? You're not full! A big man like you, full! Maybe you're hot? Would you like to take off your jacket? Look how much more there is; Shpresa will be upset if you don't try her kadaifi too, it's delicious, help yourself to some baklava now, and make sure to leave some space for the kadaifi later.'

The straw that broke the camel's back was Flamur playing the traditional dance of the Napoloni, raising the volume on the stereo. At the sound of the first notes, everyone who was still sitting at the table recognized the song and hurried to the improvised dance floor with the kind of urgency one would normally associate with the need to find shelter after a natural disaster. Then some remembered that Van de Berg had been left alone at the table. A delegation of two men, one younger and one older, was sent back in a hurry, and, indicating the area where the rest of the group was singing, dancing and waving their handkerchiefs, they shouted in his ear: 'Vincent, we have to dance, it's the Napoloni, you have to learn it, you can't live in Albania without learning the Napoloni, come!'

Van de Berg made a gesture to indicate that he wasn't too keen on dancing. The men pulled at his chair and shouted again: 'Come, don't be shy, it's the Napoloni, you must dance to this; here, here's a handkerchief!' Van de Berg made a movement with his shoulders to release himself from the hold. 'I can't dance,' he said. 'I'm not a good dancer. I enjoy watching. The Napoloni looks a bit like Zorba's dance.' As the dance progressed and the music moved towards its last notes, the men, slightly irritated that they might miss out on their favourite song, urged him even more emphatically.

'Vincent!' the younger of the two men shouted almost with despair. 'Quickly, quickly, Vincent, it's almost finished, the Napoloni is almost finished. What do you mean, you can't dance! Of course you can dance, everyone can dance the Napoloni; look here, you just hold the handkerchief like this and wave it in the air, and you keep your arms open like an aeroplane, and hold them like this, up, up, up, and open, without moving your arms, and you only need to move your belly . . .'

To show what a dancing aeroplane looked like, the older of the two men grabbed Vincent's left arm, and the younger his right arm, and both tried to hold them up. Van de Berg turned bright red. Small drops of sweat dripped from his forehead. He shoved both men out of his way, regained his place on the chair, and, just as the music was coming to a stop, he banged his fist on the table, causing a glass of raki to spill to the ground. He was beside himself with rage. 'Look, I am free!' he shouted. 'Do you understand? I am free!'

Everyone on the dance floor froze. They turned towards the tables. Donika's husband, Mihal, who was sitting on the opposite side of the circle and could not see very clearly, stood up and went to check if a fight between drunken men had broken out. Then he noticed that something was wrong with Van de Berg, remembered he couldn't communicate in any language other than his own, and asked for help with translation. Vincent, who had regained control of his nerves, gathered his things, stood up from his chair, and said to Mihal: 'I apologize. I must go. I'm very tired. Thank you for the lovely dinner.'

There was a murmur through the crowd as people returned to their tables, and Mihal accompanied Van de Berg to the door. 'He did say he was full,' Shpresa commented after he'd left, 'but I thought he wanted to save us food and was worried about our expenses. The poor man.'

'The poor man,' Donika confirmed. 'It's probably the mosquitoes. Or the heat. These tourists, they just can't take it. I told him many times, but he wouldn't take his jacket off.'

'The poor man,' my father repeated. 'He did tell me once he wasn't a good dancer, that he didn't enjoy it.'

'*I am free!*' repeated the two men who had tried to teach Vincent to dance the Napoloni. They rolled their eyes and shrugged. 'What does that even mean? As if anyone's trying to take away your freedom. We're all free here. If you want to dance, fine. If you don't want to dance, fine. Just make it clear, no need to bang your fist on the table. The poor man. He must have been so hot.'

There was a tacit agreement, after that dinner, that no matter how hard we tried to integrate Van de Berg, he would never be one of us. My father was the only one in the street to remain in regular contact with him, either because he wanted to practise numbers in English by discussing football scores across the gate, or because they were forced to see each other regularly in meetings to discuss privatization. As for the other neighbours, they greeted him courteously from a distance while they continued to gossip about 'the poor man', sometimes 'the poor Dutchman', or, more rarely, 'the Crocodile'. When he appeared at the end of the road, the women chatting on their doorstep disappeared, only to reconvene a few minutes later. They resumed their detailed analysis of the habits of 'the poor man', like a group of therapists conducting a psychoanalytic session in the absence of their patient. Did you notice, they would say, how he goes jogging every morning, almost as if he'd been brought up in the Cultural Revolution? Could he be a spy? And isn't it weird how he never hugs or shakes hands with anyone? I wonder if his parents are still alive. Probably in a care home somewhere, that's how they do it. He must be making lots of money to want to live with all these queues and power cuts. A hundred a day, perhaps? A thousand?

On weekends, Van de Berg explored the countryside. He kept the crocodile shirts, but swapped the laptop bag for a rucksack, wore beige shorts instead of dark jeans, carried a straw hat which had 'Ecuador' written on it, and brought along a camera, which made him look like all the other tourists.

'Vincent, have you been up to Mount Dajti yet?' my father would ask him while exchanging pleasantries across the gate. 'Not yet,' Van de Berg would reply, 'but I am planning to go soon, also to that other place, I can't remember the name now. I can't remember it exactly, it was hard to pronounce, I won't even try!'

Of all the habits Van de Berg had, this was the one that perplexed people the most. He was never able to recall the exact names of the places he had seen, or the people he had met and the things he had done. Different sounds, flavours and encounters were all filed in his mind like documents in a chaotic desk of which only the owner knew the order. Whenever we suggested a new dish to try, or a tourist site he might like to visit, or whenever we wanted to teach him a common word in our language, he welcomed the recommendation without surprise, thought of another experience he could compare it to, and let himself be guided without showing signs of disorientation. Likewise, when we tried to warn him of challenges, or to help him cope with difficulties. Vincent was grateful to receive the tips, but one was always left with the impression that he didn't strictly need them.

With the exception of the one dinner at which he lost his temper, I never saw a trace of anxiety. 'Vincent,' we would say, 'there may be a power cut in the evening; there hasn't been one all day. Have you got candles?' Or: 'Vincent, it's 2 p.m.; the water tends to come back around now, it's best to store it in bottles or you'll run out again in half an hour.' To which Vincent would reply: 'I see! Thank you for letting me know. We had the same when I used to stay in . . . in wherever it was in the Middle East, we had water supply issues there too, and frequent power cuts. At least there are no bombs here!' Replicability was Vincent's secret weapon; the impression of déjà vu he conveyed was like a magic power, a trick that helped him to domesticate all that was new, to reduce the foreign to familiar categories.

This had the opposite effect on us. When Vincent evoked those associations with places he had been to, sharing experiences from his past life, the familiar became foreign. It didn't offend us to learn that we weren't teaching Vincent anything new, but there was something troubling about the discovery that what we thought was uniquely ours wasn't so distinctive after all; that everything we had assumed stood out was part of a familiar pattern for those who knew the ways of the world. The dishes we shared with other cuisines, the rhythms of traditional songs and dances, the sounds of our language, all seemed to belong not just to us but to others too; it was our fault for not knowing this. Our heroes were ordinary people, and there were millions of others like them in the world; our language was a patchwork of words that had emerged from who knows where. We existed not as a product of our efforts but of the mercy of others, more powerful enemies perhaps, who had decided to let us be, whose marks of victory were a thousand smaller places in their own image, which all looked like one another, and all thought themselves to be different.

Van de Berg's capacity to draw parallels between the most disparate experiences, to identify commonalities between people in different parts of the world, to make you realize, for example, that a byrek in Albania tasted no different from a non-spicy samosa, or that a rubbish dump in Durrës looked just like a rubbish dump in Bogotá, sometimes reminded me of my teacher Nora. There was no overlap in the content of what they said, but there was a certain similarity in their attitude to generalization, in their ability to abstract from minute details, in the way they compared situations and used the comparison to explain a broader vision of the world, to reveal their knowledge of a whole system. Nora used to say that we had more in common with our brothers and sisters in other parts of the world than we realized. Everyone, she explained, unless they had liberated themselves, like we had done, was subject to the same capitalist exploitation; we were all part of the same global anti-imperialist struggle. Oppression, she told us, has the same face everywhere.

Van de Berg did not recognize capitalism, or at least he did not think that capitalism was a plausible term to refer to any kind of historical development. It was no more a useful label for a phenomenon than the precise names of the places where he had lived. The only distinction he accepted was that between societies in transition and those that had already transitioned; between the people on the move and those who had moved in the past. Of course, he had a vague sense of the destination. But catching up mattered more than explaining where one was heading. And, unlike my primary school teacher Nora, who'd insisted on the necessity of organizing global proletarian struggle, Van de Berg was there not to mobilize any resistance but to 'foster transparency', 'defend human rights' and 'fight corruption'. He had other agents of change, like 'the international community', and 'civil society actors'. And he had other intentions.

18.

Structural Reforms

'Do you know what the hardest thing I've done in my life is?' my father asked one gusty November morning before going to work. He stood in front of the closed curtains in our living room, listening to the sound of the window frame rattling from the draught, stirring his coffee.

'Was it when you had to lie to me about our relation to Ypi the prime minister?' I asked. 'That must have been hard.'

He shook his head.

'Wait, I know,' I said. 'Remember when I was desperate to have a photo of Enver Hoxha on the bookshelf? You told me we needed a nice frame for it, and we had to wait until it would be ready. I almost believed that.' I chuckled.

Five years after the fall of socialism, episodes of our life back then had become part of the repertoire of amusing family anecdotes. It didn't matter if the memories were absurd, hilarious or painful, or all of these at once. We would joke about them over meals, like drunken sailors who had survived a shipwreck and relished showing one another the scars. My father joked more than anyone else. He joked all the time, so much so that it was often difficult to infer from the tone of his questions if they were intended seriously or if he wanted to make us laugh. At one point in his life, he had figured out that irony was more than a rhetorical device, it was a mode of survival. He made ample use of it and was usually pleased when my brother and I tried to mimic him.

'Or was it when I—'

'The world doesn't always revolve around you, Leushka,' he curtly interrupted me. He was not in his usual playful mood.

He had recently been promoted to general director of the port, the biggest port in the country and one of the largest in the Adriatic Sea. We'd had a telephone line installed in our house, and the first thing he did each morning was call the Harbour Office. He worried about storms preventing ferries from docking, cranes threatened by the wind, queues forming in the customs office. After he'd spent two years running Plantex, amassing a proven record of cutting costs and reducing debt, someone high-up must have thought he was ready for even greater responsibilities. He received a higher salary, was assigned a personal driver who picked him up in a Mercedes Benz each morning to go to work, and doubled the dose of Valium he normally swallowed to go to sleep.

I made other guesses, correcting the tone of my replies. Was it the time when as a little boy of six or seven he tried to protect his mother from being kicked by a police officer? Or when he had to give away his pet dog because the family was being deported? Or when he first met his father, after he was released from prison, and wondered about the stranger who'd come to live with them? Was it suspecting that his best friend was a spy?

He shook his head and kept staring at the bottom of

his small coffee cup, as if he expected the concentrated dark liquid to wash away his even darker thoughts.

'It is this,' he said, slowly moving the curtain to reveal a group of twenty or thirty Roma gathered in the garden. Some of the women had toddlers tied to their backs; others nursed babies while sitting on the ground. More were crowded outside the gate, their faces pressed against the metal rails, like frozen prisoners behind bars. When they noticed my father behind the open curtain, a sudden movement spread in the courtyard; everyone pointed their finger towards our window and started to shout: 'There he is! He's there! He's up! He's going to come out!'

My father closed the curtain. He sat on the sofa and reached out for his pump, taking a few deep breaths to inhale the medicine. His hands always trembled; the result of years of anti-histaminic medicines for the asthma he had contracted as a child. This time, they trembled more.

'They work in the port,' he said after a pause. 'Do you know what we call them? Structural reforms.'

His face was twisted by an expression of pain that he tried to contain, like someone due to appear on stage who has just got their fingers trapped in the dressing-room doors. From the start of his contract at the harbour, he had been in negotiations with foreign experts like Van de Berg to discuss what the World Bank called 'structural reforms'. Like every other state enterprise, the port was in deficit and had been urged to cut costs. This time, nobody promised there would be no redundancies. The experts charted what they called a 'road map', the first step of which involved a series of lay-offs, mostly of low-skilled workers. Hundreds of Roma worked at the port: cargo loaders, cleaners, freight transporters, warehouse operatives. My father was responsible for firing them all.

When those working in the port heard they were about to lose their jobs, they began to visit our house in the early hours of the morning, waiting patiently outside until my father left. At first, there were only four or five, but as news of the structural reforms spread, the crowds grew bigger. They stood in the courtyard until my father appeared at the door, then shouted at him, begging him to think twice. 'Good morning, boss. You're a good man, boss, don't do it, don't listen to them thieves.' 'Is it about drinking, boss? Is it that? I can quit drinking tomorrow, if that's the problem. Tomorrow I can quit drinking, and I can quit smoking too, if you want. Who has money for raki these days? I've cut so much, boss, really cut down, you know.' 'I only have a couple of years until retirement, boss. Just two more years. I have worked in the port since I was thirteen.' 'Boss, I never stole anything. You know, they say gypsies steal everything. Maybe someone told you I stole from the warehouse. I've never stolen a penny, boss. I swear on my children's heads, I've never stolen anything.' 'Let me do my job. I like my job. It's a hard job, but I like it. I know everyone in the port. The port is like my house. I sleep there, I eat there, I do everything at the port. When I go home, my children are sleeping.'

'I don't know how to go out there,' my father said that morning. 'Every day, there are more people. Yesterday, I had another meeting with them in the office. I have meetings all the time. First with the World Bank, then with them, then again with the World Bank. Take a look at these people, standing there. They think it depends on me. They think I can do something. I don't know what to say to them. There are new rules now. Things work differently, companies are run differently. Parts of the port will need to be privatized. Someone has to do it. It just happens to be me, but if it wasn't me, it would have to be someone else, whoever, doesn't matter who, someone has to do it.'

'Why do you have to do it?' I asked.

'We can't keep them all on the payroll,' he said. 'Van de Berg says we need to modernize, save money, buy new equipment. He talks about replacing them, as if they were machines. Like you get rid of some old machine and buy a faster one. Bang, just like that. I don't know how to do it. I'm not a machine. I wish I were a machine, so someone could program me to just do it. Van de Berg says they've done it in Bolivia. I've never been to Bolivia. These people don't even know where Bolivia is. What does that even mean, they've done it in Bolivia – so what? Look at them. They're not machines. They're people. They have tears in their eyes, and sweat on their brows. They would have hope too, if there was any left. Go to the window. Stand there and take a look. Structural reforms, they are called. Structural reforms.'

My father nervously pulled his raincoat from the hanger and left the house, slamming the door. I did as I was told. I returned to the window and opened it to listen. When he showed up in the courtyard, the crowd remained silent. The gate opened and a man appeared; a man the same height as a five-year old, who used his hands to hop along the ground and dangled his amputated thighs left and right like a fish tail. From the window, I recognized Ziku, the Roma cripple I used to see as a child, who begged for money at the cemetery entrance.

Ziku smiled and waved like someone seeing an old friend. I had never noticed his front teeth were missing, just like his legs. I had never seen him smile before. It was a contorted smile, almost like a grimace.

'You remember me, boss!' Ziku exclaimed. 'I told them you wouldn't have the heart to do it. You never walked past this cripple without giving him a little something. Sometimes more, sometimes less, but a little something each time. I told them you're a man of the people. I know you won't let them down. There aren't many people who love gypsies, and who love cripples, but you do. I know you do. You never let me go without bread. You won't let these children go hungry. I told them you won't. You're a good man. I told them.'

My father searched for my eyes on the other side of the window. *It's not Ziku's fault for being a cripple,* he would say to me when I was little. *It's not my fault,* his face was saying now. He inserted his hand in the right pocket of his trousers, as if looking for spare change. This time, he found no coins, only a handkerchief, with which he wiped his face. Ziku spotted him, and dragged himself closer to my father's feet. 'He's crying.' He turned to the others. 'You see, he's crying,' he repeated pointing his finger at my father. 'I told them, boss, I told them you would do anything you could.' 'We know you're a good man, boss,' the other men joined in. 'Don't do it, don't listen. They only want to make money for themselves. You don't want to make money, you want to give it to the poor, you don't want to keep it.' Two women nursing their toddlers threw themselves at his feet, sobbing, begging him to save their husbands' jobs. When the toddlers saw their mothers crying, they cried too. It was not a protest; it looked more like bereavement. There was no anger, only despair.

'Not here, not here, please,' my father said to Ziku with a dying voice. 'This is my house. We can discuss it in the office. If I . . . if I . . . the money is not mine. I would keep everyone at work, it's not about me, I'm not the one who makes the decision. I mean . . . yes, I make the decision, but the decision is . . . well, it's not mine.' He noticed he was rambling, and tried to organize his thoughts. 'You see' – he turned to the crowd – 'this is not like giving money to Ziku, it's not the same thing. We're given a *ratmat*, you see. You must understand, there are rules. We need to get the market economy going. There's a path that must be followed. If we do it properly, it will be better for everyone, for all of us. These are structural reforms. Everything needs to change, and we need to change how we do things – we can't keep everyone at work, it's not possible. Soon, there will be jobs for everyone, it will be better. But now we have no choice, we all have to make sacrifices, we just have to do it. It must be done.'

He promised his bosses he would do it, but never did. He never signed off on the redundancies. He kept repeating that structural reforms were inevitable, but he avoided them for as long as he could. 'It's about politics,' he would say. 'These are political decisions, I'm just an administrator, a bureaucrat. I can only delay things. I can't stop them.' He spent long evenings staring at numbers, charts and graphs, trying to work out how to cut costs without firing people. He was not proud of the results. A part of him felt embarrassed, ashamed even, that he couldn't find the courage to fulfil the duties he had been given. He had worked conscientiously all his life. My grandmother had taught all of us to put our best effort even into the most meaningless tasks, to always try to own the consequences even if we couldn't own the causes. He could not admit to failure in his role. 'Soon, very soon,' he would say.

He had meetings with the deputy minister, then the minister, then the prime minister. They all repeated Van de Berg's warning. 'Structural reform is like going to the dentist: you can postpone it, but the more you postpone it, the more painful it will get.' But my father had never wanted to be a dentist; he'd wanted to be something other than what he was, although he had never had a chance to discover what. He remained a dissident at heart. He was critical of capitalism. He had never believed in the rules he was now asked to enact. He did not have much faith in socialism either. He hated authority in all its forms. Now that he represented that authority, he resented the role. He would neither endorse structural reforms nor obstruct them. He hated wrecking people's lives, and he hated leaving the dirty work to others.

My father had been proud of his promotions at first. After years of depending on the goodwill of his superiors, and a lifetime of relying on the mercy of Party officials, he cherished the independence he presumed the new role would give him. Soon he came to realize that independence had its limits; that he was not as free as he had imagined. He wanted to change things but

discovered there was little left for him to do. The world
had acquired a definitive shape before anyone could
understand what that shape was. Moral imperatives and
personal convictions mattered very little. He discovered that, although nobody ordered him what to say and
where to go, he needed to say something and be somewhere before he had time to reflect on it, to consider
the benefits and weigh up the costs. In the past, when
dilemmas arose and he failed to live up to his commitments, he could blame the system. Now it was different.
The system had changed. He had not tried to stop the
changes; he had welcomed them, encouraged them.

Or perhaps not. My father assumed, like many in his
generation, that freedom was lost when other people tell
us how to think, what to do, where to go. He soon realized that coercion need not always take such a direct
form. Socialism had denied him the possibility to be
who he wanted, to make mistakes and learn from them,
and to explore the world on his own terms. Capitalism
was denying it to others, the people who depended on
his decisions, who worked in the port. Class struggle was
not over. He could understand as much. He did not want
the world to remain a place where solidarity is destroyed,
where only the fittest survive, and where the price of
achievement for some is the destruction of hope in others. Unlike my mother, who thought that human beings
were naturally inclined to harm one another, he believed
there was a kernel of goodness in everyone, and that the
only reason it failed to emerge was that we lived in the
wrong societies.

But he could not name the right societies: he could
bring up no examples of any existing place where

things worked out. He distrusted big theories. 'Stop philosophizing!' he would often admonish me. He had grown up with socialist realist novels, and Soviet films that explained what was right and wrong, how justice comes about, how freedom is realized. He admired the intentions, but hesitated to endorse their prescriptions. The world he wanted to see was always different from the one he lived in. When he noticed the beginnings of a movement that resisted the way things were, he thought there was promise. But as soon as that movement became concrete, as soon as it had its own leaders, its own set of constraints and conventions, as soon as it became something as opposed to the rejection of something else, he lost faith. He knew there was a cost to everything, but he was not prepared to accept that cost. The people he admired were nihilists and rebels, men and women who spent their lives merely condemning the world they inhabited, but without committing to any alternatives.

When confronted with the same decisions about structural reforms, his colleagues became cynical. 'Oh, well,' they would say. 'We survived the Turks. We survived the fascists and the Nazis. We survived the Soviets and the Chinese. We'll survive the World Bank.' He was terrified of forgetting what that survival had cost. Now that he was safe, now that our family was no longer at risk of being killed, imprisoned or deported, he was anxious that he might soon no longer remember what it was like to wake up in the morning and worry about what the day would bring. He tried to recall the names of all the people who worked in the port, even though there were hundreds of them. 'If I forget their names, I will forget about their lives,' he said. 'They will no longer be people; they'll become numbers. Their aspirations, their fears, will no longer matter. We will only remember the rules, not those to whom they apply. Only think about orders, not about the purpose they serve. That's probably what the Mule thought as she informed on her pupils' families. What Haki repeated to himself when reaching out for his torture instruments.'

The sole thought of being like them, of complying with rules in the same abstract and heartless way, was enough to leave my father sleepless at night. He didn't share Van de Berg's ideas of how everything would work out once the transition was complete. He knew something like a market economy would be needed, but had never given much thought to the form it would take. Like many in his generation, he was more preoccupied by freedom of thought, the right to protest, the possibility of living in accordance with one's moral conscience.

Even if he had shared the theory, even if he was convinced of the truths everyone now accepted, he would have worried about believing too much. He had met too many people for whom theories came first; he knew that one can injure others by acting in good faith. Ideals now looked different; perhaps even calling them ideals would be an exaggeration, perhaps they were simply prudential prescriptions. They still required human intervention to be turned into practice. He had been innocent in the past. He had been a victim. How could he suddenly become the offender?

19.

Don't Cry

In the mid-nineties, I had my own share of torment to contend with. My teenage years were mostly ones of misery, a predicament which intensified the more my family denied that it had cause to exist. They seemed to assume that one was entitled to feel wretched only when there were objective grounds: if you were at risk of starving or freezing or had no place to sleep, or lived under the threat of violence. These were absolute thresholds. If something could be done to raise yourself above the threshold, you forfeited your right to protest; otherwise, it would be an insult to those less fortunate. It was a bit like with food vouchers under socialism. Since everyone had a share of something, hunger couldn't possibly exist. If you said you were hungry, you became an enemy of the people.

I was urged to feel grateful, to show my appreciation for the bliss of freedom, which had arrived too late for my parents to enjoy and therefore required me to exercise it all the more responsibly. When I failed to sympathize with their predicament, I was scolded for my selfishness, for being insensitive to the suffering of my ancestors, for erasing the memory of their plight with the lightness of my behaviour. I did not feel free at all. I felt especially constrained in the winter. It got dark early, and I was not allowed to go outside after the sun had set. 'You'll get into trouble,' my parents would say, without feeling the need to specify what kind of trouble they anticipated, just as I didn't feel the need to ask them to clarify.

Trouble could take many forms. One might get killed by a car, like my classmate Dritan, who was walking by the beach one evening and got run over by a young man teaching himself to drive his uncle's Audi. Or one might disappear without a trace, like Sokrat, Besa's father, who suffered from a limp and worked with a dinghy. Each night, he helped smuggle people to Italy, then returned to sleep in his bed, except for the night he didn't. And all sorts of small accidents could happen to you, like hitting a broken lamppost in a dark street while walking, or falling into a manhole whose cover had just been stolen for its steel. Or one could be harassed all the way home by hungry stray dogs. Or it could be drunken men, or boys placing bets on how girls would respond to catcalling. For my parents, these were not real problems. We were in transition, after all. We just had to be patient. And there was always something one could do to avoid those misfortunes. One could simply stay indoors.

And so I did. I locked myself up in my bedroom and spent long afternoons chewing on sunflower seeds. To say that I was bored would risk making the condition interesting by qualifying it, by attaching a description to a mass of events in which nothing deserved to stand out. Time was the eternal return of the same. The clubs I used to attend as a child, for poetry, theatre, singing, maths, natural science, music or chess, had all come to an abrupt end in December 1990. In school, the only subjects to be taken seriously were the hard sciences: physics, chemistry, maths. For the humanities, either new classes were introduced, such as when Market Economy replaced Dialectical Materialism, and we had no textbooks at all, or, as with the history and geography material, they still described our country as 'the lighthouse of anti-imperialist struggles around the world'. I finished my homework quickly and was left wondering how to kill the time that remained. We now had a telephone line, and I spoke to friends, then read novels in bed, often shivering under a blanket, with a candle lit above my head. The electricity continued to run out, and on some winter evenings the cold bit harder than the sadness.

Every forty-five minutes my grandmother would walk in without knocking, carrying a glass of milk or a piece of fruit. 'Are you OK?' she would enquire. I'd nod. She'd heard of a new Western disease called ano-rexia, which struck teenage girls. She had no idea how it spread or why, but decided that if she forced me to eat at regular intervals I would be safe. When I negotiated to swap her snacks with my own supplies of sunflower seeds, she demanded to see the shells. The intervals got extended to ninety minutes. 'We're so lucky,' she would say to herself, apropos of nothing, as she left the room. I guessed she was referring to the glass of milk, for which we were no longer required to queue.

A few pubs and clubs had started to open. Most of them belonged to people-smugglers, drug-dealers or sex-traffickers. These were all mentioned as normal occupations, in the same way one would have explained in the past that so-and-so was a cooperative worker, a factory employee, a bus driver or a hospital nurse. Often labels from different eras attached to the same people.

'That one, the man in the BMW with the dark windows, that one is Hafize's son,' neighbours would gossip while sipping coffee on the balcony. 'He used to work in the biscuit factory. He was laid off before they closed for good. He managed to cross into Switzerland. He's in business now. He does imports–exports. Cannabis, cocaine, that sort of thing.'

I was allowed to visit clubs only for daytime parties, where the curtains were brought down so that we could act as if it was dark, punch and cigarettes were smuggled in, and my peers played a new game imported from abroad called Spin the Bottle. I joined in, and pretended not to notice the contorted faces of the boys when the bottle pointed in my direction, or not to hear their moaning voices when my turn to kiss them finally came: 'I don't kiss men!' they would say. 'I'm not gay!'

I didn't know yet who or what gay was, but felt embarrassed to ask. That I looked like a boy, there was no doubt. We were no longer required to wear uniforms in school; we could do what we wanted. Just as the other girls were smuggling make-up into the school toilets and reducing the length of their skirts, I embraced oversized trousers and my father's checked socialist shirts. Just as they started straightening their hair and dying it blonde, I asked the barber to cut mine short. They rebelled against their families by mimicking Madonna in 'Material Girl'; I rebelled against the ribbons and laces mine had imposed by turning into a poster girl for the Cultural Revolution. My nickname at home switched from Brigatista to Gavroche. At school it went from Mamuazel to the Vase (for the word 'qypi', which rhymes with Ypi), not so much on account of my body shape, which was as slim and frail as always, as the clothes in which it swam.

I often wondered if things would be different if Elona were still around. I sometimes saw her father with his new wife and his new child, and I saw how he pretended not to recognize me. Perhaps Elona too had embraced heavy make-up, false nails and miniskirts. Perhaps she too had dyed her blonde hair even blonder. Perhaps she was allowed to be outside after sunset. Perhaps she had recently discovered *Crime and Punishment* or *The Brothers Karamazov*.

In the winter of 1996, I saw Arian, the boy – now a young man – who used to live on my street and with whom Elona had run away. His parents had extended their house by purchasing the next one along, which used to belong to Marsida's family; they, in turn, had left the neighbourhood to rent a smaller place in a different part of town. There was something eerie about the sight of him, standing by the door of the same house where Marsida and I used to find shelter as children whenever Arian appeared on the street. He had grown long hair that covered his shoulders, and wore a thick gold necklace, a dark leather jacket with a skull stamped on the back, leather trousers and heavy black boots covered in silver chains. He drove a large Mercedes Benz, which he had brought back from Italy to leave with his parents. The car started with a loud, grating sound. There were now fewer children playing in the streets, but when they heard the sound of the car they all ran back inside, just as children had always done when Arian appeared. There was no sign of Elona. I didn't dare ask.

I missed my friend. I wanted to tell her that the

woman from whom we'd bought sunflower seeds near our school had disappeared, but that her place had been taken by a cute boy of around ten who sold bananas and cigarette packets. I wanted to tell her that the valuta shop had closed but you could buy the red bra she liked everywhere; and in the second-hand market you could buy it for the price of two bananas or five cups of sunflower seeds. I wanted to tell her that even I needed a bra now, just as my grandmother had warned us that it would happen soon, that our bodies would change, just like our minds. My grandmother had also said we might start to develop what she called *des amitiés amoureuses*. I wanted to ask Elona if she had managed to figure out what an *amitié amoureuse* was, if that was what she had with Arian, or if she had ever heard of a much more raw, lonely and painful thing, something the books called love.

Life was less constrained but no less grim in the summer, when the school closed. In June 1995, after a week of the same ritual of going to the beach, returning home for lunch, taking a siesta in the afternoon, and the obligatory early-evening walk along the waterfront to see my friends, who gossiped while parading their new summer dresses, a disaster occurred. My grandmother had warned me that there was only one category of boys I must never, under any circumstances, fall in love with: children of former secret service agents. That summer it happened, twice. I felt so guilty that I decided to increase my visits to the mosque. I contemplated wearing a veil, but my family prohibited that too. There is a difference between religion and fanaticism, Nini said. Since more girls were turning up at the mosque wearing veils and I did not want to stand out, I switched to a new

religion: Buddhism. I discovered it by reading my grandfather's old Larousse dictionary when I ran out of books.
I added meditation sessions to my daily schedule, but I
never learned to meditate without crying. I was haunted
by tales of the persecution my family had endured at
the hands of Sigurimi agents, a thought which not only
didn't help me fall out of love with their sons but made
that love more desperate.

'Our Leushka has become like young Werther,' my
father joked, ignorant of the cause of my tears. 'Don't cry,'
Nini reproached. 'Crying never helped anyone. If I had
ever thought about crying, I wouldn't be here. I would
have thrown myself under a train, or joined my cousins
in the mental asylum. Do something. Read another book.
Learn a new language. Find some activity.'

I started to volunteer for the Red Cross, and got
involved in a project at the local orphanage. Every
morning, we would take the children to the beach and,
along with the carers, look after them while they messed
around in the sand or splashed in the sea. 'It will help
you put your life into perspective,' my grandmother
encouraged me. 'You don't realize how lucky you are.
There's a lot of misery out there.'

'Remember,' my mother told me, the day I started my
volunteer work at the Red Cross, 'the orphanage is not
where it used to be. The old building has been returned
to the owners.'

Whenever my mother said 'owners', she meant the
previous owners. The state, for her, could never be considered an owner of anything, only a criminal entity
built on the violent appropriation of other people's hard
work. I remembered the surname of those owners from

the boundary maps of her family properties scattered across the floor of our house. 'These maps make such a big mess,' my grandmother would complain while cleaning. 'They make Zafo's asthma worse. He's allergic to dust. A hundred times I told Doli, a hundred times. She brings them from the land registry and leaves them lying around. If you want to take them to court, fine. Nothing is going to come out of these properties. They're just lines drawn on paper.'

But the orphanage was not just lines drawn on paper. The previous owners had successfully reclaimed the building from the state, then sold it to some kind of church. The orphanage had moved to new premises: three rooms in a derelict two-floor building. It possessed little natural light, a distinctive smell of sour milk and an unnatural silence in the hour of the afternoon nap that was broken only by the gnawing of mice on the ground floor. The number of abandoned children had grown in recent years, ranging from newborns to pre-schoolers. They came from the local area, and when they reached the age of six, if they had not already been adopted, they would either be returned to their parents, if they were willing to take them back, or sent to an orphanage for older children in the north.

Many of the carers I remembered from my previous visits with Elona had been made redundant or had left the country. I recognized only one of them, Teta Aspasia, a bubbly middle-aged woman who used to be in charge of the babies' room and gave Elona and me water with sugar as a treat when we went to see her sister. 'You've grown up!' she exclaimed. 'Baby Mimi is so grown up too. She's in a different orphanage now, up in Shkodra. The father never shows up. Her grandparents visit her every now and then. They agreed to her adoption by a Canadian couple. Then the Canadian couple decided to take the gypsy twins. Remember the little gypsies in the babies' room, the ones with the parents in prison? The parents came out after an amnesty in 1990 but they were accused of trying to sell the twins as soon as they were released. They went straight back in. They've got no chance. It's very hard to place gypsy children. Nobody wants them. People will say, "Please, no gypsies; they're hard to control, they steal everything." One of the twins turned out to have some kind of handicap, a mental problem, I can't remember exactly what. The ones with disabilities are even harder to place. The Canadians were seeing Mimi, but then they got asked if they would like the twins. We asked everyone; nobody wanted them. It was incredible when they agreed. They were probably religious people. The director thought Mimi would be easier to place, but she's still in Shkodra. Your friend, her sister, also used to send letters—'

'Elona?' I exclaimed. 'Do you know where she is? What she does?'

'We haven't heard from her for a while,' she said. 'Letters take forever now, if they make it. She called a couple of times. Yes, I know what she does. One of the carers who now lives in Milan recognized her near a train station. She works. Up and down the pavements. You know what I mean. She left with the *exodus*, with some boy from here. He works too. He is involved in some kind of trafficking, women I guess, he probably started with her . . . You have to go, sweetheart, the Red Cross van is downstairs, they're waiting. The van is like new. It's a donation from the French. The little ones are so excited. They've never seen the sea before. They've hardly been out in the sun, poor things. We have no garden in this building. You have to be careful they don't get sunburned. I brought some olive oil from home. Don't take their clothes off immediately, we should wait a couple of days. Here, take Ilir. He's all ready to go. Drita will be coming with you.' She pointed to her colleague. 'Ilir is in the morning shift. You will like him; he's very sweet. His mum is like your old friend. She looks a bit like her too, she does the same work. Ilir, come here, meet Lea, she's going to take you to the beach.'

I was still digesting the news about Elona, but had no time to ask. Ilir was hiding outside the door. When he heard his name, he walked in, shyly at first, then with more confidence. He was a chubby little boy of around two, with curly hair and big brown eyes. 'Mama,' he whispered when he came closer, as if he was about to let me into his deepest secret. His face lit up, and his pupils dilated. 'Mama here . . . Mama—'

'No, not Mama,' Aspasia interrupted him. 'Not Mama, darling. Mama is still in Greece. This is Lea, she will take you to the beach.' She turned towards me. 'I'm surprised he remembers her; last year is the only time he's seen her, she came to visit regularly every day for a week or so. She sends pictures, though, we've shown him. You don't look like her, maybe just the age. How old are you, remind me? Fifteen, yes, that's what I thought, his mum is a little older, perhaps seventeen. Same age as your friend. Like Elona, but she works in Greece, not in Italy.'

Later that day, I also learned the full story of Ilir's mother, as she had told it earlier to the carers. She was raped by her boyfriend, then her boyfriend's friends. She was smuggled out to Greece soon after delivering the baby, which she insisted on keeping. She dropped Ilir at the bottom of the stairs of the orphanage when he was around three weeks old, wrapped up in a blanket, with a box of clothes, some bottles of milk and a letter in which she promised to collect him on his sixth birthday. She called and wrote regularly, and sent money to buy presents. The carers were confident she would come back. Ilir was not on the adoption list. He, too, knew that his mother would return to collect him one day. When he saw me, he must have decided the day had come.

'Ilir go Mama,' he insisted. 'Ilir go Mama beach.'

'Not Mama, darling. You will go to the beach with Lea. This is Lea, not Mama, Mama is in Greece. Mama will be back soon,' Aspasia corrected him again. Then she turned to me. 'You need to insist on this. Explain you're not his mama, okay, just one of us. They do this sometimes; they call us Mama. We have to be very strict. Otherwise, they become attached, they don't let you go home at the end of the day, it's very difficult. Try to explain it to him, okay? Tell him Mama is in Greece; she left us money to buy a toy for his birthday, and for the New Year. He understands that.'

But Ilir never understood. Or perhaps he never accepted it. After a few visits in which I would play with him, read stories or take him to the beach, he became more insistent. 'Mama here!' he would shout every time he saw me. 'Go Mama beach!' Then, when it was time for me to leave, he would cling on to my leg, throw himself to the floor and kick his carers, insisting that I should either stay with him or take him with me. 'Bring Ilir home,' he would cry. 'Mama take Ilir.' He became increasingly difficult to handle in my presence: he refused to come out of the water at the beach, eat his food or go down for his naps. When I tried to leave, I noticed that my bag was missing, or my sandals had disappeared. It could have been normal toddler behaviour, except that babies at the orphanage never cried, and toddlers never threw tantrums. The problem, the carers explained, consisted in my presence, in his attachment to me. Ilir didn't have to be miserable like that; he would be fine if I just kept out of sight. I was asked to reduce my visits to the toddler room and moved to a different area of the building, one with younger babies, who forgot people more easily.

Then the summer came to an end. The weather changed, the project ran out of funding, and I stopped my visits. I don't know what happened to Ilir, nor did I ever hear anything else about Elona or her sister. I sometimes wondered if Elona was still on the streets, and if Mimi had found Canadian parents. I returned to my bedroom, where my grandmother walked in without knocking, at regular intervals of ninety minutes, carrying a glass of milk or a piece of fruit. 'We're so lucky,' she would say to herself each time as she left the room.

20.

Like the Rest of Europe

At first, it was going to be my mother who would run to become an MP in 1996. She had been a member of the party since the day it was founded. She knew everyone in party circles, she'd even read the manifesto. We called it the party, even though it wasn't the Party: it was the Democratic Party of Albania, the former communists' main opponent in elections. Still, everyone understood what we meant. There was no danger of my family supporting the former communists. There was only one party for us, just as there was only one party for them.

At that point, my mother had been politically active for five years. She endorsed the party's main slogan, whose disarming simplicity concealed decades of frustrated aspiration: 'We want Albania to be like the rest of Europe.' When my mother was asked what 'the rest of Europe' stood for, she summarized it in a few words: fighting corruption, promoting free enterprise, respecting private property, encouraging individual initiative. In short: freedom.

Yet, as my mother soon realized, explaining the slogan was not enough to make her a successful parliamentary candidate. Other virtues were needed. She had charisma on stage, but lost her patience in meetings. She was possessed with the zeal of the prophet, and although her speeches enthused in the short term, in the long run they frightened people. The seriousness with which she took her commitments made her reluctant to compromise. Her manners remained those of the strict maths teacher.

She volunteered my father to take her place. 'He is a man. That helps,' she explained while pitching him. 'And he is loved as if he were a woman. That helps too.' In general, my father was much more popular than my mother. Not many candidates could appeal both to the Roma workers fighting to keep their jobs at the port and to former dissident families fighting to reclaim the properties of their grandfathers. He had a good reputation even among his socialist opponents because he did not interrupt them in debates and he tried to put his views forward without personalizing the critique. 'He can fight too, if he needs to,' my mother hastened to add, as if it had just occurred to her that my father's affable manners might end up compromising his chances. 'He can fight corruption. There is so much corruption out there. We need honest politicians.'

'Corruption' was a new buzzword. It was a generic explanation for all sorts of evils, both present and past, personal and political, a problem of humans and a deficiency of institutions. It was where economic liberalization and political reform met and, instead of integrating harmoniously, as promised, started to rot. Described sometimes as a dereliction of moral duty, sometimes as an abuse of office, more often it was seen as a failure of human nature, after its attempted socialist transformation. It was, moreover, extremely difficult to fight. Like the Hydra, for every head you chopped, two more would grow. Corruption had its own logic, but nobody tried to decipher it, much less challenge the premise. The word itself was enough to account for the problem.

Initially, my father was reluctant to run for office. He had never been a member of the party. He worried his views were too obscure, even controversial. He wasn't sure about privatization and free markets. He wasn't sure that the country should join NATO. He wasn't even sure our biggest problem was corruption. He did not know where his opinions placed him, on the left or on the right. He felt 'left' on justice but 'right' on freedom.

My mother corrected him. In a former communist country, she said, there was no left or right, only 'communist nostalgics' and 'liberal hopefuls'. He did not necessarily fit the category of hopefuls either. But he had grown frustrated with his life as a bureaucrat. Every day, he came home from the port increasingly anxious and resentful, with tales of efforts that had gone awry, with papers that shouldn't have been signed. It was easy to persuade him, as my mother did, that if he cared, if he wanted to do some good, or limit the bad, he shouldn't stay idle. That he should take action, and that to be active meant to be involved in politics. Politics matters, she said, because you don't just implement other people's decisions, you get to make them. That's what democracy is about.

Yet no party would have been able to prevent structural reforms. They were intrinsically bound up with what was now called, in candid tones of self-congratulation: 'the process of integration into the European family'. There may have been times and places in the history of my country where politics made a difference, where being an activist rather than a bureaucrat meant that you could try to change the rules by intervening at the level at which laws were made rather than applied. This was not one of them. Structural reforms were as inevitable as the weather. They were adopted everywhere in the same form, because the past had failed, and we had never learned how to shape the future. There was no politics left, only policy. And the purpose of policy was to prepare the state for the new era of freedom, and to make people feel as if they belonged to 'the rest of Europe'.

During those years, 'the rest of Europe' was more than a campaign slogan. It stood for a specific way of life, one which was imitated more often than understood, and absorbed more often than justified. Europe was like a long tunnel with an entrance illuminated by bright lights and flashing signs, and with a dark interior, invisible at first. When the journey started, it didn't occur to anyone to ask where the tunnel ended, whether the light would fail, and what there was on the other side. It didn't occur to anyone to bring torches, or to draw maps, or to ask whether anyone ever makes it out of the tunnel, or if there is only one exit or several, and if everybody goes out the same way. Instead, we just marched on, and hoped the tunnel would remain bright, assuming we worked hard enough, and waited long enough, just as we used to wait in socialist queues – without minding the time that passed, without losing hope.

'Like the rest of Europe,' the local imam, Murat, repeated one balmy May afternoon, when we visited him to ask whether my father could count on his support for the upcoming election. 'Of course, of course we will support you, Zafo,' Murat said. 'You need money, though. Can't do these things without money.'

After selling the house to Arian's parents, Murat's family had moved out of our neighbourhood and rented a small flat near the cemetery. The flat was cramped, with furniture piled up like a barricade. I recognized the same green polyester curtains with printed flowers and butterflies. The bookshelf had been removed to make space for a colour television. On the floor there were scattered copies of the Koran in different languages, and several pairs of shoes wrapped in newspaper, because Murat still did repairs in his spare time.

'I watched an interview with Berlusconi the other day,' he continued. 'You know Berlusconi. What a man. He looks so fit. Like a twenty-something. Always smiling. I watched an interview where Berlusconi told his life story. He started with construction. Then he played music on a boat. Then he bought a private television channel. One has to try different things; you never know what works. He said this himself. He's a businessman. Now other people take care of his business; he is in politics. If he knows how to make money, he knows how to win elections. Of course, he has many enemies, people are envious, they always are. But he can just ignore them; he's got his own television stations, his own newspapers. If you want to win, you need money. One always needs money. If you don't have money for yourself, you can't give it to others. Where's your money?'

'In my father's coat pocket,' my father joked.

Murat giggled.

'You will need a lot of money, Zafo, a lot of money,' he continued. 'I know how these things work. I've seen

it with the Arabs who make donations to the mosque.'
He paused to light a cigarette. 'When Flutura's factory
closed down' – he looked in the direction of his wife –
'I thought, what are we going to do? We're all going to
starve. I thought: Allah Qerim.* But Allah helps those
who help themselves. Then, fortunately, things took a
turn for the better. The firms started. You know what I
mean. The firms—'

'Xhaxhi Murat, I have a question,' I interrupted. 'Do
you actually sing "Allahu-akbar" from the minaret every
morning and afternoon, or is it a recording? We have a
bet going on at school. Some people say you do it every
day. I said it's a recording.'

'It's a recording, Leushka,' he answered. 'It's a recording. Now you owe me 10,000 leks.' He winked. Then he
turned to my father again with a serious look on his face.
'Sude, Populli, Kamberi, Vefa. The firms. You have to
put some money in, so you can get more money out. We
didn't have any money to put in. What could we do? We
tried to leave the country. We were on the *Vlora*, remember. All we got from our trip to Italy was a few bruises.
That's when we decided to sell the house. The kids were
sad to leave our street. We were sad too, we had good
neighbours. I built that house with my own hands. The
same hands that have made all your shoes.' He paused
briefly, and raised his hands, as if holding all the shoes
that he had made.

'One has to make sacrifices. The Bakis, our neighbours, they bought the house and paid us in cash. We
could do anything we liked with it. We could spend it,

* Allah is the most generous.

or we could . . .' He thought for a moment. 'What's the word? Invest it. We invested it. We didn't keep anything. What do you think the rest of Europe does with money? They invest it. They invest it so it can grow.'

My father was thinking. He had a vaguely guilty expression on his face. We had recently talked about the new firms at home. Sude, Kamberi, Populli, Vefa were the names of companies that had begun to appear, promising high rates of interest in return for savings. At the height of their activity, more than two thirds of the population was involved in investments that amounted to half of the country's GDP. Some of the companies also built hotels, restaurants, clubs and shopping centres. But my family was reluctant to deposit the cash we kept at home.

Murat blew out the smoke, stubbed out the cigarette he held between his fingers and lit another one.

'Zafo, listen to me,' he said with a serious air. 'You can't keep all your savings in a coat pocket. Times have changed. You need to invest it. Like the rest of Europe. What are you waiting for? We had all our savings in Kamberi, but they only gave ten per cent each month, so we switched the money to Populli, where you get thirty per cent. Then we discovered Sude, and they've been doubling our savings each month. Even more. Of course, we don't take it all out, we leave it there so it can grow. Like the rest of Europe. You have to save and invest. Save, and invest, so the money can grow.'

My father smiled, and nodded. Whenever we discussed the firms at home, my parents argued. My mother said we should forget about the coat pocket and put our savings in the firms. The rest of the family was reluctant.

'I don't understand how you can just deposit 100,000 leks in a firm,' my father said, 'and receive double that amount after a couple of months. It sounds like gambling.'

'We could try it with a small sum,' my mother replied, 'and see how it goes. We can take it slowly. I'm not saying we should sell our house or anything.'

'But where does all the money come from?' my father insisted. 'There are no factories here, there's no production.'

'Just because you're not used to it, it doesn't mean it's something dirty,' my mother argued. 'The firms make investments too. They have restaurants, clubs, hotels. The money circulates. People send money back from Italy, from Greece, a lot of immigrants help their parents. Most of it is from honest work. That's where the money comes from. They send it to their parents, their parents save it in the firms, and the firms keep it all safe together, invest it and pay people interest. Then, if you need it, if you need to make a purchase, they can give it to you or lend you money. It's not nuclear science. You have a university diploma. What's there not to understand?'

'What *I* don't understand,' Nini joined in, 'is what happens if everyone demands their money back at the same time? How can the firms pay everyone?' This last remark proved especially irritating to my mother. 'Why should people all ask for money at the same time?' she replied. 'Why should they want it all back? It's not like you can spend it all at once. Why would you prefer to keep your money under your mattress rather than in a firm?'

'Why would you keep your money in your father's pocket?' Murat also repeated to my father. 'My family, we're doing okay now. One day we may be able to buy our house back. *Positive thinking,*' he said in English. 'Like the rest of Europe. We were never taught *positive thinking.* I tell you, that's our problem.'

In the end, *positive thinking* won. We did not sell our house, but we did 'invest' most of our savings in one of the firms, Populli, whose full name was Demokracia Popullore (Popular Democracy). My grandmother never got used to it; she kept confusing the firm with Fronti Demokratik (Democratic Front), the local council unit from which we'd received our food vouchers before 1990. 'Did you get our interest from the Democratic Front?' she asked my father at the end of the first trimester, when he returned from Populli's offices with the interest on the savings he had deposited. 'I did,' he replied. 'It's all in the pocket.'

Positive thinking also won with regard to my father's election as an MP. He obtained more than sixty per cent of the vote. This was the only success he recorded in his short career as an MP. The rest of the months spent in parliament were an unmitigated failure. He soon discovered he had neither the fearless instinct of a leader nor the calculated patience of an adviser. He lacked party discipline. He hesitated to make decisions but was unwilling to endorse those of others. He had neither the ambition to guide, nor the inclination to follow.

It was a cursed time to become an MP. The elections that year ended up being some of the most contested in the history of the country. The socialist opposition accused the sitting government of fraud. They did not recognize the result, and never took up their seats in parliament. The country was flooded with international observers, diplomatic mediators and political advisers.

It was also flooded with financial experts who specialized in popularizing technical names in English for problems they considered in need of urgent solutions: *emerging markets, investor confidence, governance structures, transparency to fight corruption, transitional reforms.* The only technical term they failed to popularize was the one for the 'firms' to which the overwhelming majority of my fellow-countrymen had entrusted their savings: *pyramid schemes.* These had started to emerge in the early nineties, to compensate for the country's underdeveloped financial sector, and in the context of an informal credit market based on family ties and supported by emigrant remittances. After the United Nations suspended sanctions to the former Yugoslavia in 1995, there were fewer opportunities for smuggling and more people sitting on cash, which meant that the pyramid companies could promise increasingly high interest rates in return for deposits. The 1996 elections compounded the problem: several of the firms donated to the campaign of the governing Democratic Party, raising their profile and contributing to the general hype about investing in order to profit *like the rest of Europe.*

A few months later, it emerged that these pyramid schemes were unable to keep up with their promised high-interest payments. They all became insolvent. More than half of the population, including my family, lost their savings. People accused the government of colluding with the owners of the companies and took to the streets to demand their money back. The protests, which started in the south, with its strong traditional base of Socialist Party support, soon extended to the rest of the country. Looting, civilian assaults on military garrisons and an unprecedented wave of emigration followed. More than two thousand people lost their lives. These events are recorded in the history books as the Albanian Civil War. For us, it is enough to mention the year: 1997.

21.

1997

How does one write about civil war? Below is what I wrote in my diary between January and April 1997.

1 January 1997

I don't know why people always try to convince me that a new year will bring a new life. Even the tree lights are recycled. Even the fireworks are the same as the year before.

9 January

We had a test in Electro-technics.* I got 10.

14 January

School is useless. I don't enjoy it. But it's the end of term, and this year is the last. I need to focus on the grades. I spent the whole day on Maths and Physics.

* A compulsory subject in secondary school focused on machines and engineering, a remnant of the Soviet-oriented curriculum.

1997

27 January 1997

Sude failed.* The government has frozen the accounts of all the other firms. There are protests in the south. I miss K. I think I'm falling in love with him. He ignores me, though.

7 February

It's dark and I'm in bed listening to the new Metallica album. I bet someone is going to come and complain it's too loud.

10 February

Gjallica failed.† People are demanding their money back. There has been some unrest in Vlora.‡ The protesters want the government to resign.

13 February

We did an event with the Mule in school, for Valentine's Day. There were visitors from the French embassy, I didn't understand why. K. was wearing a tracksuit, like he

* One of the first pyramid schemes to collapse.
† Another pyramid scheme, especially widespread in the south of the country.
‡ A town in the south of the country, traditionally left-leaning.

275

couldn't be bothered. He asked what my father thinks of the political situation. I told him he signed some motion in parliament asking for the government to resign. K.'s father is dead. He died in mysterious circumstances in the early nineties. He used to be a Sigurimi agent. So annoying.

14 February

[Very long love letter to K. which he will never receive and never know was written]

15 February

We won the national Soros debate. The motion was 'Open societies require open borders.'

24 February

I went for the Physics Olympiad today. I looked at the problems, spent three hours inside, then wrote a poem about boredom.

25 February

The political situation continues to be tense. The students in Vlora are on a hunger strike. The motion Babi*

* An affectionate term for 'Dad' in Albanian.

signed with thirteen other MPs was published in all the newspapers. It made a big splash. They were accused by the party of being 'red opportunists'.

There will be a vote in parliament to confirm Berisha* as president on 9 March. The European Union held a meeting yesterday and declared their support for him. Babi says that the signatories of the motion have written that they are pro-Europe so this puts them in a difficult position. Since the EU is supporting Berisha, they would consider the open opposition to him 'destabilizing'. I told him that if he votes in favour of Berisha, he's a coward. He says politics is complicated. I think people should do what they think is right, not what the circumstances dictate.

26 February

I didn't do any homework today. Tomorrow we're going to boycott school in solidarity with the hunger strike in Vlora. Everyone is very excited to miss classes.

27 February

The headteacher didn't object to the boycott but said that to avoid disciplinary repercussions on him personally,

* Sali Berisha (1944–), a cardiologist and former Party member, was one of the historic leaders of the student movement that overthrew socialism in the nineties. He was the head of the Democratic Party of Albania for which my father was an MP, and which was in government at the time when the events took place.

we must present a petition signed by the whole school. We drafted this: 'In solidarity with the students in Vlora, and while distancing ourselves from the acts of violence of the last few weeks, we declare that we are going to boycott classes indefinitely.' Not everyone signed.

When I went home in the afternoon, the secretary of the youth league of the Democratic Party called to ask if I knew who had organized the walkout. I said I didn't know anything, it was all spontaneous, and we had no leaders. Then he said that if we wanted an extra holiday, they could fix this, but what we had done was very unpleasant. I replied it wasn't only done to get a holiday. He asked if I knew any of the names of the organizers. I said it's everyone. Then he asked if there were other people like me, close to the party, who could convince the others to return to school. I said I wasn't planning on convincing anyone to go back. Why are you so keen on protest, he said, your mum is in the party, your dad is an MP, your party is in government, when the prime minister resigns what are you going to eat, your own shit? I didn't give names. Do I look like a spy or what?

28 February

K. was annoyed that the article on school boycotts was on page five of *Koha Jonë*,* he said it should have been on page two. Most of the time he ignores me, but we had a nice chat today. He joked that of the people who go to school, eighty per cent can't speak proper Albanian, ten

* A left-leaning newspaper critical of the government.

per cent can speak Albanian but don't read newspapers, and five per cent read newspapers but don't understand them. He's nice as a friend. I don't think it was a good idea to fall in love with him. He's weird.

There were more phone calls from the youth league to put pressure on me to support the party in school. What's the point? Power has slipped away; they can't hold on to it with strands of hair.

1 March

Nine people died in Vlora during fights with the police. Babi received a phone call at 1 a.m. last night to summon him to an extraordinary session in parliament this morning. There has been more unrest in other towns. Many roads to the south are blocked by barricades. They say a 'civil war' is about to break out. I don't understand who would fight who. Everyone has lost their money. We were wise not to sell our house. Mami said it's fine to go and stand outside the school, but I need to shut up and not stir up the protests. I saw K. I also met up with Besa. She was going to a house party. This whole school boycott has been cool. We get to hang out a lot.

2 March

8 p.m.

It's weird. The prime minister resigned. Berisha has organized a round table with all the parties. Yesterday the

socialists agreed to a new government, led by the democrats. Today they withdrew from the agreement. The
south is in chaos. In Saranda and Himarë,* five weapons
warehouses were attacked and one naval warehouse was
blown up. All the convicts sentenced for murder have
escaped from the prison.

10 p.m.

I stopped writing to watch the news. Babi came back from
the parliament, then left again. He called while he was
on the way to Tirana to warn me not to leave the house.
He says it's not safe, and if people are angry with him,
they could retaliate on me. The president has declared a
state of emergency and transferred powers to the military.
Military rule sounds awful. You're not allowed to go out
in groups of more than four, there's a curfew, there can be
no organized activities, including for cultural purposes,
and soldiers are entitled to open fire if they see you break
the law. People from Vlora are marching to Tirana to over-
throw the government. Everyone around me whispers. I
got a phone call today from some Italian journalists I'd
met before in school. '*È grave*,' was all I could say. I'm
scared. It's all quiet here, though. Maybe it's just the words.
Military rule. State of emergency. They sound terrifying.

3 March

This morning we watched on television the presiden-
tial election farce. Of the 118 Democratic Party MPs,

* Towns in the south, traditionally left-leaning.

113 voted in favour, one against, four abstained. Babi was among the four. This morning in Tirana, the offices of *Koha Jonë* were burned down, and one journalist disappeared. I don't think the military is strong enough to take down the rebels. Last night at 2 a.m. the students in Vlora abandoned the hunger strike. They didn't know who to negotiate with. Different gangs have been assaulting military barracks, stealing weapons, looting shops. Our tanks are so old. I don't know if they even work.

I'm scared. Babi said I must categorically not leave the house, and if we find a way, they will send me to Italy. He heard that if you get good grades, there are university scholarships you can apply for. Bashkim Gazidede, the general in charge, announced the closure of schools today. He looks like he has no clue. There's a curfew between 8 p.m. and 7 a.m. Shops close at 3 p.m. Durrës is quiet. Maybe it's okay to leave. I'll miss it here. Everything is broken. I don't want to go.

4 March

1.40 p.m.

Mami just came back from a party meeting. She said the party is registering names to hand out guns so that people can defend themselves if they need to. Babi says he doesn't want a gun at home. He wouldn't use it anyway. Mami says it can be a deterrent. She says she would use it. Cars with Vlora number plates were seen in Durrës today. The government sent tanks to the south. Apparently, the tanks still work. The protesters fled to the mountains and all the journalists were evacuated by helicopter. I don't know what we're going to do if the protests reach Durrës. It's all fine here. I play chess and cards at home. I don't want to leave. I want to finish school.

5 March

I miss K. I want to see him before I leave. I don't want to leave. Leaving makes you forget things. It makes you forget people.

7 March

12.30 p.m.

The president said that if people surrender their weapons there will be a coalition government and an amnesty within 48 hours. There was a round table between the parties yesterday. I thought the atmosphere in parliament was civilized. I'm still not allowed outside the house. It's just me. Everyone else is going out. People from school are still meeting outside curfew hours. I don't know why I'm not allowed. I don't get it.

8.40 p.m.

European experts advised drafting a new constitution and holding new elections. They didn't say anything about whether the government can use any means necessary to suppress the insurrections.

8 March

There is an armistice for 48 hours. The rebels have taken Gjirokastra.* Lots of delegations coming and going.

9 March

The situation is improving. There was another round table yesterday and the parties agreed to a coalition government, new elections in June, amnesty for people who hand back their weapons within a week. Maybe I won't need to leave. I was allowed to go out this afternoon. The state of emergency should be over soon, and the school will reopen. I'm so happy. It was becoming unbearable. We got so close to war. I miss K. I hope everything will be fine with my exams. I'm looking forward to starting again. Babi is in such a state. You can't talk to him. I'm sorry his life in politics was so short. I don't know if he will run again in the new elections. I guess it depends on whether they restructure the party.

10 March

So boring. I haven't seen K. for ten days. Ten days.

* A left-leaning town in the south, the birthplace of Enver Hoxha.

11 March

Despite the agreement between parties, despite the technical government with a socialist prime minister, despite all the 'bilateral' efforts to solve the crisis, the protests continue. I just heard on the news that a few northern towns, Shkodra, Kukës and Tropoja, are now also in the hands of insurgents. Parliament approved an amnesty for people who return their weapons. I don't think it's stopped the lootings.

13 March

I can't see through my tears. I'm in my bedroom. The only thing I hear apart from my own sobbing is the thundering of machine guns. I don't even know where it comes from. I hear it everywhere. Nobody thought the mess would get here. Yesterday we heard blasts here and there, and helicopter sounds, but we didn't really think anything of it. There were rumours of troubles having reached Tirana and we assumed the noises we heard were echoes. Then I sat by the window in the kitchen and I saw people running around. All the men on our street were walking up the hill carrying weapons: some people had Kalashnikovs, some pistols, some were carrying barrel bombs. I saw our neighbour Ismail, he's so old, he walks with a stick. He was struggling to drag a big metallic thing on a wooden wheelbarrow. He said it was a medium-range RS-82 rocket. It made a scraping sound. People complimented him: Ismail, that looks great, have you got the launch pad too? He said he didn't have it, but maybe someone else would find it. You never know when you need a rocket, he said.

Later on, there were rumours of a new exodus; word spread that the boats in the port would carry people to Italy. Some managed to jump on the Adriatica passenger ferry, opened fire, and forced the captain to leave. I went in our bedroom and found Nini shaking. She said Babi is stuck in parliament, and there's probably a fight going on right now, the parliament is in flames. The phone line is broken. She was so pale.

Mami is at the beach with Lani, they went there this morning before things got out of control. They still haven't come back. I started to cry, then Besa came and said she was going out with her mother to check if they could find a boat in the port. Her mother asked Nini if she would let me go with them, but she refused. I cried even harder. Then I opened my mouth to say I wanted to go, but no sound would come out. I tried again. Nothing. I couldn't say anything.

I lost my voice. I haven't tried again. I don't know if I can speak any more. I don't want to try it in case my voice doesn't come out. There's so much noise around. All I can hear is Kalashnikovs. Donika came here to be with Nini. I don't understand why everyone is asking me to talk, to use my voice. What if it doesn't come out? I don't want to try it. Nini said that when Babi is back, they will send me to see a doctor. As soon as they ask me to speak, I get tears. I can't stop the tears. They just flow. I try to stop them, but I can't. I can't speak. I don't know what to do. I'm on my own now, and I want to try, but what if it doesn't come out? What if it's gone for good? If I cry, maybe it will come back.

14 March

9.50 a.m.

I can only hear machine guns. Mami and Lani left for Italy yesterday. A man came to tell us. They were at the beach and saw a boat stop at the pier and they jumped on it. The man who told us, he was at the pier too with his family, but he decided not to go. The people inside had Kalashnikovs, and they were shooting. Mami tried to convince him there was shooting everywhere so you might as well go to Italy, but he said his family was too scared. He said they are probably in a refugee camp in Bari now. I don't know if they made it, though, they haven't called. I don't know how they paid for the sailing. They had no money with them. They probably won't even be let out of the camp. They'll be kept there for two weeks and sent back. The phone started working again. Then it stopped. Now I think it works, but nobody's called. The roads are blocked but I think the television would report if someone died in parliament so I guess Babi is okay.

I still can't talk, though. I don't think my voice is back. I don't know if it will ever come back. Nini says to try and speak so that when Babi comes back he doesn't get a shock. She gave me Valium. She said it would help. It didn't do anything. She then gave me another one. I still can't speak. I haven't tried, but what if I try and my voice is gone for ever? Nini says the situation is not too bad. She says I need to be strong; I need to find some strength. I don't know when she thinks it will get really bad. My voice is gone. I'm feeling sleepy.

3.30 p.m.

Kalashnikovs have become like fireworks for New Year's Eve. They just go on and on and on. Day and night. Who could have predicted it? The state of emergency is backfiring. There's talk of bringing in NATO troops. I worry that it will make things worse, it will start massive bloodshed. Like the peacekeepers in Bosnia. Just wait for it. Nini is right, I probably need to get used to this. I'm trying. I get a shiver down my spine when I think about yesterday, people running around, cars driving at top speed, shooting on the street. Today is a bit better. I think I'm getting better at coping. It's like everyone has gone mad at the same time, they destroy everything.

Babi made it back from Tirana. He said the port has been completely destroyed. All the offices were burned. Very few shops are left standing and the owners are defending them with Kalashnikovs. I can only hear guns. The country is in the hands of gangsters. It's total anarchy. Nobody is even talking about political solutions any more. It's not about socialists versus democrats. Now all political powers are completely powerless. Nobody understands anything. It's like a whole country committing suicide. Just when it looked like things were getting better it all went downhill. Now that we are all falling from a precipice, there's no way back. It's so much worse than 1990. At least there was hope in democracy then. Now there is nothing, just a curse.

5 p.m.

I can't stand this. I'd rather go out and catch a bullet than just sit here. There is nobody to talk to. I always thought that if there was going to be a war, I would be strong. I never thought I would just keep crying. It's the waiting. The waiting strangles me.

Nini said to move my bed away from the window. We get lots of Kalashnikov bullets falling on the window sill. I don't know where they come from, but if they get shot not too far from here and they have retained most of their speed, they can kill. That's what she said. Just move the bed.

6 p.m.

These gunshots. It's like they explode in my head. I just can't stop the tears. Every time I try to speak, I get tears in my eyes instead.

15 March

Nini gave me more tranquillizers earlier. I just woke up. I'm feeling a bit better. I don't know if things are really bad or if it's my imagination that makes them worse. Now that Besa has also left, I don't have anyone to talk to. I can't talk anyway. I've heard fewer gunshots today. Apparently, there will be an international police force. I want to go back to school.

12.30 p.m.

I thought about killing myself but was sorry for Nini. It only lasted fifteen minutes. I need to find a new book to read.

8.50 p.m.

The afternoon was fine. Mami called earlier, for the first time. They're in a refugee camp in Bari. Babi is angry with her. He says she shouldn't have left without asking. Nini spoke to her then passed the phone to Babi, and he said nothing, just passed the phone to me, but I couldn't say anything. I haven't tried but I don't think I can talk. I don't think my voice is back. Mami said she just saw the boat and went on it. She was trying to save Lani. Nini said you don't take one child and leave the other. Babi swears he is never going to talk to her again.

16 March

I went out today. I left the house when Nini was sleeping. I couldn't stand it any more. I thought, if I'm killed, so what. I went to the top of the hill, to see the old Royal Palace. There's nothing left. The rails are broken. The tiles have been stolen. The flowers have all been plucked. The chandeliers are gone. The ceiling looks like it's about to fall on your head. When I was there, I tried to shout. My voice came out. I knew it was there, I just didn't want to use it. It was all so empty. Completely empty. There was no furniture left.

I started reading *War and Peace*. There are a lot of characters. It's like you get to know them. It's probably better to spend time with fictional characters than miss the real ones you will never see again. I've stopped thinking about school. I've stopped thinking about K.

17 March

Flamur killed himself. He was playing with a Tokarev TT-33 and he thought it wasn't loaded. His mother was there. He pulled the trigger and there was a bullet left inside. Just one. People on the street said they heard a blast, but I didn't hear anything. There are so many blasts. I only heard Shpresa screaming, like a dry roar, like an animal. She came out on the street, pulling her hair, she just lost it. She kept saying someone needed to go inside and cover him. That was the only thing she said. Go inside and cover him.

18 March

It's so much fun to hang out with Babi. We went to the shops together today. He does talk a lot, though. He also meets too many people, it takes ages. There were people outside today. Things looked a bit better. I think everything will be fine. I just need to be brave. Nini is so brave. I don't know how she does it. There's a cuckoo stuck inside our house. We keep looking for it, but we haven't found it. You can hear it, though, it's really loud. Nini says they bring bad luck.

19 March

I talked to Mami on the phone today. She said they're going to leave the camp soon. She found a job in Rome looking after some elderly woman who is paralysed. Mami says she will apply for political asylum. They give her food and lodging and 500,000 lire, and she can keep Lani with her. She says maybe after a while she will find a job as a maths tutor. Then she will apply for citizenship and get family reunification. She has no clue. She doesn't watch television. I saw a programme about Albanians in Italy. She's more likely to find a man than get citizenship. Babi still won't talk to her.

20 March

I couldn't write last night. We had a power cut at 5 p.m. and we only got the light back this morning. Then it went again, but I've just managed to find a candle. Yesterday there was nobody on the streets. The port is full of people trying to leave. There was such a crazy wind, it felt like it was going to lift the house up and hurl it away. I don't know where they think they're going with that wind. I finished *War and Peace*. Turgenev apparently wrote that it's got some things that are unbearable and others that are wonderful, and the wonderful ones dominate. I didn't find anything unbearable. By the end, I couldn't put it down. Babi said if Mami ever comes back he will take her to court. He says he will never forgive her. There's still fighting. My head is exploding. It's like there's something inside my head but I haven't figured out what it is. It's so noisy in my head. It's so noisy outside. There are no people on the streets but it's really noisy. The gunshots never stop.

25 March

I don't think the school will reopen this year. I have no idea what will happen to my final exams. So much for starting university. I haven't even decided what I want to study. Soon there will be foreign soldiers: Italian, Greek, Spanish, Polish. International peacekeepers. I guess it's going to be good for the economy, good for prostitution.

29 March

A boat sailing from Vlora to Italy sank last night near Otranto. It carried around one hundred people and was hit by an Italian military vessel which was patrolling the waters. The Italians made a manoeuvre to try and stop the boat and it capsized. There are around eighty bodies dispersed at sea, they're still searching, mostly women and children, some as young as three months old. Our prime minister had signed an agreement with Prodi* the day before, he agreed to the use of force to ensure Italian control of territorial waters, including hitting vessels

* Romano Prodi, then the Italian prime minister (centre-left).

at sea as a way of sending them back. I'm not taking Valium any more, I'm taking valerian, it's meant to be milder.

6 April

The education minister has come up with some ridiculous idea called 'Schooling through television'. They're not going to reopen the schools. It's not safe. They will give classes on television so that 'nobody misses out'. I don't know what will happen with the final exams. Maybe they'll hold those on television.

22.

Philosophers Have Only Interpreted the World; the Point is to Change It

The schools remained closed until late June 1997, when they opened for a few days to enable final-year students like me to take their exams. International peacekeeping troops had arrived a few weeks before, in an effort to stabilize the country – not so much to stop the violence as to help the state regain the monopoly on it. Foreign soldiers were scattered everywhere, wearing the same green uniforms and grey helmets, distinguished only by the colour of the flags sewn on to their sleeves. Operation 'Alba' ('Dawn') was led by Italy; the second time since the Second World War that a 'civilizing' mission had brought Italian soldiers to Albanian soil.

Soon there would be new elections. There would also be a referendum to decide whether the country should remain a republic or restore the monarchy. Descendants of the king, that same King Zog whose ruling powers were briefly transferred to my great-grandfather as the country became a fascist protectorate, returned to try their hand at managing the country's collapse. Having fled Albania carrying gold from the national bank in 1939, they bought an advertising slot on television to campaign in favour of voting for the monarchy. Every evening, a split screen showed images of Albania in flames alongside photos of landmarks in Oslo, Copenhagen and Stockholm. Written in blue under the photos one could read: 'Norway: Constitutional Monarchy'; 'Denmark: Constitutional Monarchy'; 'Sweden: Constitutional Monarchy'.

The advert had the instant capacity to ruin my grandmother's mood, more so than the thundering of Kalashnikovs outside the window. 'Zog!' she would snort. 'Don't tell me about Zog. I went to his wedding. Zog! What is this madness? I can't believe it!'

My father's interventions were less emotionally charged but just as perplexing. 'Sweden,' he would say each time the advert appeared, without explaining. 'Olof Palme. Leushka, have you ever heard of Olof Palme? He was a good man. You should read about him. He was a social democrat. A real one. You would have liked him. Olof Palme was a good man.' Years later, I learned more about Olof Palme, his fierce critiques of both the United States and the Soviet Union, his support for decolonization, and his assassination. Only then did it occur to me that all his life my father had admired politicians only once they were dead.

The night before my last test, in physics, I sat in front of an atlas, trying to memorize the capitals of the world. I found it difficult to motivate myself to go over the physics book again. I was exhausted. I had been studying without interruption every night for months, the same way I would have done during the day if school had been open. At night, the sound of Kalashnikovs became sporadic. You could still hear dogs barking; you could even hear the occasional cricket in the garden. Power cuts became more predictable: either there was going to be electricity for the night, or there wasn't. By midnight, you knew. In the dark, life almost returned to normal, except for my grandmother stirring in her sleep and then waking up to warn me that if I studied too much, I would make myself sick. That bit was unusual: she'd never before told me to stop reading.

In school, we were informed that anything we did during the exams was unlikely to make a difference. Final marks would most likely be assigned to match one's predicted grades. I found it difficult to let go. I wanted to be prepared for all contingencies. There was no guarantee that all of the exams would take place, or that the advice we were given would remain the same. I might be about to repeat the year. Or I might be about to finish school without ever having learned the capitals of the world.

On the day of the last exam, my teacher, Kujtim, opened the envelope containing the list of questions sent by the Ministry of Education. There was a solemn silence in the school sports hall, where single desks had been placed one metre apart to prevent us from cheating. He read out what we called the 'exam theses' with the gravity one would expect in ordinary circumstances. His tone made me think that, despite the extraordinary context, I had been right to take the preparation seriously. He read out: 'A space shuttle which flies towards Earth with velocity V emits light signals in the direction in which it is flying. What—'

Before Kujtim could finish reading the question, the headteacher walked into the hall. Kujtim took his glasses off, and waited. The headteacher whispered something in Kujtim's ear, and he whispered back, then the headteacher nodded, and left. Kujtim stared out of the window, coughed, swallowed and, without putting his glasses back on, started reading again: 'A space shuttle which flies towards Earth with velocity V emits light signals in the direction in which it is flying. What is the velocity of the photons in relation to Earth?'

When he had finished with the questions, he turned to the blackboard and filled both sides of it with graphs and equations. Then he turned to us, holding the A4 sheet close to his face like a shield. 'Here are the answers,' he said, surrounded by a cloud of chalk dust. 'Nobody is going to fail. If your predicted grade is 6, you must only copy two answers. If it's 8, you need to copy three. If it's 10, you have to copy all four. Don't try to answer them yourself. The headteacher has received an anonymous phone call. A bomb may have been placed in the school, and may explode in two hours. Two hours, he was told. The police have already been to search for it; they can't see anything. It could be one of your friends playing a joke. You don't need to panic. But you do need to be quick.'

That was my last exam. The school did not explode; it was a false alarm. When I reported the episode back home, my father laughed – he laughed deliriously, banging on the table repeatedly with his open hand and wiping the tears that rolled from his cheeks. 'A bomb!' he screamed. 'A bomb! I told you to sleep, Leushka! I told you it was going to be a formality! A bomb! That's genius! A bomb! And they let you carry on! Masters! Genius!'

In the afternoon, I fretted that the silky turquoise dress I had bought for my end-of-school party was too long, and I couldn't find a seamstress to help me adjust the length at short notice. 'It's already way above your knees,' my grandmother said when I tried it on. 'I've got the curtain in my eyes,' she added apologetically, referring to her cataract, 'I can't do anything.'

It was the kind of small clothing alteration my mother specialized in. I resented that she wasn't there. I had only ever worn trousers in school, and I wanted to mark the occasion. My father rolled his eyes with his usual helpless air, a vaguely guilty look passing across his face. At least he had the grace not to suggest the dress was already short.

The next day, we held our end-of-school party in a romantic hotel by the beach called Hotel California. It belonged to the main local gang, the same gang who had smuggled my mother to Italy, and who controlled most of the looted weapons. Hotel California was surrounded by gunmen who regularly fired bullets into the air, both to warn rival gangs that the hotel was well defended, and to contribute to the festive atmosphere inside the main hall, following the old Balkan tradition of shooting during weddings. The party did resemble a wedding: the boys wore suits and ties, and all the girls except me turned up in long evening dresses. The waiters brought out meze throughout the day, and the line dancing continued until about 4 p.m., when the gun men came inside to inform us that the curfew was about to start. They played 'Hotel California', as a finale, and as we packed our things to leave the hall we sang, 'Welcome to the Hotel California! Such a lovely place, such a lovely face!' with guns pointing at us. 'I hate it,' a girl in my class said when we were out of the door. 'I hate this heat! Look what it's done to my make-up, it's all dripping on my face, like I'm some dead person covered in mud.'

When I think about the end of school now, I remember feeling relieved that we got away with the exams so lightly, and resentful that my nights preparing for them had been wasted. My effort to retain order in that one dimension of my life, despite everything else going on around me, now seems like its own kind of pathology.

There was so much I had come to accept during those months. I accepted that my father would be regularly stuck in parliament without knowing when he would make it home, if he would make it at all. I accepted my mother's enthusiastic updates about the fate of her Italian work permit, and her comical reassurances that she didn't at all mind cleaning strangers' bathrooms for a while; she said it took her mind off politics. I accepted losing my voice. I accepted that I might have to resort to expressing my thoughts in writing from now on. I accepted that my childhood friend, Flamur, who had once killed a cat in front of me, killed himself in front of his mother while playing with that Tokarev TT-33. I accepted the clinking sound of Kalashnikov bullets falling on my window sill. I learned to fall asleep with them. I accepted bombs during the exam, and guns at the school prom.

I learned to live with the feeling of the precariousness of my existence. I accepted the meaninglessness of performing everyday actions like eating, or reading, or going to sleep, when you don't know if, the next day, you will be able to do the same. I accepted the anonymity of all the tragedies unfolding before me, and how it suddenly became pointless to find out what kind of death a neighbour or relative had suffered – intentional or accidental, solitary or surrounded by family, violent or peaceful, comical or dignified.

I accepted the different explanations of what had caused this or that, how the international community had warned about such-and-such decision, how the Balkans had long had an explosive history – how one must factor in the ethnic and religious divisions that pervaded that corner of the world, and the legacy of socialism too. I accepted the story I heard on foreign media: that the Albanian civil war could be explained not by the collapse of a flawed financial system but by the long-standing animosities between different ethnic groups, the Ghegs in the north and the Tosks in the south. I accepted it despite its absurdity, despite the fact that I didn't know what *I* counted as, whether both or neither. I accepted it although my mother was a Gheg and my father a Tosk, and throughout their married life only their political and class divisions had ever mattered, never the accents with which they spoke. I accepted it, as we all did, as we accepted the liberal *road map* we had followed like a religious calling, as we accepted that its plan could be disrupted only by outside factors – like the backwardness of our own community norms – and never be beset by its own contradictions.

I accepted that history repeats itself. I remember thinking: is this what my parents experienced? Is this what they wanted me to experience? Is this what losing hope looks like, becoming indifferent to categorization, to nuance, to making distinctions, to assessing the plausibility of different interpretations, to truth?

It was like being back in 1990. There was the same chaos, the same sense of uncertainty, the same collapse of the state, the same economic disaster. But with one difference. In 1990, we had nothing but hope. In 1997, we lost that too. The future looked bleak. And yet I had to act as if there was still a future, and I had to make decisions featuring myself in it. I had to decide what I wanted to be as a grown-up, and choose my topic of study at university. I found the choice excruciatingly difficult. I found it hard to assess the options, to imagine myself in one kind of life rather than another, and to think about my future in each. I found it impossible to think about isolated fields of study like law, medicine, economics, physics, engineering, about what they were and how one could become an expert. I kept reflecting on their shared value, whether there was anything they had in common, and what purpose they all served. I wondered about their role in helping us make sense of this thing called history, which we take to be more than a chaotic sequence of characters and events, and on which we project meaning, a sense of direction, and the possibility of learning about the past and using that knowledge to shape the future. I didn't know what to pick. All I had were doubts.

But the doubts helped me decide. I announced the outcome of the decision over dinner with my father and grandmother one evening, while eating some olives. My father was alarmed.

'Philosophy,' he said. 'Philosophy, like the Mule?'

'The Mule?' I asked, surprised that he had brought up my teacher.

'Philosophy. Marxism,' he insisted. 'That's what the Mule studied. Same thing. Even Marx knew it wasn't worth it. Do you know what he said? He said that philosophers have only interpreted the world. The point is to change it. He said it in the *Eleventh Thesis on Feuerbach*. Do you want to be like the Mule? Not many truths came out of Marx, but that may well have been one.'

My father recited the *Eleventh Thesis on Feuerbach* as if he were reciting a verse from the Koran or the Bible. Thou shalt not covet. Thou shalt not study philosophy.

'I've never heard that sentence before,' I replied. 'And anyway, you can change the world by studying philosophy,' I continued, still chewing on an olive.

'That's Marx's point,' my father replied. 'Philosophy is dead. Philosophers come up with theories, one theory after the other, but they all contradict each other. There's just no way of telling who is right and who is wrong. You should pick an exact science, something that can be verified or falsified, like chemistry or physics. Or pick a subject that gives you skills you can use to improve people's lives. Like becoming a doctor, or a lawyer, anything really.'

'Of course, there is a way,' I argued, still thinking about my father's quote.

He looked perplexed.

'You said that the point is not to interpret the world, but to change it. Perhaps Marx meant that the philosophical theory that changes the world in the right direction is the right one,' I mumbled, twisting my tongue around the olive in my mouth, trying to get the stone out.

'You're already talking like a Marxist,' he said. 'They think they know what the right direction is.'

This second reference to Marx was more alarming than the first. Whenever my parents said that 'so-and-so was a Marxist' or that 'so-and-so is still a Marxist', what they meant was anything from 'so-and-so is stupid' to 'one ought not to trust them' to 'so-and-so is a criminal.' Being called a Marxist was never meant as praise.

'Philosophy is not a profession!' he exclaimed. 'The most you will end up as is a secondary school teacher, explaining the history of the Party to apathetic sixteen-year-olds.'

'What Party?' I said, munching more olives. 'There is no Party. We don't do any history of the Party.'

'Whatever it is that the Mule teaches these days,' he conceded, correcting himself.

'I didn't bring up Marx.' I said, starting to raise my voice. 'You did. That's all you know about philosophy. You're all obsessed with Marxism. Maybe Marxism is dead.' At that point, my voice began faltering. 'But there is so much more to philosophy. I don't know anything about Marxism. I can see how it ruined your lives. But—'

'It would have ruined yours too, had you been born a few years earlier,' my father interrupted.

'It's ruined enough as it is. Marxism isn't going to make it worse.'

My grandmother stood up to collect the dinner plates, then turned to my father, as if having second thoughts. 'You didn't study what you wanted at university,' she said calmly. 'Why do you want to inflict the same on your daughter? What's the point of doing to your child something you yourself resented all your life?'

Her tone was in striking contrast to her words. She spoke without enthusiasm, as if she was helping diagnose an illness rather than discussing options for the future. I decided to remain silent.

'I don't understand,' my father said nervously. 'They never studied any philosophy at school. Not even Marx. How am I going to ask people to lend me money for her to study? To study what? PHI-LO-SO-PHY. People will think we have lost our minds. What does she know about philosophy?' There was anger in his voice.

That night, we made a pact. They promised to let me study philosophy, and I promised to stay away from Marx. My father let me go. I left Albania and crossed the Adriatic. I waved goodbye to my father and my grand-mother on the shore and travelled to Italy on a boat that sailed over thousands of drowned bodies, bodies that had once carried souls more hopeful than mine, but who met fates less fortunate. I never returned.

Epilogue

Each year, I begin my Marx courses at the London School of Economics by telling students that many people think of socialism as a theory of material relations, class struggle or economic justice but that, in reality, something more fundamental animates it. Socialism, I tell them, is above all a theory of human freedom, of how to think about progress in history, of how we adapt to circumstances, but also try to rise above them. Freedom is not sacrificed only when others tell us what to say, where to go, how to behave. A society that claims to enable people to realize their potential, but fails to change the structures that prevent everyone from flourishing, is also oppressive. And yet, despite all the constraints, we never lose our inner freedom: the freedom to do what is right.

My father and my grandmother did not live to see what became of my studies. After quitting his career as an MP, my father was thrust from one private employer to another, each time blaming the dismissal on his poor English and, increasingly, his rudimentary computer skills. To facilitate his job searches, the family moved to a flat in the capital, close to the old Botanical Gardens, now one of the most polluted areas in the country. His asthma deteriorated. One summer evening, shortly after his sixtieth birthday, he had a violent asthma attack. He rushed to the window and opened it to breathe but was wrapped in a cloud of carbon monoxide and dust. The ambulance found him dead.

My mother was in Italy when it happened. My parents had reconciled, but she worked there seasonally as a carer or cleaner to help offset some of our new debts, while her siblings in Albania chased their old confiscated properties. Those efforts, which Nini had always deemed a 'waste of time', came to fruition a few months after her death, following that of my father. A large chunk of coastal land was sold to an Arab property developer, and our fortunes changed overnight.

I no longer needed to count my last pennies until the next scholarship instalment. I could enjoy meals out and drink late in bars discussing politics with my new university friends. Many of those friends were self-declared socialists – Western socialists, that is. They spoke about Rosa Luxemburg, Leon Trotsky, Salvador Allende or Ernesto 'Che' Guevara as secular saints. It occurred to me that they were like my father in this respect: the only revolutionaries they considered worthy of admiration had been murdered. These icons showed up on posters, T-shirts and coffee cups, much like the way photos of Enver Hoxha would show up in people's living rooms when I was growing up. When I pointed this out, my friends wanted to know more about my country. But they did not think that my stories from the eighties were in any way significant to their political beliefs. Sometimes, my appropriating the label of socialist to describe both my experiences and their commitments was considered a dangerous provocation. We used to go to a large open-air concert in Rome for 1 May, and I could not help but reminisce about the parades of my childhood on

Workers' Day. 'What you had was not *really* socialism,' they would say, barely concealing their irritation.

My stories about socialism in Albania and references to all the other socialist countries against which our socialism had measured itself were, at best, tolerated as the embarrassing remarks of a foreigner still learning to integrate. The Soviet Union, China, the German Democratic Republic, Yugoslavia, Vietnam, Cuba; there was nothing socialist about them either. They were seen as the deserving losers of a historical battle that the real, authentic bearers of that title had yet to join. My friends' socialism was clear, bright and in the future. Mine was messy, bloody and of the past.

And yet, the future that they sought, and that which socialist states had once embodied, found inspiration in the same books, the same critiques of society, the same historical characters. But, to my surprise, they treated this as an unfortunate coincidence. Everything that went wrong on my side of the world could be explained by the cruelty of our leaders, or the uniquely backward nature of our institutions. They believed there was little for them to learn. There was no risk of repeating the same mistakes, no reason to ponder what had been achieved, and why it had been destroyed. Their socialism was characterized by the triumph of freedom and justice; mine by their failure. Their socialism would be brought about by the right people, with the right motives, under the right circumstances, with the right combination of theory and practice. There was only one thing to do about mine: forget it.

But I was reluctant to forget. It is not that I felt nostalgic. It is not that I romanticized my childhood. It is not that the concepts I had grown up with were so deeply rooted in me that it was impossible to disentangle myself. But if there was one lesson to take away from the history of my family, and of my country, it was that people never make history under circumstances they choose. It is easy to say, 'What you had was not the real thing', applying that to socialism or liberalism, to any complex hybrid of ideas and reality. It releases us from the burden of responsibility. We are no longer complicit in moral tragedies created in the name of great ideas, and we don't have to reflect, apologize and learn.

'We are doing a reading group on *Das Kapital*,' a friend told me one day. 'If you join it, you will learn about real socialism.' And so I did. When I read the opening pages of the preface, it felt a bit like hearing French: a foreign language I had been taught as a child but rarely practised. I remembered many of the keywords – capitalists, workers, landlords, value, profit – and they echoed inside my head in the voice and simplified formulations of my teacher Nora, adapted for schoolchildren. Individuals, Marx wrote in the opening pages, 'are dealt with only in so far as they are the personifications of economic categories, embodiments of particular class relations and class interests'. But, for me, behind every personification of an economic category, there was the flesh and blood of a real person. Behind the capitalist and the landlord there were my great-grandfathers; behind the workers there were the Roma who worked at the port; behind the peasants, the people with whom my grandmother was sent to work in the fields when my grandfather went to prison, and about whom she spoke condescendingly. It was impossible to finish reading and just move on.

My mother finds it difficult to understand why I teach and research Marx, why I write about the dictatorship of the proletariat. She sometimes reads my articles and finds them baffling. She has learned to weather awkward questions from relatives. Do I really believe these ideas are convincing? Or feasible? How is it possible? Mostly, she keeps her criticisms to herself. Only once did she draw attention to a cousin's remarks that my grand-father did not spend fifteen years locked up in prison so that I would leave Albania to defend socialism. We both laughed awkwardly, then paused and changed the topic. It left me feeling like someone who is involved in murder, as if the mere association with the ideas of a system that destroyed so many lives in my family were enough to make me the person responsible for pulling the trig-ger. Deep down, I knew this was what she thought. I always wanted to clarify, but didn't know where to start. I thought that it would take a book to answer.

This is that book. At first, it was going to be a philo-sophical book about the overlapping ideas of freedom in the liberal and socialist traditions. But when I started writing, just like when I started reading *Das Kapital*, ideas turned into people; the people who made me who I am. They loved and fought each other, they had different conceptions of themselves, and of their obligations to other people. They were, as Marx writes, the product of social relations for which they were not responsible, but they still tried to rise above them. They thought they'd succeeded. But when their aspirations became reality, their dreams turned into my disillusionment. We lived in the same place, but in different worlds. These worlds overlapped only briefly; when they did, we saw things through different eyes. My family equated socialism with denial: the denial of who they wanted to be, of the right to make mistakes and learn from them, to explore the world on one's own terms. I equated liberalism with broken promises, the destruction of solidarity, the right to inherit privilege, turning a blind eye to injustice.

In some ways, I have gone full circle. When you see a system change once, it's not that difficult to believe that it can change again. Fighting cynicism and political apathy turns into what some might call a moral duty; to me, it is more of a debt that I feel I owe to all the people of the past who sacrificed everything because *they* were not apathetic, *they* were not cynical, *they* did not believe that things fall into place if you just let them take their course. If I do nothing, their efforts will have been wasted, their lives will have been meaningless.

My world is as far from freedom as the one my parents tried to escape. Both fall short of that ideal. But their failures took distinctive forms, and without being able to understand them, we will remain for ever divided. I wrote my story to explain, to reconcile, and to continue the struggle.

Acknowledgements

This book was written mostly from a cupboard in Berlin during the Covid-19 pandemic. It turned out to be the perfect location to hide from the children I was supposed to home-school (my own) and to muse about my grandmother's words: 'When it's difficult to see clearly into the future, you have to think about what you can learn from the past.' Thank you to my mother, Doli, and my brother, Lani, for being willing to revisit that past with me, for letting me share *their* stories in *my* words, and for always telling the truth.

Thank you to my editor, Casiana Ionita, for being the first person to ask if I had ever thought about bringing my academic writing to a wide audience, and to my agent, Sarah Chalfant, for giving me the confidence to pursue a project which ended up being very different from how it was initially envisaged. Without their intelligence, questions, comments, patience and good humour at various stages, the book would not exist.

Thank you to Alane Mason at Norton and to Edward Kirke at Penguin for excellent editorial suggestions on the manuscript as a whole, and to the incredibly talented and passionate teams that turned the book into material reality: Sarah Chalfant, Emma Smith and Rebecca Nagel at the Wylie Agency; Casiana Ionita, Edward Kirke, Sarah Day, Richard Duguid, Thi Dinh, Ania Gordon, Olga Kominek, Ingrid Matts and Corina Romonti at

Penguin Press; and Alane Mason, Mo Crist, Bonnie Thompson, Beth Steidle, Jessica Murphy and Sarahmay Wilkinson at Norton.

Thank you to Chris Armstrong, Rainer Forst, Bob Goodin, Stefan Gosepath, Chandran Kukathas, Tamara Jugov, Catherine Lu, Valentina Nicolini, Claus Offe, David Owen, Mario Reale, Paola Rodano and David Runciman for excellent comments on early drafts of the book, and for their ongoing support and friendship.

Thank you to my friends from Albania, and from the 'other' side of the Iron Curtain more generally, who shared their childhoods with me, helped me reconstruct events and impressions, and gave me praise and criticism in due proportion. I am especially grateful to Uran Ferizi and Shqiponja Telhaj (my unofficial editors!) and to Odeta Barbullushi, Migena Bregu, Eris Duro, Borana Lushaj, Xhoana Papakostandini and the Secret Pioneer for excellent comments on the manuscript and for invaluable comparative perspectives both geographical and political.

Thank you also to Joni Baboci, Tsveti Georgieva, Anila Kadija, Bledar Kurti, Viliem Kurtulaj, Gjyze Magrini, Adlej Pici, Roland Qafoku, Fatos Rosa, Flora Sula and Neritan Sejamini for help with different aspects of the project, or for sending material from Tirana at short notice even during the lockdowns.

Thank you to my wonderfully supportive colleagues and my brilliant students at the London School of Economics for many inspiring conversations on freedom, to all the members of the Normative Orders colloquium in Frankfurt for an excellent early discussion of my ideas for the book, and to the Leverhulme Trust and the

Humboldt Foundation for funding the research leave that enabled me to write these pages.

Thank you to my family: Jonathan (another unofficial editor!), Arbien, Rubin, Hana, Doli, Lani and Noana, for sharing all the torments and joys of this book, and for everything else.

My father, Zafo, and my grandmother, Nini, have been with me all along. Zafo would have found a joke to make at this point, probably about me claiming to be a Marxist while saying 'thank you' so many times. Nini taught me how to live, and how to think about living. I miss her every day. The book is dedicated to her memory.

ALLEN LANE
an imprint of
PENGUIN BOOKS

Also Published

Emma Smith, *Portable Magic: A History of Books and their Readers*

Kris Manjapra, *Black Ghost of Empire: The Long Death of Slavery and the Failure of Emancipation*

Andrew Scull, *Desperate Remedies: Psychiatry and the Mysteries of Mental Illness*

James Bridle, *Ways of Being: Beyond Human Intelligence*

Eugene Linden, *Fire and Flood: A People's History of Climate Change, from 1979 to the Present*

Cathy O'Neil, *The Shame Machine: Who Profits in the New Age of Humiliation*

Peter Hennessy, *A Duty of Care: Britain Before and After Covid*

Gerd Gigerenzer, *How to Stay Smart in a Smart World: Why Human Intelligence Still Beats Algorithms*

Halik Kochanski, *Resistance: The Undergroud War in Europe, 1939-1945*

Joseph Sassoon, *The Global Merchants: The Enterprise and Extravagance of the Sassoon Dynasty*

Clare Chambers, *Intact: A Defence of the Unmodified Body*

Nina Power, *What Do Men Want?: Masculinity and Its Discontents*

Ivan Jablonka, *A History of Masculinity: From Patriarchy to Gender Justice*

Thomas Halliday, *Otherlands: A World in the Making*

Sofi Thanhauser, *Worn: A People's History of Clothing*

Sebastian Mallaby, *The Power Law: Venture Capital and the Art of Disruption*

David J. Chalmers, *Reality+: Virtual Worlds and the Problems of Philosophy*

Jing Tsu, *Kingdom of Characters: A Tale of Language, Obsession and Genius in Modern China*

Lewis R. Gordon, *Fear of Black Consciousness*

Leonard Mlodinow, *Emotional: The New Thinking About Feelings*

Kevin Birmingham, *The Sinner and the Saint: Dostoevsky, a Crime and Its Punishment*

Roberto Calasso, *The Book of All Books*

Marit Kapla, *Osebol: Voices from a Swedish Village*

Malcolm Gaskill, *The Ruin of All Witches: Life and Death in the New World*

Mark Mazower, *The Greek Revolution: 1821 and the Making of Modern Europe*

Paul McCartney, *The Lyrics: 1956 to the Present*

Brendan Simms and Charlie Laderman, *Hitler's American Gamble: Pearl Harbor and the German March to Global War*

Lea Ypi, *Free: Coming of Age at the End of History*

David Graeber and David Wengrow, *The Dawn of Everything: A New History of Humanity*

Ananyo Bhattacharya, *The Man from the Future: The Visionary Life of John von Neumann*

Andrew Roberts, *George III: The Life and Reign of Britain's Most Misunderstood Monarch*

James Fox, *The World According to Colour: A Cultural History*

Clare Jackson, *Devil-Land: England Under Siege, 1588-1688*

Steven Pinker, *Rationality: Why It Is, Why It Seems Scarce, Why It Matters*

Volker Ullrich, *Eight Days in May: How Germany's War Ended*

Adam Tooze, *Shutdown: How Covide Shook the World's Economy*

Tristram Hunt, *The Radical Potter: Josiah Wedgwood and the Transformation of Britain*

Paul Davies, *What's Eating the Universe: And Other Cosmic Questions*

Shon Faye, *The Transgender Issue: An Argument for Justice*

Dennis Duncan, *Index, A History of the*

Richard Overy, *Blood and Ruins: The Great Imperial War, 1931-1945*

Paul Mason, *How to Stop Fascism: History, Ideology, Resistance*

Cass R. Sunstein and Richard H. Thaler, *Nudge: Improving Decisions About Health, Wealth and Happiness*

Lisa Miller, *The Awakened Brain: The Psychology of Spirituality and Our Search for Meaning*

Michael Pye, *Antwerp: The Glory Years*

Christopher Clark, *Prisoners of Time: Prussians, Germans and Other Humans*

Rupa Marya and Raj Patel, *Inflamed: Deep Medicine and the Anatomy of Injustice*

Richard Zenith, *Pessoa: An Experimental Life*

Michael Pollan, *This Is Your Mind On Plants: Opium—Caffeine—Mescaline*

Amartya Sen, *Home in the World: A Memoir*

Jan-Werner Müller, *Democracy Rules*

Robin DiAngelo, *Nice Racism: How Progressive White People Perpetuate Racial Harm*

Rosemary Hill, *Time's Witness: History in the Age of Romanticism*

Lawrence Wright, *The Plague Year: America in the Time of Covid*

Adrian Wooldridge, *The Aristocracy of Talent: How Meritocracy Made the Modern World*

Julian Hoppit, *The Dreadful Monster and its Poor Relations: Taxing, Spending and the United Kingdom, 1707-2021*

Jordan Ellenberg, *Shape: The Hidden Geometry of Absolutely Everything*

Duncan Campbell-Smith, *Crossing Continents: A History of Standard Chartered Bank*

Jemma Wadham, *Ice Rivers*

Niall Ferguson, *Doom: The Politics of Catastrophe*

Michael Lewis, *The Premonition: A Pandemic Story*

Chiara Marletto, *The Science of Can and Can't: A Physicist's Journey Through the Land of Counterfactuals*

Suzanne Simard, *Finding the Mother Tree: Uncovering the Wisdom and Intelligence of the Forest*

Giles Fraser, *Chosen: Lost and Found between Christianity and Judaism*

Malcolm Gladwell, *The Bomber Mafia: A Story Set in War*

Kate Darling, *The New Breed: How to Think About Robots*

Serhii Plokhy, *Nuclear Folly: A New History of the Cuban Missile Crisis*

Sean McMeekin, *Stalin's War*

Michio Kaku, *The God Equation: The Quest for a Theory of Everything*

Michael Barber, *Accomplishment: How to Achieve Ambitious and Challenging Things*

Charles Townshend, *The Partition: Ireland Divided, 1885-1925*

Hanif Abdurraqib, *A Little Devil in America: In Priase of Black Performance*

Carlo Rovelli, *Helgoland*

Herman Pontzer, *Burn: The Misunderstood Science of Metabolism*

Jordan B. Peterson, *Beyond Order: 12 More Rules for Life*

Bill Gates, *How to Avoid a Climate Disaster: The Solutions We Have and the Breakthroughs We Need*

Kehinde Andrews, *The New Age of Empire: How Racism and Colonialism Still Rule the World*

Veronica O'Keane, *The Rag and Bone Shop: How We Make Memories and Memories Make Us*

Robert Tombs, *This Sovereign Isle: Britain In and Out of Europe*

Mariana Mazzucato, *Mission Economy: A Moonshot Guide to Changing Capitalism*

Frank Wilczek, *Fundamentals: Ten Keys to Reality*

Milo Beckman, *Math Without Numbers*

John Sellars, *The Fourfold Remedy: Epicurus and the Art of Happiness*

T. G. Otte, *Statesman of Europe: A Life of Sir Edward Grey*

Alex Kerr, *Finding the Heart Sutra: Guided by a Magician, an Art Collector and Buddhist Sages from Tibet to Japan*

Edwin Gale, *The Species That Changed Itself: How Prosperity Reshaped Humanity*

Simon Baron-Cohen, *The Pattern Seekers: A New Theory of Human Invention*

Christopher Harding, *The Japanese: A History of Twenty Lives*

Carlo Rovelli, *There Are Places in the World Where Rules Are Less Important Than Kindness*

Ritchie Robertson, *The Enlightenment: The Pursuit of Happiness 1680-1790*

Ivan Krastev, *Is It Tomorrow Yet?: Paradoxes of the Pandemic*

Tim Harper, *Underground Asia: Global Revolutionaries and the Assault on Empire*

John Gray, *Feline Philosophy: Cats and the Meaning of Life*

Priya Satia, *Time's Monster: History, Conscience and Britain's Empire*

Fareed Zakaria, *Ten Lessons for a Post-Pandemic World*

David Sumpter, *The Ten Equations that Rule the World: And How You Can Use Them Too*

Richard J. Evans, *The Hitler Conspiracies: The Third Reich and the Paranoid Imagination*

Fernando Cervantes, *Conquistadores*

John Darwin, *Unlocking the World: Port Cities and Globalization in the Age of Steam, 1830-1930*

Michael Strevens, *The Knowledge Machine: How an Unreasonable Idea Created Modern Science*

Owen Jones, *This Land: The Story of a Movement*

Seb Falk, *The Light Ages: A Medieval Journey of Discovery*

Daniel Yergin, *The New Map: Energy, Climate, and the Clash of Nations*

Michael J. Sandel, *The Tyranny of Merit: What's Become of the Common Good?*

Joseph Henrich, *The Weirdest People in the World: How the West Became Psychologically Peculiar and Particularly Prosperous*

Leonard Mlodinow, *Stephen Hawking: A Memoir of Friendship and Physics*

David Goodhart, *Head Hand Heart: The Struggle for Dignity and Status in the 21st Century*

Claudia Rankine, *Just Us: An American Conversation*

James Rebanks, *English Pastoral: An Inheritance*

Robin Lane Fox, *The Invention of Medicine: From Homer to Hippocrates*

Daniel Lieberman, *Exercised: The Science of Physical Activity, Rest and Health*

Sudhir Hazareesingh, *Black Spartacus: The Epic Life of Touissaint Louverture*

Judith Herrin, *Ravenna: Capital of Empire, Crucible of Europe*

Samantha Cristoforetti, *Diary of an Apprentice Astronaut*

Neil Price, *The Children of Ash and Elm: A History of the Vikings*

George Dyson, *Analogia: The Entangled Destinies of Nature, Human Beings and Machines*

Wolfram Eilenberger, *Time of the Magicians: The Invention of Modern Thought, 1919-1929*

Kate Manne, *Entitled: How Male Privilege Hurts Women*

Christopher de Hamel, *The Book in the Cathedral: The Last Relic of Thomas Becket*

Isabel Wilkerson, *Caste: The International Bestseller*

Bradley Garrett, *Bunker: Building for the End Times*

Katie Mack, *The End of Everything: (Astrophysically Speaking)*

Jonathan C. Slaght, *Owls of the Eastern Ice: The Quest to Find and Save the World's Largest Owl*

Carl T. Bergstrom and Jevin D. West, *Calling Bullshit: The Art of Scepticism in a Data-Driven World*

Paul Collier and John Kay, *Greed Is Dead: Politics After Individualism*

Anne Applebaum, *Twilight of Democracy: The Failure of Politics and the Parting of Friends*

Sarah Stewart Johnson, *The Sirens of Mars: Searching for Life on Another World*

Martyn Rady, *The Habsburgs: The Rise and Fall of a World Power*

John Gooch, *Mussolini's War: Fascist Italy from Triumph to Collapse, 1935-1943*

Roger Scruton, *Wagner's Parsifal: The Music of Redemption*

Roberto Calasso, *The Celestial Hunter*

Benjamin R. Teitelbaum, *War for Eternity: The Return of Traditionalism and the Rise of the Populist Right*

Laurence C. Smith, *Rivers of Power: How a Natural Force Raised Kingdoms, Destroyed Civilizations, and Shapes Our World*

Sharon Moalem, *The Better Half: On the Genetic Superiority of Women*

Augustine Sedgwick, *Coffeeland: A History*

Daniel Todman, *Britain's War: A New World, 1942-1947*

Anatol Lieven, *Climate Change and the Nation State: The Realist Case*

Blake Gopnik, *Warhol: A Life as Art*

Malena and Beata Ernman, Svante and Greta Thunberg, *Our House is on Fire: Scenes of a Family and a Planet in Crisis*

Paolo Zellini, *The Mathematics of the Gods and the Algorithms of Men: A Cultural History*

Bari Weiss, *How to Fight Anti-Semitism*

Lucy Jones, *Losing Eden: Why Our Minds Need the Wild*

Brian Greene, *Until the End of Time: Mind, Matter, and Our Search for Meaning in an Evolving Universe*

Anastasia Nesvetailova and Ronen Palan, *Sabotage: The Business of Finance*

Albert Costa, *The Bilingual Brain: And What It Tells Us about the Science of Language*

Stanislas Dehaene, *How We Learn: The New Science of Education and the Brain*

Daniel Susskind, *A World Without Work: Technology, Automation and How We Should Respond*

John Tierney and Roy F. Baumeister, *The Power of Bad: And How to Overcome It*

Greta Thunberg, *No One Is Too Small to Make a Difference: Illustrated Edition*

Glenn Simpson and Peter Fritsch, *Crime in Progress: The Secret History of the Trump-Russia Investigation*

Abhijit V. Banerjee and Esther Duflo, *Good Economics for Hard Times: Better Answers to Our Biggest Problems*

Gaia Vince, *Transcendence: How Humans Evolved through Fire, Language, Beauty and Time*

Roderick Floud, *An Economic History of the English Garden*

Rana Foroohar, *Don't Be Evil: The Case Against Big Tech*

Ivan Krastev and Stephen Holmes, *The Light that Failed: A Reckoning*

Andrew Roberts, *Leadership in War: Lessons from Those Who Made History*

Alexander Watson, *The Fortress: The Great Siege of Przemysl*

Stuart Russell, *Human Compatible: AI and the Problem of Control*

Serhii Plokhy, *Forgotten Bastards of the Eastern Front: An Untold Story of World War II*

Dominic Sandbrook, *Who Dares Wins: Britain, 1979-1982*

Charles Moore, *Margaret Thatcher: The Authorized Biography, Volume Three: Herself Alone*

Thomas Penn, *The Brothers York: An English Tragedy*